U^the^nofficial Guide®
Color Companion
to Walt Disney World®

Bob Sehlinger and Len Testa

WILEY

Wiley Publishing, Inc.

Produced by Menasha Ridge Press
Cover design by Paul Dinovo
Interior design by Steveco International

For information on our other products and services or to obtain technical support, please contact our Customer Care Department within the United States at 800-762-2974, outside the United States at 317-572-3993, or by fax at 317-572-4002. John Wiley & Sons, Inc., also publishes its books in a variety of electronic formats. Some content that appears in print may not be available in electronic formats.

ISBN 978-0-470-49774-6
Manufactured in the United States of America
5 4 3 2 1

CONTENTS

South Orlando and Walt Disney World Area

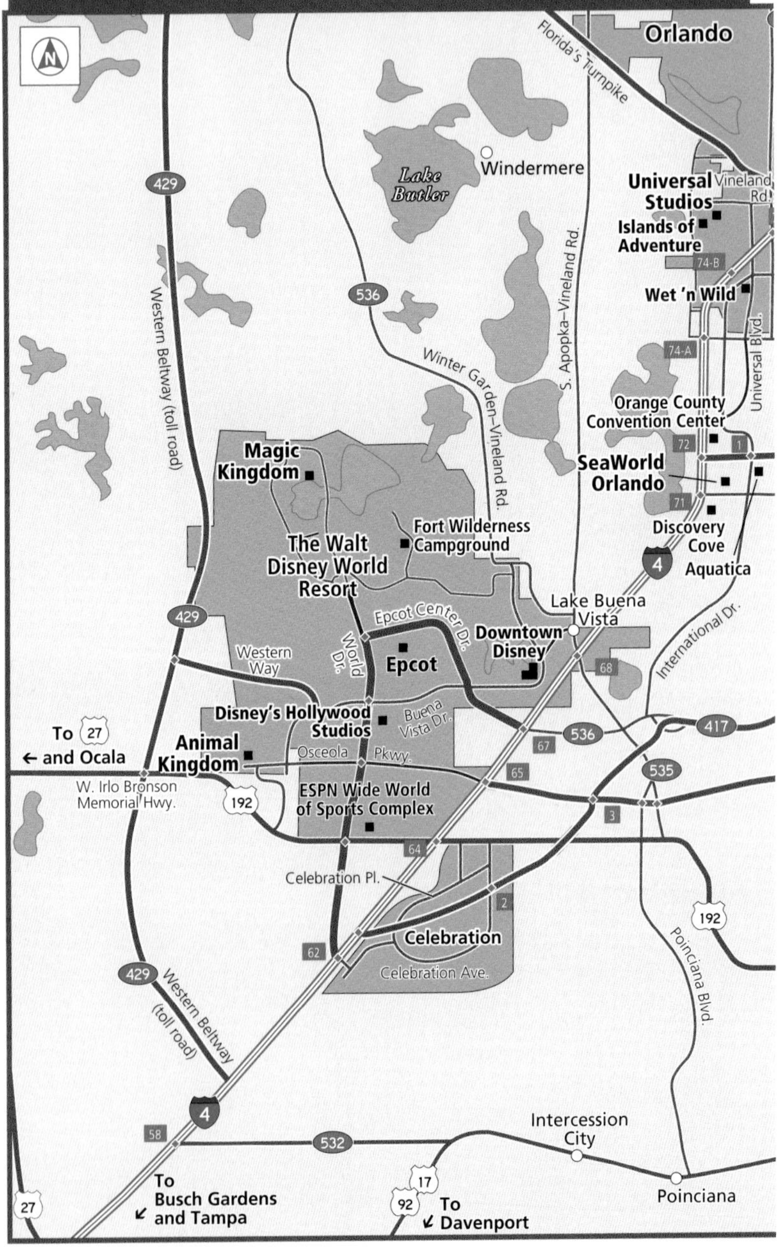

Orlando

Florida's Turnpike

429

Windermere

Lake Butler

536

Winter Garden-Vineland Rd.

S. Apopka-Vineland Rd

Western Beltway (toll road)

Universal Studios
Vineland Rd.

Islands of Adventure

74-B

Wet 'n Wild

74-A

Universal Blvd.

Orange County Convention Center

72

Magic Kingdom

SeaWorld Orlando

Fort Wilderness Campground

The Walt Disney World Resort

429

Epcot Center Dr.

Western Way

World Dr.

Epcot

Downtown Disney

Lake Buena Vista

Discovery Cove

Aquatica

4

International Dr.

68

To 27
← and Ocala

Disney's Hollywood Studios

Animal Kingdom

Buena Vista Dr.

Osceola Pkwy.

67

536

417

W. Irlo Bronson Memorial Hwy.

192

ESPN Wide World of Sports Complex

65

64

535

3

Celebration Pl.

2

192

Celebration

62

Celebration Ave.

Poinciana Blvd.

429 Western Beltway (toll road)

4

58

532

Intercession City

27

To Busch Gardens ↙ and Tampa

17
92 To ↙ Davenport

Poinciana

v

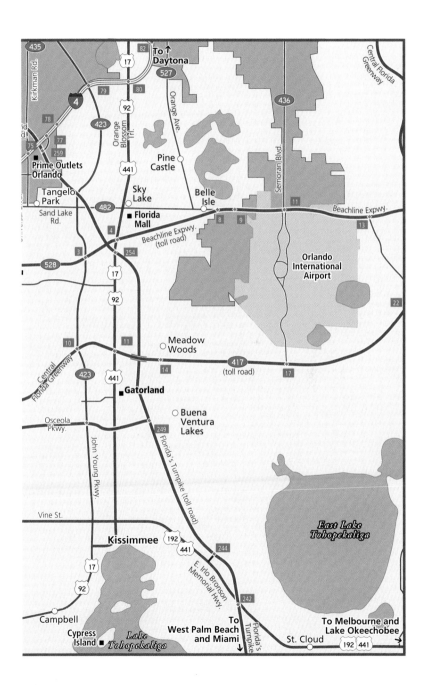

Walt Disney World

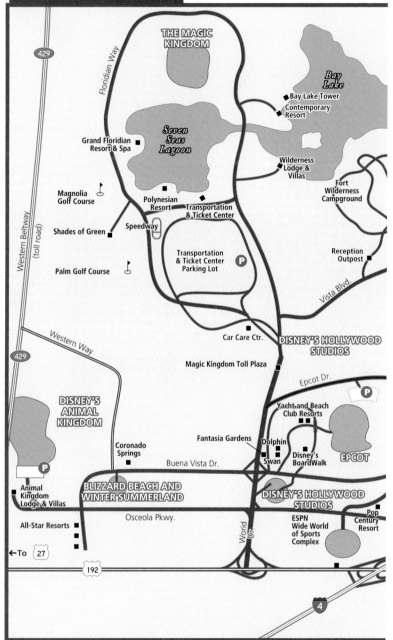

429

THE MAGIC
KINGDOM

Bay Lake

Bay Lake Tower
Contemporary
Resort

Floridian Way

Seven Seas Lagoon

Grand Floridian
Resort & Spa

Wilderness
Lodge &
Villas

Fort
Wilderness
Campground

Magnolia
Golf Course

Polynesian
Resort

Transportation
& Ticket Center

Western Beltway
(toll road)

Shades of Green

Speedway

Reception
Outpost

Palm Golf Course

Transportation
& Ticket Center
Parking Lot

P

Vista Blvd.

Western Way

Car Care Ctr.

DISNEY'S HOLLYWOOD
STUDIOS

429

Magic Kingdom Toll Plaza

Epcot Dr.

P

DISNEY'S
ANIMAL
KINGDOM

Coronado
Springs

Fantasia Gardens

Yacht and Beach
Club Resorts

Dolphin

Swan

Disney's
BoardWalk

EPCOT

Buena Vista Dr.

P

Animal
Kingdom
Lodge & Villas

BLIZZARD BEACH AND
WINTER SUMMERLAND

DISNEY'S HOLLYWOOD
STUDIOS

Pop
Century
Resort

All-Star Resorts

Osceola Pkwy.

World Dr.

ESPN
Wide World
of Sports
Complex

←To 27

192

4

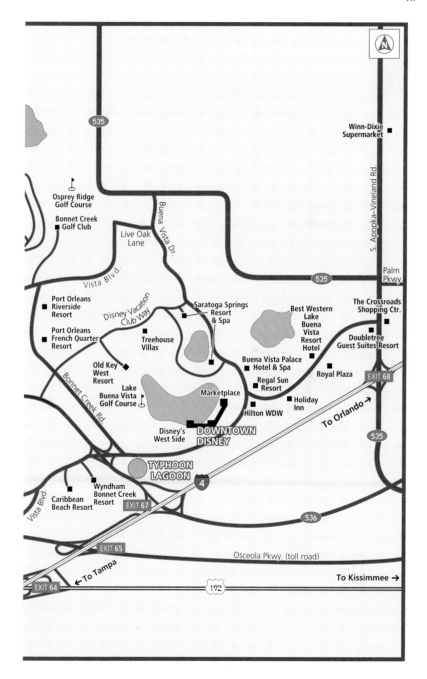

DECLARATION OF INDEPENDENCE

The authors and researchers of this guide specifically and categorically declare that they are and always have been **TOTALLY INDEPENDENT** of the Walt Disney Company, Inc.; of Disneyland, Inc.; of Walt Disney World, Inc.; and of any and all other members of the Disney corporate family not listed. The material in this guide has not been reviewed, edited, or approved by the Walt Disney Company, Inc.; Disneyland, Inc.; or Walt Disney World, Inc.

In this guide, we represent and serve you. If a restaurant serves bad food, or a gift item is overpriced, or a ride isn't worth the wait, we say so, and in the process we hope to make your visit more fun and rewarding.

Don't Tread On Me

THE UNOFFICIAL TEAM

It takes a big team to create an *Unofficial Guide*. Allow me to introduce our crew except for our dining critic, who shall remain totally anonymous, and our onsite researchers who, as you can see, shall remain kinda anonymous:

★ BOB SEHLINGER Author and executive publisher

★ LEN TESTA Coauthor, touring-plans software developer, data-collection director, and TouringPlans.com Webmaster

★ EVE ZIBART Contributing writer and author of *The Unofficial Guide To Walt Disney World for Grown-Ups*

★ FRED HAZELTON Statistician

★ KRISTEN HELMSTETTER Survey collator

★ KAREN TURNBOW, Ph.D. Child psychologist

★ JIM HILL Disney historian

★ PAM BRANDON Shopping guru

★ LARRY OLMSTED Golf expert

★ STEVE JONES and SCOTT MCGREW Cartographers

★ TAMI KNIGHT Cartoonist

★ MARIE HILLIN, STEVE MILLBURG, and DARCIE VANCE Research editors

Data Collectors	Hotel Inspectors	Editorial and Production
Rob Sutton, *supervisor*	Sarah Biggs	Molly B. Merkle, *production manager*
Chantale Brazeau	Joshua Carver	Ritchey Halphen, Holly Cross,
Kai Brückerhoff	Chantale Brazeau	and Amber Kaye Henderson,
Kenny Cottrell	Jenn Gorman	*managing editors*
Guy Garguilo	Ritchey Halphen	Amber Kaye Henderson, *photo coordinator*
Lillian Macko	Kristen Helmstetter	Stephen Sullivan, *design and layout*
Richard Macko	Darcie Vance	Steve Jones, Scott McGrew, and
Cliff Myers	Megan Parks	Travis Bryant, *chief creative guys*
Robert Pederson		Ann Cassar, *indexer*
Julie Saunders	**Contributing Writers**	
Linda Sutton	Megan Parks	
Christine Testa	Sue Pisaturo	
Mais Testa	Grant Rafter	
Darcie Vance	Darcie Vance	
Rich Vosburgh	Mary Waring	
Kelly Whitman	Deb Wills	

MORE KUDOS

The *Unofficial Guides* have always been a team effort. It all begins with our friends at Wiley Publishing, Ensley Eikenburg and Paul Kruger, who provided direction and support and who tolerate our, shall we say, unorthodox sense of humor. Wiley is a conservative publisher, but one that does remarkably well teaming up with what to them must seem like Monty Python.

Our heartfelt appreciation goes to the dozens of *Unofficial Guide* readers who provided photos for the *Walt Disney World Color Companion*.

Many thanks to Sam Gennawey for providing the interesting "Disney Design" sidebars in our parks chapters. Sam is an urban planner in Pasadena, California. His past projects include designs for Walt Disney World. In his spare time he plans the future of California's urban landscapes. Visit Sam's blog at **SamLandDisney.blogspot.com**.

Thanks to Sara Moore for her logistic support of the research team; to Carol Damsky, Larry Bleiberg, and Lisa Schultz Smith for their good humor and creative contributions; to Jol Silversmith for his keen proofreading skills; to intellectual property counsels Andrew Norwood and Deirdre Silver; and to models Anna and Claire Merkle.

THE PHOTOGRAPHERS

The work of the following photographers have come together as a symphony of color and excitement in this first all-color *Unofficial Guide*.

Gail Mooney If our photographers create a visual symphony, Gail Mooney is our first chair violin. Co-partner of Kelly/Mooney Productions in the NYC area, she has over 30 years of experience in still photography. Her work has appeared regularly in *National Geographic*, *Smithsonian*, *Islands*, and *Travel & Leisure*, among many other publications. She has published books on Martha's Vineyard and Nantucket, Provence, and *Down on the Delta* about the Delta blues musicians. She is also a documentary videographer.

Richard Macko *Unofficial Guide* Research Team photographer Richard Macko lives in Orlando. Working at Walt Disney World almost every week on a shoot or research project, Richard is a retired newspaper executive. An avid golfer, he and his wife, Lillian (also an *Unofficial Guide* researcher), have two sons and two grandchildren.

Stefan Zwanzger Born in 1979 in Germany, Stefan became an entrepreneur at age 19, was lucky with affiliate marketing, and then pursued his passion for filmmaking. In 2007 he chose to dedicate all his energy to **thethemeparkguy.com.** Stefan lives in a different country every other year, with Bratislava, Dubai, and London being his latest residential encounters. His favorite theme park in the world is Tokyo DisneySea.

Matt Pasant Matt's first trip to Walt Disney World was in 1992 and forever sparked a passion in the magic of Disney. For many years he has sought to share the magic memories of Disney through his photography. Matt now enjoys trips to Walt Disney World with his wife, Aubrey, and their daughter, Allison.

Tom Bricker Yearly vacations with his parents, Don and Beth, sparked Tom's interest in Walt Disney World. After a long absence, Tom was drawn back to the World and became engaged to his fiancée, Sarah, on the beach of Disney's Polynesian Resort in 2007. Tom and Sarah now visit bi-yearly, combining Tom's expertise in photography with their passion for the Disney theme parks.

Joe Penniston Although he lives in Iowa, Joe Penniston's heart lies in Walt Disney World. With wife Bridget and daughters Olivia and Anna, the Pennistons are always looking forward to their next Disney trip. When not visiting WDW, Joe enjoys practicing all aspects of photography—from initial capture to final edit. For more of Joe's work, log on to **flickr.com/expressmonorail**.

Jon Fiedler A lifelong Disney fan, Jon Fiedler took his first trip to WDW at the age of 3. Not surprisingly, Disney parks and characters are his favorite subjects to photograph. He has visited WDW more than 30 times, Disneyland around 10 times, and Disneyland Paris twice (and counting).

Jay B. Parker A Mississippi native and digital photography enthusiast, Jay B. Parker lives in central Arkansas with his wife, Lauren, and their three children. He works as an information technology manager at the University of Arkansas at Little Rock. You can view more of his photography at **flickr.com/photos/jbparker**.

Tim Gerdes Tim Gerdes is an accomplished photographer whose work has appeared in a variety of publications. Recently, Tim has focused his artistic talent on documenting the Walt Disney World theme parks. Working mostly with available light, Tim strives to replicate the Disney World experience in photos. Tim lives in New Jersey with his wife, daughter, and their two bulldogs.

Other Contributing Photographers (listed alphabetically)

J. David Adams	Carolina Gondoputro	Thomas Damgaard Sabo
Jeff Bergman	Paul Gowder	Cody Sims
Daniel M. Brace	Lyman Green	Neil Staeck
Barrie Brewer	Vanessa L. Guzan	Carol Stokes
Travis Bryant	Josh Hallet	Rob Sutton
Gary Burke	Thomas Jung	*Unofficial Guide* Readers
Mona Collentine	Chuck Kramer	Darren Wittko
Chris Cornwell	Jennifer Lazzaro	Allie Wojtaszek
Cory Disbrow	Linda O'Keefe	
Rusty Gaul	Dave Oranchak	
Meghan Gerc	Andrew Petersen	
Dana Gillin	Bri Sabin	

Note: For a complete list of photo credits, see page 367.

INTRODUCTION
WHEN YOU WISH UPON A STAR . .

2

When the Magic Kingdom opened its door in 1971, it was the only theme park on the vast acreage that Walt Disney cagily acquired near the sleepy central Florida city of Orlando. Every year since then, the park's turnstiles rotate nearly 50 million times. Tourists from all corners of the world travel to Walt Disney World to participate in the most successful amusement concept in history: part playground, part schoolroom, and part sugar plum fairy. Many of them bring their children, of course; many have been coming since they themselves were children.

What these multigenerational, multinational, and multicultural visitors all have in common is a lack of self-consciousness, a sense of playfulness, and perhaps also a sense of relief in escaping what seems to be an increasingly dark and complex real world for the instant gratifications of the Magic Kingdom and its sister parks. Other resorts may bill themselves as "antidotes to civilization," but Disney World offers an antidote to incivility; a respite from violence, squalor, hunger, and environmental depredation; and even a sort of inoculation against aging. Like Peter Pan, the international citizens of Disney World never really grow up. In many ways, it is Walt Disney's greatest gift, as close to eternal youth as we will ever get. Ponce de León may have failed to find his fountain of youth in Florida, but only because he was in the right place at the wrong time.

4

FROM WHENCE IT CAME

The vastness of Walt Disney World was no happy accident. Disney had made one mistake building his first kingdom—not building a big enough "moat" around it—and he wasn't about to make such a mistake with the second one. "One thing I learned from Disneyland," Walt Disney once groused, "was to control the environment." Almost as soon as Disneyland opened in 1955, motel operators, fast-food franchises, and tacky souvenir shops tried to camp as close to the castle door as possible. The entrance to the Anaheim park is on Harbor Boulevard, and that jerry-built, neon-splattered strip became the company's version of the Alamo: "Never again!"

After watching what happened to the periphery of Disneyland once the get-rich-quick jackals moved in, Walt Disney was determined that the next time he began such an endeavor, he would control the visual horizon in every direction, no matter how much land it took. The illusion, the controlled perspective, would not blur even at the

edges. That has remained one of the most remarkable aspects of Walt Disney World today. Despite its (now) urbanized location, Walt Disney World seems to exist entirely apart from any city. Once inside the perimeter, no concrete skyscrapers, no truck exhaust, no billboards, and no power lines interrupt the perfect sky.

An unblemished vista wasn't the only consideration, of course: Disney wanted to hold enough territory to exercise total control over development in the practical sense as well. For one thing, in Disneyland's first decade the merchants in the area just outside the park bled off an incredible amount of the entertainment dollars that would otherwise have been spent inside. By one estimate, the exploiters made twice the money Disney did. Dealing with Anaheim's local utilities cost him a fortune as well: He had to pay for installing power lines a second time in order to have them buried underground.

So, for Disney, aesthetics and economics went hand in hand. That meant finding a large enough tract of undeveloped, or at least minimally developed, land

that at the same time would be accessible—under Disney's own terms—to the millions of people he needed to attract. The site needed to be in a fairly warm climate, so it could operate year-round. That eliminated such early suggestions as Niagara Falls, Baltimore, and Washington, D.C.

It was the beauty of the area itself—the mixture of pasture, orange groves, forest, and marsh—that finally sold Walt Disney on his future kingdom. In 1964, when Disney had his pilots swing the corporate Gulfstream over the pine swamps of central Florida, he pointed out a spot about 15 miles south of Orlando where an unfinished expressway (soon to be the Florida Turnpike) was scraping toward I-4. Then Disney caught a glimpse of a little island in the blue of Bay Lake. "Great," he pronounced. "Buy it." (That island is now the abandoned Discovery Island, working its way back to the natural state it was in when Walt first admired it.)

Disney also quickly dispensed with the Harbor Boulevard problem. When at one meeting early in the planning stages his brother Roy, the financial fall guy, objected to buying yet more land, saying, "We already own about 12,500 acres," Walt shot back: "Two questions: Is the price right? Do we have the money?"

"Yes to both," his brother conceded.

"OK," Walt said, ending the discussion. "How would you like to own 10,000 acres next to Disneyland right now?"

But even that didn't quite satisfy Walt. "If he could have," one of his key staffers said later, "he would have bought 50,000 acres."

6

YOUNG AT HEART

Walt Disney died on December 15, 1966, which means that the vast majority of park guests don't really remember him, or only know a video ghost. But that doesn't mean he isn't visible: To a great extent, the "character" of Disney World reflects the personality of Walt Disney himself. Even in his 50s, when Walt started work on the original Disneyland, he was building it as much for himself—for if there was ever a man who cherished his inner child, it was he—as for his children.

What a man cherishes, he hopes to preserve and pass to his children. It was the settings and stories, the fairy tales, and young people's adventures that he remembered from his own childhood, such as *Kidnapped, Tom Sawyer, Wind in the Willows, Peter Pan, The Jungle Book and Just-So Stories, Tarzan of the Apes, The Arabian Nights, 20,000 Leagues under the Sea*, and Howard Pyle's rousing versions of *Robin Hood* and *King Arthur*, that Walt re-created in the original Adventureland, Fantasyland, and Tomorrowland and in his first movies.

When Disney was still a toddler, the Wright brothers made the dream of flight a reality, in a clumsy-winged box far less graceful than Dumbo the Flying Elephant. When he was in his mid-20s, Charles Lindbergh made the first nonstop solo Atlantic air crossing and inspired the very first Mickey Mouse cartoon, *Plane Crazy*. (It was the first Mickey cartoon made, though it wasn't released until after the better-known *Steamboat Willie*, in which Mickey's alter ego echoed Mark Twain as much as it played on the contemporary popularity of Edna Ferber's *Show Boat*.) In fact, as Walt himself not only scripted Mickey's adventures but also provided his actual voice until 1946, one can plausibly argue that all of Mickey's roles reenacted Walt's own childhood fantasies.

Walt Disney's first full-length feature was a version of *Snow White and the Seven Dwarves*, a fairy tale he'd seen in a silent version in his early teens. Tchaikovsky's *Nutcracker* and *Sleeping Beauty* ballets were instantly classics, and he remembered them, too. All these images, all these national obsessions, romances, and heroes, and in particular all the explorers and inventors—everything except the plagues and the wars—reappear in the part of Walt's amusement park that was closest to his own vision: the Magic Kingdom. The symbols of various other countries that appear in It's a Small World—which foreshadow many of the icons at the World Showcase—are straight out of early newsreels that featured the Eiffel Tower, the Sphinx, the Acropolis, the Taj Mahal, and Big Ben.

Because Disney grew up in the age of such inventors as Thomas Edison and Alexander Graham Bell and photographers George Eastman and Eadweard Muybridge, and in a time when the medical research of Walter Reed, Louis Pasteur, and their colleagues seemed to promise a future free of disease, he remained fascinated by and absolutely confident of the advances of science and technology. Like Muybridge and Eastman, he pushed camera technology forward; like Karl Benz and Bell, he dreamed of impulsive travel and instantaneous communication. These images and ideas pop up again and again throughout the Disney kingdom.

The three-part *Men in Space* series that began airing as a Disneyland TV show in the mid-1950s, and that featured such eminent scientists as Wernher von Braun, was so forward-looking—and so convincing—that it helped push the Pentagon into backing the space program. Walt's original vision for Epcot, the Experimental Prototype Community of Tomorrow, was of the sort of technological utopia Jules Verne would have welcomed. And for many of the original Disney generation—those uncynical post–World War II baby boomers who could remember iceboxes and operator-assisted telephones—the rapid transformation of American culture was just as magical as it seemed to Disney. Even the phrase "Atomic Age" conjured notions of progress rather than debate.

So, though the actual Epcot is not a living city but a sort of permanent world exposition, it nevertheless echoes the unquestioning faith Disney's generation grew up placing in the captains of industry. "Progress equals prosperity" is the credo; dreams, especially the American dream, can come true if you're young at heart.

Walt Disney and Wernher von Braun at the Redstone Arsenal in 1954.

NASA

And the young at heart, like Super Bowl quarterbacks and Olympic heroines, go to Walt Disney World, where they are joined by their children, grandchildren, and thousands of their peers in a mini-nation. For the 20-somethings who throng to Disney World, the continual barrage of music, lights, lasers, and special effects provides a three-dimensional ambience that's as stimulating as a computer game. For the 30- and 40-somethings, the movie references that make up the Disney vocabulary are as familiar as their real-life friends. For older visitors, the international pavilions of Epcot's World Showcase and the safaris of Animal Kingdom are as close to foreign travel as possible without need of a passport. For the self-indulgent, a few days at the resorts can supply the delights of three or four holidays in one: beach time, wilderness hiking, club hopping, chore-free dining, sports, spa services, and shopping.

None of this is purely coincidental. So broad a potential audience doesn't go unnoticed, or unexploited. Neither does the ever-greater proportion of disposable income and increased leisure time of young and old alike. Self-fulfillment is no longer considered selfish; it's spiritual. It may require years to achieve. The Disney Company is notoriously clever at creating both demand and supply, and over the past decade it has deliberately targeted middle-aged professionals (supplying business services in the hotels and offering management and efficiency seminars to companies), sports fans (purchasing ESPN and constructing the huge Wide World of Sports complex), active retirees (offering part- and full-time jobs to seniors as well as emphasizing golfing vacations), young lovers (constructing a fairy-tale wedding pavilion and offering a wide range of fantasy ceremonies), and trend-savvy yuppies (offering expensive restaurants and wine bars). It was ahead of the curve on taking special notice of military personnel, working with the Department of Defense to establish a whole resort (Shades of Green) for armed service members and their families.

Under former CEO Michael Eisner, who, during his 20-year reign, used his own very broad interests as the litmus test for Disney programs, the company went from being amenable to all age groups to specifically targeting each age group. The advertising campaigns proclaim, "It's time to remember the magic," and "It's just not the same without the kids"—which can be read two ways. Golf and tennis facilities abound, along with luxurious spa services and ever-more expensive merchandise, not to mention a cruise line and a rapidly expanding adventure travel service. Seniors are so important to Disney economics that an entire branch of the Guest Services department is geared to silver-age visitors. And teens, always Disney's weakest market, will in the future be lured by characters and attractions drawn from Marvel Comics, which Disney acquired in 2009.

OK, I'LL BITE. HOW BIG IS IT?

It was almost kismet—Kismet, Florida. But even then, it might not have been big enough for Walt Disney's dream. Walt Disney World comprises more than 25,000 acres, or 43 square miles. That's about the size of Boston, two times larger than Manhattan, and 60 times the size of Monaco; Grace Kelly would have been queen of a larger and wealthier kingdom if she'd married Uncle Walt instead of Prince Rainier. (And, in fact, until the development of the town of Celebration, Walt Disney World actually contained 30,000 acres.) Situated hither and yon in this vast expanse are the Magic Kingdom, Epcot, Disney's Hollywood Studios, and the Animal Kingdom theme parks; two swimming theme parks; 34 hotels; a campground; more than 100 restaurants; a shopping complex; seven convention venues; a nature preserve; a series of interconnected lakes, streams, and canals; and a transportation system consisting

of four-lane highways, elevated monorails, and a network of canals.

Walt Disney World has more than 50,000 employees, or cast members, making it the largest single-site employer in the United States. Keeping the costumes of those cast members clean requires the equivalent of 16,000 loads of laundry a day and the dry-cleaning of 30,000 garments daily. Mickey Mouse alone has 175 different sets of duds, ranging from a scuba wet suit to a tux. (Minnie's wardrobe tops Mickey's with more than 200 outfits.) Each year, Disney restaurants serve 10 million burgers, 7 million hot dogs, 50 million Cokes, 9 million pounds of French fries, and 150 tons of popcorn. In the state of Florida, only Miami and Jacksonville have bus systems larger than Disney World's.

A QUICK TRIP AROUND THE MAJOR THEME PARKS

MAGIC KINGDOM

When people think of Walt Disney World, most think of the Magic Kingdom, which opened in 1971. The Magic Kingdom consists of adventures, rides, and shows featuring Disney cartoon characters, and, of course, Cinderella Castle. This park is only one element of Disney World, but it remains the heart.

The Magic Kingdom is subdivided into seven lands, six of which are arranged around a central hub. First encountered is Main Street, U.S.A., which connects the Magic Kingdom entrance with the hub. Clockwise around the hub are Adventureland, Frontierland, Liberty Square, Fantasyland, and Tomorrowland. Mickey's Toontown Fair, the first new land added since the Magic Kingdom opened (and soon to be the first land that goes the way of the passenger pigeon), is situated along the Walt Disney World Railroad on three acres between Fantasyland and Tomorrowland. Access to Toontown Fair is through Fantasyland or Tomorrowland or via the railroad. Main Street and the six lands will be detailed later.

Four hotels (Bay Lake Tower and the Contemporary, Polynesian, and Grand Floridian resorts) are near the Magic Kingdom and directly connected to it by monorail and boat. Two other hotels, Shades of Green and Disney's Wilderness Lodge Resort and Villas, are nearby but not served by the monorail.

EPCOT

Opened in October 1982, Epcot is twice as big as the Magic Kingdom and comparable in scope. It has two major areas: Future World consists of pavilions that exhibit human creativity and technological advancement; World Showcase, arranged around a 40-acre lagoon, presents the architectural, social, and cultural heritages of almost a dozen nations, including Mexico, Norway, China, Germany, Italy, United States, Japan, Morocco, France, United Kingdom, and Canada. Each country is represented by replicas of its famous landmarks and settings. Epcot is more educational than the Magic Kingdom and has been characterized as a permanent world's fair.

Recognize right up front that Epcot is huge—larger than the Magic Kingdom and Disney's Hollywood Studios combined—and time-consuming. Even good walkers should plan on a return visit. Also remember that Future World opens earlier and (with a few exceptions) closes earlier than the World Showcase, so plan your time accordingly. Look for the Tip Board near the entrances.

The Epcot resort hotels—Disney's Beach Club Resort and Villas, Disney's Yacht Club, Disney's BoardWalk Inn and Villas Resort, the Walt Disney World Swan, and the Walt Disney World Dolphin—are within a 5- to 15-minute walk of the International Gateway (backdoor) entrance to the theme park. The hotels are also linked to Epcot and Disney's Hollywood Studios by canal. Epcot is connected to the Magic Kingdom and its hotels by monorail.

ANIMAL KINGDOM

About five times the size of the Magic Kingdom, Animal Kingdom combines zoological exhibits with rides, shows, and live entertainment. The park is arranged somewhat like the Magic Kingdom, in a hub-and-spoke configuration. A lush tropical rain forest serves as Main Street, funneling visitors to Discovery Island, the park's hub. Dominated by the park's central icon, the 14-story-tall, hand-carved Tree of Life, Discovery Island offers services, shopping, and dining. From there, guests can access the themed areas: Africa, Asia, DinoLand U.S.A., and Camp Minnie-Mickey. Discovery Island, Africa, Camp Minnie-Mickey, and DinoLand U.S.A. opened in 1998, followed by Asia in 1999. Africa, the largest themed area at 100 acres, features free-roaming herds in a re-creation of the Serengeti Plain. Guests tour in open-air safari vehicles.

The Animal Kingdom has its own pay parking lot and is connected to other Disney World destinations by the Disney bus system. Although there are no hotels within Animal Kingdom proper, the All-Star Resorts, Animal Kingdom Lodge and Villas, and Coronado Springs Resort are nearby.

DISNEY'S HOLLYWOOD STUDIOS

Opened in 1989 and about the size of the Magic Kingdom, Disney's Hollywood Studios is divided into two areas. The first is a theme park focused on the past, present, and future of the motion-picture and television industries. This section contains movie- and TV-inspired rides and shows and covers about two-thirds of the complex. The second area, formerly a working motion-picture and television production facility, encompasses soundstages, a back lot of streets and sets, and support services. Public access to this area is limited to tours that take visitors behind the scenes for crash courses on Disney animation and moviemaking, including (on occasion) the opportunity to witness the shooting of a film, television show, or commercial.

Disney's Hollywood Studios is connected to other Walt Disney World areas by highway and canal but not by monorail. Guests can park in the Studios' pay parking lot or commute by bus. Guests at Epcot resort hotels can reach the Studios by boat or on foot.

DISNEY-SPEAK POCKET TRANSLATOR

Although it may come as a surprise to many, Walt Disney World has its own somewhat peculiar language. See the following chart for some terms you are likely to bump into:

DISNEY-SPEAK	ENGLISH DEFINITION
Adventure	Ride
Attraction	Ride or theater show
Attraction host	Ride operator
Audience	Crowd
Backstage	Behind the scenes, out of view of customers
Bullpen	Queuing area
Cast member	Employee
Character	Disney character impersonated by an employee
Costume	Work attire or uniform
Dark ride	Indoor ride
Day guest	Any customer not staying at a Disney resort
Face character	A character who does not wear a head-covering costume (Snow White, Cinderella, Jasmine, Aladdin, and the like)
Fur	A character who wears a head-covering costume
General public	Same as day guest
Greeter	Employee positioned at an attraction entrance
Guest	Customer
Hidden Mickeys	Frontal silhouette of Mickey's head worked subtly into the design of buildings, railings, vehicles, golf greens, attractions, and just about anything else
In rehearsal	Operating, though not officially open
Lead	Foreman or manager, the person in charge of an attraction
On stage	In full view of customers
Preshow	Entertainment at an attraction prior to the feature presentation
Resort guest	A customer staying at a Disney resort
Role	An employee's job
Security host	Security guard
Soft opening	Opening a park or attraction before its stated opening date
Transitional experience	An element of the queuing area and/or preshow that provides a story line or information essential to understanding the attraction

Fur

Backstage

Face characters

Hidden Mickey

Bullpen

PHOTOS AND COMMENTS FROM READERS

Many who use *The Unofficial Guide Color Companion to Walt Disney World* write us to comment or share their own photos of their Disney World visit. Their comments and photos are frequently incorporated into revised editions of the *Unofficial Guides*. If you write us or send a photo, rest assured that we won't release your name and address to any mailing-list companies, direct-mail advertisers, or other third party. Unless you instruct us otherwise, we'll assume that you don't object to being quoted or having your photo appear in *The Unofficial Guide Color Companion to Walt Disney World*. If you're up for having your comments or photos appear in the guide, please be sure to tell us your hometown.

How to contact the authors:
Bob Sehlinger and Len Testa
The Unofficial Guide Color Companion to Walt Disney World
P.O. Box 43673
Birmingham, AL 35243
unofficialguides@menasharidge.com

When you write, put your address on both your letter and envelope; the two sometimes get separated. It's also a good idea to include your phone number. If you e-mail us, please tell us where you're from. Remember, as travel writers, we're often out of the office for long periods of time, so forgive us if our response is slow. *Unofficial Guide* e-mail isn't forwarded to us when we're traveling, but we'll respond as soon as possible after we return.

PART 1

PRACTICAL STUFF

PLANNING BEFORE YOU LEAVE HOME

There's certainly no scarcity of information on Walt Disney World. There are more than 8,000 books in print (according to Amazon.com), hundreds of dedicated Web sites and blogs, numerous videos and DVDs, and a growing phalanx of podcasts pertaining to this well-known destination. And then, of course, there are "alternative methods" for finding out what you want to know.

We've boiled down the best sources of information on Walt Disney World to a manageable few, each described in this chapter. If you're interested in "alternative methods," we recommend *The Unofficial Guide to Channeling Deceased Members of the Disney Family.*

In addition to this guide, we recommend the following resources:

1. *THE UNOFFICIAL GUIDE TO WALT DISNEY WORLD* by Bob Sehlinger and Len Testa is the most comprehensive guide to Walt Disney World in print and contains field-tested touring plans that will save you more than four hours a day standing in line. The *Color Companion* is designed to work in conjunction with *The Unofficial Guide to Walt Disney World.*

2. THE WALT DISNEY TRAVEL COMPANY FLORIDA VACATIONS BROCHURE AND VIDEO/DVD This resource describes Walt Disney World in its entirety, lists rates for all Disney resort hotels and campgrounds, and describes Disney World package vacations. The brochure and video/DVD are available from most travel agents or by calling the Walt Disney Travel Company at ☎ 407-828-8101 or 407-934-7639, or by visiting **disneyworld.com.** Be prepared to hold if you inquire by phone.

3. THE DISNEY CRUISE LINE BROCHURE AND DVD This brochure provides details on vacation packages that combine a cruise on the Disney Cruise Line with a stay at Walt Disney World. Disney Cruise Line also offers a free DVD that tells all you need to know about Disney cruises and then some. To obtain a copy, call ☎ 800-951-3532 or order online at **disneycruise.com.**

4. *THE UNOFFICIAL GUIDE TO WALT DISNEY WORLD* WEB SITE Our Web site, **TouringPlans.com,** offers a free online trip organizer, more than 100 different touring plans, and updates on changes at Walt Disney World, among other features. The site is described more fully later in this chapter.

5. ORLANDO MAGICARD If you're considering lodging outside Walt Disney World or if you think you might patronize attractions and restaurants outside the World, it's worthwhile to obtain an Orlando Magicard, an Orlando Vacation Planning Kit, and the *Orlando Official Vacation Guide* (all free) from the Orlando Visitors Center. The Orlando Magicard can be conveniently downloaded from a new Web site, **orlandoinfo.com/magicard.** To order the *Official Vacation Guide,* call ☎ 800-643-9492 (allow four weeks for delivery). For more information and materials, call ☎ 407-363-5872 or visit **visitorlando.com.** Both telephone numbers are staffed during weekday business hours.

6. FLORIDA *ROOMSAVER GUIDE* Another good source of discounts on lodging, restaurants, and attractions throughout the state is the Florida *RoomSaver Guide,* published by Exit Information Guide. The guide is free, but you will be charged $3 ($5 shipping to Canada) for handling. To order, call ☎ 352-371-3948 Monday through Friday, 8 a.m. to 5 p.m. EST, or go to **travelerdiscountguide.com.** Similar guides to other states are available at the same number. The **roomsaver.com** Web site has hotel coupons that you can print off your computer.

22   7. *KISSIMMEE VISITOR'S GUIDE* This full-color visitors guide is one of the most complete available and is of particular interest to those who intend to book lodging outside Walt Disney World. The guide features ads for rental houses, time-shares, and condominiums, as well as a directory of attractions, restaurants, and other useful info. To receive a copy, call the Kissimmee Convention and Visitors Bureau at ☎ 800-327-9159, or check out **floridakiss.com.**

8. *GUIDEBOOK FOR GUESTS WITH DISABILITIES* If you have disabled individuals in your family or group, check out each park's *Guidebook for Guests with Disabilities*, available online at **disneyworld.com.**

Request information as far in advance as possible, and allow four weeks for delivery. Follow up if you haven't received your materials within six weeks.

Walt Disney World on the Web

Disney's official Web site, **disneyworld.com,** offers much of the same information as the Walt Disney Travel Company's vacation brochure, but the brochure has better pictures. Now you can purchase theme-park admission and make resort and dining reservations on the Internet. The site also offers online shopping, weather forecasts, and information on renovations and special events. Supposedly the Disney Web site is updated daily, but we frequently find errors on it.

Other Recommended Web Sites

Unofficial Guide coauthor Len Testa combs the Web looking for the best Disney sites. Here are his recommendations. If you surf while ironing, try not to incinerate the clothes.

BEST OFFICIAL THEME-PARK SITE The official Walt Disney World Web site (**disneyworld.com** or **disneyworld.disney.go.com**) recently underwent its third major overhaul in four years. It gets our nod as the best official park Web site over the official sites for Universal Studios (**universalorlando.com**) and SeaWorld (**seaworld.com**). All three sites contain information on ticket options, park hours, and the like, but Disney's site is the most comprehensive and best organized. On the minus side, however, the site remains bogged down by multimedia gimmickry that causes pages to load slower than Space Mountain's standby line in July.

BEST GENERAL UNOFFICIAL WALT DISNEY WORLD WEB SITE Deb Wills's **AllEars. net** is the first Web site we recommend to friends who are interested in making a trip to Disney World. It contains information on virtually every hotel, restaurant, and activity in the World. Want to know what a room at a Disney resort looks like before you book one? This site has photos—sometimes for each floor of a resort. The site is updated several times per week and includes menus from Disney restaurants, ticketing information, maps, and such.

TOURINGPLANS.COM The Web companion to our Disney World *Unofficial Guides* is chock-full of useful features. For instance, we've designed 140 Disney–theme-park touring plans, in addition to those featured in this book, that include variations for holidays, seniors, Extra Magic Hours, and those who like to sleep in. If our plans aren't quite what you're looking for, **TouringPlans.com** lets you create your own, either from scratch or by using one of ours as a template (we'll automatically include restaurant information, hidden Mickeys, attraction trivia, park hours, and weather forecasts), and share it with family and friends. As of this writing, around 30,000 reader-contributed plans are available on the Web site free of charge.

BEST MONEY-SAVING SITE We humbly suggest that Mary Waring's **mousesavers** .com is the kind of Web site for which the Internet was invented. The site keeps an updated list of discounts and reservation codes for use at Disney resorts. The codes are separated into categories such as "For anyone," "For residents of certain states," and so on. The site also lists discount codes for rental cars and non-Disney hotels in the Orlando area.

BEST DISNEY DISCUSSION BOARDS The best online discussions of all things Disney can be found at **mousepad.mouseplanet.com** and **disboards.com**. With tens of thousands of members and millions of posts, these discussion boards are the most active and popular on the Web. Posting a question on any aspect of an upcoming trip is likely to get you helpful responses from lots of folks who've been in the same situation.

Walt Disney World Main Information Number

When you call the main information number, you will be offered a menu of options for recorded information on theme-park operating hours, recreation areas, shopping, entertainment complexes, tickets and admissions, resort reservations, and directions by highway and from the airport. If you are using a rotary telephone, your call will be forwarded to a Disney information representative. If you are using a touch-tone phone and have a question not covered by recorded information, press eight (8) at any time to speak to a Disney representative.

Important Walt Disney World Addresses

Compliments, Complaints, and Suggestions
Walt Disney World Guest Communications
P. O. Box 10040
Lake Buena Vista, FL 32830-1000

Walt Disney World Info/
Guest Letters/Letters to Mickey
P.O. Box 10040
Lake Buena Vista, FL 32830-0040

Convention and Banquet Information
Walt Disney World Resort South
P.O. Box 10000
Lake Buena Vista, FL 32830-1000

Walt Disney World
Educational Programs
P.O. Box 10000
Lake Buena Vista, FL 32830-1000

Merchandise Mail Order
(Guest Service Mail Order)
P.O. Box 10070
Lake Buena Vista, FL 32830-0070

Walt Disney World Ticket
Mail Order
P.O. Box 10140
Lake Buena Vista, FL 32830-0140

Walt Disney World
Central Reservations
P.O. Box 10100
Lake Buena Vista, FL 32830-0100

Important Walt Disney World Telephone Numbers

General Information	☎ 407-824-4321
Accommodations/Reservations	☎ 407-934-7639 *or* 407-824-8000
Convention Information	☎ 407-828-3200
Dining Advance Reservations	☎ 407-939-3463
Disabled Guests Special Requests	☎ 407-939-7807
Lost and Found	☎ 407-824-4245
Merchandise Guest Services Department	☎ 407-363-6200
Resort Dining and Recreational Information	☎ 407-939-3463
Telecommunication for the Deaf Reservations	☎ 407-939-7670
WDW Information	☎ 407-939-8255
Walt Disney Travel Company	☎ 407-828-3232

WHEN TO GO TO WALT DISNEY WORLD
Selecting the Time of Year for Your Visit

Walt Disney World is busiest Christmas Day through New Year's Day. Also extremely busy are Thanksgiving weekend, the week of Presidents' Day, the first full week of November, spring break for colleges, and the two weeks around Easter. What does busy mean? As many as 92,000 people have toured the Magic Kingdom alone on a single day during these peak times! While this level of attendance isn't typical, it is possible, and only those who absolutely cannot go at any other time should challenge the Disney parks at their peak periods.

The least busy time to visit is from after the Thanksgiving weekend until the week before Christmas. The next slowest times are November through the weekend preceding Thanksgiving, January 4 through the first week of February, and the week after Easter through early June. Late February, March, and early April are dicey. Though crowds have grown markedly in September and October as a result of special promotions aimed at locals and the international market, these months continue to be good for weekday touring at the Magic Kingdom, Disney's Hollywood Studios, and the Animal Kingdom, and for weekend visits to Epcot.

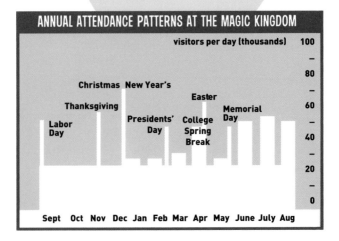

ANNUAL ATTENDANCE PATTERNS AT THE MAGIC KINGDOM

visitors per day (thousands) 100 — 80 — 60 — 40 — 20 — 0

Labor Day · Thanksgiving · Christmas · New Year's · Presidents' Day · College Spring Break · Easter · Memorial Day

Sept Oct Nov Dec Jan Feb Mar Apr May June July Aug

The Downside of Off-season Touring

Though we strongly recommend going to Walt Disney World in the fall, winter, or spring, there are trade-offs for visiting at these times. The parks often open late and close early during the off-season. When they open as late as 9 a.m., everyone arrives at about the same time, which makes it hard to beat the crowds. A late opening coupled with an early closing drastically reduces the hours available to tour. Even when crowds are small, it's difficult to see a big park like the Magic Kingdom or Epcot between 9 a.m. and 6 p.m. Early closing (before 8 p.m.) also usually means that evening parades or fireworks are eliminated. And, because these are slow times at Disney World, some rides and attractions may be closed for maintenance or renovation. Finally, central Florida temperatures fluctuate wildly during the late fall, winter, and early spring; daytime lows in the 40s and 50s are not uncommon.

Given the choice, however, small crowds, bargain prices, and stress-free touring are well worth risking a little cold weather or a couple of closed attractions. So much easier is touring in the fall and other off periods that our research team, at the risk of being blasphemous, would advise taking children out of school for a week at those times rather than battling the summer crowds. We should tell you, however, that teachers don't like this idea one little bit.

Crowd Conditions and the Best and Worst Parks to Visit for Each Day of the Year

Each year we receive more than 1,000 e-mails and letters inquiring about crowd conditions on specific dates throughout the year. Readers also want to know which park is best to visit on each day of their stay. To make things easier for you (and us!), we provide a calendar on our Web site, **TouringPlans.com**, and keep it totally updated for you. For each date, we offer a crowd-level index based on a scale of one (1) to ten (10), with 1 being least crowded and 10 being most crowded. Our calendar takes into account all holidays, special events, and more, as described below. The same calendar lists the best and worst park(s) to visit in terms of crowd conditions on any given day. All you have to do is look up the days of your intended visit on the calendar.

Extra Magic Hours

Extra magic hours is a perk for families staying at a Walt Disney World resort, including the Swan, Dolphin, and Shades of Green properties, and the Hilton hotel in the Downtown Disney Resort Area. On selected days of the week, Disney resort guests will be able to enter a Disney theme park one hour earlier, or stay in a particular theme park up to three hours later than the official park-operating hours. Theme-park visitors not staying at a Disney resort may remain in the park for Extra Magic Hour evenings but cannot experience any rides, attractions, or shows. In other words, they can shop and eat.

▶**UNOFFICIAL TIP** Whatever edge resort guests gain by taking advantage of early entry is offset by horrendous crowds later in the day. During busier times of year, regardless of your hotel, avoid any park on the day it's scheduled for early entry.

26 Summer and Holidays

If you visit on a nonholiday midsummer day, arrive at the turnstiles 30 minutes before the stated opening on a non-early-entry day. If you visit during a major holiday period, arrive 35 to 60 minutes ahead of the official opening time. Hit your favorite rides early using one of our touring plans, and then return to your hotel for lunch, a swim, and perhaps a nap. Don't forget to have your hand stamped for re-entry when you exit. If you are interested in the special parades and shows, return to the park in the late afternoon or early evening. Work under the assumption that, unless you use FASTPASS, early morning will be the only time you can experience the attractions without long waits. Finally, do not wait until the last minute in the evening to leave the park. The exodus at closing is truly mind-boggling.

Epcot is usually the least crowded park during holiday periods. Expect the other parks to be mobbed. To save time in the morning, purchase your admission in advance. Also, consider bringing your own stroller or wheelchair instead of renting one of Disney's. If you are touring Epcot or the Magic Kingdom and plan to spend the day, try exiting the park for lunch at one of the nearby resort hotels. Above all, bring your sense of humor and pay attention to the morale of your party. Bail out when it gets to be more work than fun.

MAKING THE MOST OF YOUR TIME AND MONEY

Allocating Money

How much you spend depends on how long you stay at Walt Disney World. But even if you only visit for an afternoon, be prepared to drop a bundle. We've already told you about some Web sites that show you how to save money on lodging, and in Part Four, you'll find tips for economizing on meals. This section will give you some sense of what you can expect to pay for admission, as well as which admission option will best meet your needs.

Walt Disney World Admission Options

In an effort to accommodate vacations of various durations and activities, Disney offers a number of different options for admission to its theme parks. These options range from the basic One-Day, One-Park ticket, good for a single entry into any one of Disney's theme parks, to the top-of-the-line Premium Annual Pass, good for 365 days of admission into every theme and water park Disney operates, as well as DisneyQuest.

The sheer number of ticket options available makes it difficult and, yes, daunting, for a family to sort out which option represents the least expensive way to see and do everything they want. Finding the optimum admission, or combination of admissions, however, could save the average family a nice chunk of change.

Magic Your Way

Magic Your Way applies to both one-day and multiday passports and begins with a Base Ticket. Features such as the ability to visit more than one park per day ("park hopping") or the inclusion of admission to Disney's minor venues (Typhoon Lagoon, Blizzard Beach, DisneyQuest, and the like) are available as individual add-ons to the Base Ticket.

There is also a volume discount. The more days of admission you purchase, the lower the cost per day. Base Tickets can be purchased for a one-day park admission or multiple days, up to ten days. You cannot use a Base Ticket to visit more than one park per day. When this guide was published, Base Tickets ran about $85 for an adult one-day ticket, $166 for a two-day ticket, and $233 for a three-day ticket. Beyond three days, ticket prices increase only a fraction. In fact, a ten-day ticket is only $25 more than a three-day ticket!

Passes expire 14 days from the first day of use. If you purchase a four-day Base Ticket on June 1 and use it that day for admission to the Magic Kingdom, you'll be able to visit a single Walt Disney World theme park on any of your three remaining days between June 2 and June 15. After that, the ticket expires and any unused days will be lost. Through another add-on, however, you can avoid the 14-day expiration and wind up with a ticket that's valid forever.

Base Ticket Add-on Options

Three add-on options are offered with the Base Ticket, each at an additional cost. All prices referenced below include sales tax. Disney raises admission prices every year, usually in late July or late February, but sometimes in both.

PARK HOPPING Adding this feature to your Base Ticket allows you to visit more than one theme park per day. The cost is about $56 on top of the price of any Base Ticket. It's an exorbitant price for one or two days, but it becomes more affordable the longer your stay. As an add-on to a Seven-day Base Ticket, the $56 flat fee (including tax) would work out to $8 per day for park-hopping privileges. If you want to visit the Magic Kingdom in the morning and dine at Epcot in the evening, this is the feature to request.

NO EXPIRATION Adding this option to your ticket means that unused admissions to the major theme parks and the swimming parks, as well as other minor venues, never expire. If you added this option to a Ten-day Base Ticket and used only four days this year, the remaining six days could be used for admission at any date in the future. The no-expiration option ranges from about $20 with tax for a Two-day Base ticket to about $224 for a Ten-day Base Ticket. This option is not available on one-day tickets.

▶ **UNOFFICIAL TIP** In our estimation, considering the time value of money, buying the no-expiration option is pretty much a sucker play.

WATER PARK FUN AND MORE (WPFAM) This option gives you a single admission to one of Disney's water parks (Typhoon Lagoon or Blizzard Beach), the ESPN

Wide World of Sports Complex, DisneyQuest, or the Oak Trail Golf Course. The cost is a flat $56 (including tax). Except for the one-day WPFAM ticket, which gives you two admissions, the number of admissions equals the number of days on your base ticket. For example, if you buy an Eight-day Base Ticket and add the WPFAM option, you get eight WPFAM admissions. What you can't do is, say, buy a Ten-day Base Ticket with only three WPFAM admissions or a Three-day Base Ticket with four WPFAM admissions. You can, however, skip the WPFAM option entirely and buy an individual admission to any of the minor parks that interest you. This option is almost always the best deal if you want to visit only one of the venues mentioned previously.

Annual Passes

An Annual Pass provides unlimited use of the major theme parks for one year. An add-on is available to provide unlimited use of the minor parks. Annual Pass holders also get perks, including free parking and seasonal offers such as room-rate discounts at Disney resorts. Tax included, Annual Passes run about $525 for adults and about $465 for children ages 3 to 9. A Premium Annual Pass, at around $660 for adults and $585 for children ages 3 to 9, provides unlimited admission to Blizzard Beach, Typhoon Lagoon, DisneyQuest, and Oak Trail Golf Course, in addition to the four major theme parks.

▶ **UNOFFICIAL TIP** The longer your Disney vacation, the more you save with the Annual Pass.

How To Get The Most From Magic Your Way

First, have a realistic idea of what you want out of your vacation. As with anything, it doesn't make sense to pay for options you'll never use. A seven-day theme-park ticket with five pluses might seem like a wonderful idea, but actually trying to visit all those parks in a week in July might end up feeling more like Navy SEAL training. If you're going to make only one visit to a water park, DisneyQuest, or ESPN Wide World of Sports, you're almost always better off purchasing that admission separately rather than in the WPFAM option.

Next, think carefully about paying for the no-expiration option. An inside source reports that fewer than one in ten admission tickets with unused days are ever reused at a Disney theme park. The rest are misplaced, discarded, or forgotten. Unless you are absolutely certain you'll be returning to Walt Disney World within the next year and have identified a safe place to keep those unused tickets, we don't think the additional cost is worth the risk. (We've lost a few of these passes ourselves.)

Where To Purchase Magic Your Way Tickets

You can buy your admission passes on arrival at Walt Disney World or purchase them in advance. Admission passes are available at Walt Disney World resorts and theme parks. Passes are also available at some non-Disney hotels and certain Walt Disney World–area grocery stores, and from independent ticket brokers. Offers of free or heavily discounted tickets abound, but they generally require you to attend a time-share sales presentation. Magic Your Way tickets are likewise available at Disney Stores and at **disneyworld.com.**

If you're trying to keep costs to an absolute minimum, consider using an online ticket wholesaler, such as **mapleleaftickets.com, theofficialticketcenter.com,** or **under covertourist.com,** especially for trips when you plan to spend five or more days in the theme parks. All tickets sold at these sites are brand-new, and savings can range from $7 to more than $25, depending on the ticket and options chosen.

The Official Ticket Center, Maple Leaf Tickets, and Undercover Tourist also offer discounts on tickets for almost all central-Florida attractions, including Disney World, Universal Orlando, SeaWorld, and Cirque du Soleil. Discounts for the major theme parks range from about 6% to 8.5%. Tickets for other attractions are more deeply discounted.

Finally, if all this is too confusing, our Web site will help you navigate all of the new choices and find you the least-expensive ticket options for your vacation. Visit **TouringPlans.com** for more details.

For Additional Information on Passes

If you have a question or concern regarding admissions that you would like addressed by a living, breathing human being, call Disney Ticket Inquiries at ☎ 407-566-4985, or e-mail wdw.ticket.inquiries@disneyworld.com. If you need current prices or routine information, you're better off calling ☎ 407-824-4321 for recorded admission info, or visiting **disneyworld.com.**

ALLOCATING TIME

Which Park To See First?

This question is less academic than it appears, especially if there are children or teenagers in your party. Children who see the Magic Kingdom first expect more of the same type of entertainment at the other parks. At Epcot, they're often disappointed by the educational orientation and more serious tone (many adults react the same way). Disney's Hollywood Studios offers some pretty wild action, but the general presentation is educational and more adult-oriented. Though most children enjoy zoos, animals can't be programmed to entertain. Thus, children may not find the Animal Kingdom as exciting as the Magic Kingdom or Disney's Hollywood Studios.

First-time visitors should see Epcot first; you will be able to enjoy it fully without having been preconditioned to think of Disney entertainment as solely fantasy or adventure in nature. See the Animal Kingdom second. Like Epcot, it's educational, but its live animals provide a change of pace. Next, see Disney's Hollywood Studios, which helps all ages make a fluid transition from the educational Epcot and Animal

Failure to plan your time well can have serious consequences—just ask Cinderella.

Kingdom to the fanciful Magic Kingdom. Also, because Disney's Hollywood Studios is smaller, you won't walk as much or stay as long. Save the Magic Kingdom for last.

Operating Hours

Disney runs a dozen or more schedules each year. Call ☎ 407-824-4321 for the exact park-operating hours in effect on the days of your visit before you arrive. Off-season, parks may be open as few as eight hours (9 a.m. to 5 p.m.) a day. At busy times (particularly holidays), they may be open from 8 a.m. until 2 a.m. the next morning.

Official Opening versus Real Opening

Operating hours quoted when you call are "official hours." Sometimes, the parks actually open earlier. If the official hours are 9 a.m. to 9 p.m., for example, Main Street in the Magic Kingdom might open at 8:30 a.m. and the remainder of the park will open at 9 a.m. Disney publishes hours of operation well in advance but allows itself the flexibility to react daily to gate conditions. Disney traffic controllers survey local hotel reservations, estimate how many visitors to expect on a given day, and open the theme parks early to avoid bottlenecks at parking facilities and ticket windows and to absorb the crowds as they arrive. At day's end, rides and attractions shut down at approximately the official closing time. Main Street in the Magic Kingdom remains open 30 minutes to one hour after the rest of the park has closed.

The Cardinal Rules For Successful Touring

Even the most time-effective touring plan won't allow you to cover two or more major theme parks in one day. Plan to allocate at least an entire day to each park (an exception to this rule is when the parks close at different times, allowing you to tour one park until closing and then proceed to another park).

One-day Touring

A comprehensive one-day tour of the Magic Kingdom, the Animal Kingdom, Epcot, or Disney's Hollywood Studios is possible but requires knowledge of the park, good planning, and plenty of energy and endurance. One-day touring doesn't leave much time for sit-down meals, prolonged browsing in shops, or lengthy breaks. One-day touring can be fun and rewarding, but allocating two days per park, especially for the Magic Kingdom and Epcot, is always preferable. Successful touring of any of the Disney parks hinges on three rules:

1. Determine in Advance What You Really Want to See

To help you set your touring priorities, we describe the theme parks and every attraction in detail in this book. In each description, we include the authors' evaluation of the attraction and the opinions of Disney World guests expressed as star ratings. Five stars is the highest rating. Finally, because attractions range from midway-type rides and horse-drawn trolleys to high-tech extravaganzas, we have developed a hierarchy of categories to pinpoint an attraction's magnitude:

Super-Headliners

The best attractions the theme park has to offer. Mind-boggling in size, scope, and imagination. Represent the cutting edge of attraction technology and design.

The Tower of Terror at Disney's Hollywood Studios is one of the park's super-headliner attractions. To house the ride, Disney built a 1930s-style hotel—complete with gardens, lobby, and gift shop—almost 200 feet tall. Inside are some of Disney's most sophisticated special effects. And, of course, the hotel's elevators go up, down, backward, and forward.

Headliners

Full-blown multimillion-dollar themed adventures and theater presentations. They are modern in technology and design and employ a full range of special effects.

Big Thunder Mountain Railroad in Frontierland is one of several headliner attractions in the Magic Kingdom. This mellow roller coaster, disguised as a runaway mine train, is a visual feast, though you have to feast fast. After writing about Big Thunder for more than 20 years, we still discover new details every time we ride.

Major Attractions

Themed adventures on a more modest scale but which incorporate state-of-the-art technologies, or larger-scale attractions of older design.

Star Tours at Disney's Hollywood Studios is a pioneer when it comes to the use of flight-simulation technology in theme parks. Featuring the robot stars of the *Star Wars* film series, Star Tours offers a wild ride, great visuals, and some big laughs.

Minor Attractions

Midway-type rides, small "dark" rides (cars on a track, zigzagging through the dark), small theater presentations, transportation rides, and walk-through attractions.

The Many Adventures of Winnie the Pooh is a dark ride, a genre that evolved from "Old Mill" and spook-house rides at amusement parks and carnival midways. Pooh at the Magic Kingdom is unique in that it's designed to be lighthearted and funny as opposed to frightening.

Diversions

Exhibits, both passive and interactive, such as playgrounds, video arcades, and street theater.

Even though it costs $1 per play, the Frontierland Shootin' Arcade is one of Walt Disney World's most enjoyable diversions.

© Barrie Brewer

▶ **UNOFFICIAL TIP** Meeting characters, posing for photos, and collecting autographs can burn hours of touring time.

34   2. Arrive Early! Arrive Early! Arrive Early!

Theme parks don't begin the day in gridlock. In fact, they usually don't hit their peak attendance until about 1 or 2 p.m. Guests arrive continuously from the time the turnstiles open through the day. As a rough approximation, about 800 guests are on hand for park opening. Once admitted, these guests will have the run of a park designed for more than 60 times that number. As the day wears on, waits of more than an hour become common at the most popular attractions. But, by that time those who arrived early will have all the big attractions in the rearview mirror.

Arriving early is the single most important key to efficient touring and avoiding long lines. First thing in the morning, there are no lines and fewer people. The same four rides you experience in one hour in early morning can take as long as three hours after 10:30 a.m. Eat breakfast before you arrive; don't waste prime touring time sitting in a restaurant.

The earlier a park opens, the greater your advantage. This is because most vacationers won't rise early and get to a park before it opens. Fewer people are willing to make an 8 a.m. opening than a 9 a.m. opening. On those rare occasions when a park opens at 10 a.m., almost everyone arrives at the same time, so it's almost impossible to beat the crowd. If you visit during midsummer, arrive at the turnstile 30 to 40 minutes before opening. During holiday periods, arrive 45 to 60 minutes early.

Many readers share their experiences about getting to the parks before opening. From a 13-year-old girl from Bloomington, Indiana:

> **Please stress this to your readers: If you want to ride anything with a short wait, you have to get up in the morning! If this is a sacrifice you aren't willing to make, reconsider a Disney World vacation. Most people say they will then be exhausted, but if [you] take a break at the hot part of the day, you'll be fine.**

3. Avoid Bottlenecks

In this guide we provide detailed information on all rides and performances, enabling you to estimate how long you may have to wait in line and allowing you to compare rides for their capacity to accommodate large crowds. In our sister guide, *The Unofficial Guide to Walt Disney World* (which is revised twice a year), we provide touring plans for the Magic Kingdom, the Animal Kingdom, Epcot, and Disney's Hollywood Studios to help you avoid bottlenecks. The step-by-step plans are scientifically derived and field-tested and can save more than four hours of time in line in a single day. The touring plans in *The Unofficial Guide to Walt Disney World* are the most time-efficient plans available anywhere.

36   FASTPASS

Your handout park map, as well as signage at respective attractions, will tell you which attractions are included in the FASTPASS program. FASTPASS attractions will have a regular line and a FASTPASS line. A sign at the entrance will tell you how long the wait is in the regular line. If the wait is acceptable to you, hop in line. If the wait seems too long, you can insert your park-admission pass into a special FASTPASS machine and receive an appointment time (for sometime later in the day) to come back and ride. When you return at the appointed time, you will enter the FASTPASS line and proceed directly to the attraction's preshow or boarding area with no further wait. There is no extra charge to use FASTPASS.

FASTPASS doesn't eliminate the need to arrive at the theme park early. Because each park offers a limited number of FASTPASS attractions, you still need to get an early start if you want to see as much as possible in a single day. Plus, as we'll discuss later, there is a limited supply of FASTPASSes available for each attraction on a given day. If you don't arrive until the middle of the afternoon, you might find that all the FASTPASSes have been distributed to other guests. FASTPASS does make it possible to see more with less waiting than ever before, and it's a great benefit to those who like to sleep late or who enjoy an afternoon or evening at the theme parks on their arrival day at Walt Disney World. It also allows you to postpone wet rides, such as Kali River Rapids at the Animal Kingdom and Splash Mountain at the Magic Kingdom, until the warmer part of the day.

▶**UNOFFICIAL TIP** FASTPASS works remarkably well, mainly because FASTPASS holders get amazingly preferential treatment.

Understanding The FASTPASS System

When you insert your admission pass into a FASTPASS time clock, the machine spits out a small slip of paper about two-thirds the size of a credit card—small enough to fit in your wallet but also small enough to lose easily. Printed on the paper is the name of the attraction and a specific one-hour time window—for example 1:15 to 2:15 p.m.—during which you can return to enjoy the ride.

WHEN TO USE FASTPASS There's no reason to use FASTPASS during the first 30 to 40 minutes a park is open. Lines for most attractions are quite manageable during this period, and this is the only time of day when FASTPASS attractions exclusively serve those in the regular line. Regardless of time of day, however, if the wait in the regular line at a FASTPASS attraction is 25 to 30 minutes or less, we recommend joining the regular line.

FASTPASS RULES Disney amended the rules so that now you can obtain a second FASTPASS soon after the first one is issued. Disney will specify on the first FASTPASS ticket how long you must wait—usually less than two hours—before getting another. Rules aside, the real lesson here is to check out the posted return time before obtaining a FASTPASS. If the return time is hours away, forgo the FASTPASS. An exception to this advice: Go ahead and get the FASTPASS if you really want to see an attraction, especially if it's a super-headliner, because sometimes those attractions run out of FASTPASSes. Especially in the Magic Kingdom, there will be a number of other FASTPASS attractions where the return time is only an hour or so away. Disney rarely enforces the expiration time on the return window, meaning that FASTPASSes are good from the beginning of the window until park closing.

DISNEY'S
FASTPASS
DISTRIBUTION
RETURN BETWEEN
11:00 AND **12:00**

STAND-BY
ENTRANCE
WAIT TIME **10** MINUTES

The Many Adventures of Winnie
the Pooh is a gentle, slow-moving
journey through the Hundred Acre Wood.
A mild rocking motion of your vehicle
will take place in some scenes.

Supervise children
at all times.

Wheelchair access

SPLASH MOUNTAIN

FASTPASS®
Return Anytime Between
10:25 AM
AND
11:25 AM

Riders must be at
least 40"(102cm)
to experience
Splash Mountain

Another FASTPASS® ticket
will be available
after 10:25am
FRI DEC 07

NX WST:CAS007 03/04/07 Tr 1 T 1
12/07/2007   TD1-H4   09:10

INSERT
PARK
TICKET
HERE

RECEIVE
YOUR
FASTPASS
HERE

INSERT
PARK
TICKET
HERE

RECEIVE
YOUR
FASTPASS
HERE

STITCH'S
GREAT ESCAPE
FASTPASS
1:40 PM
AND
2:40 PM

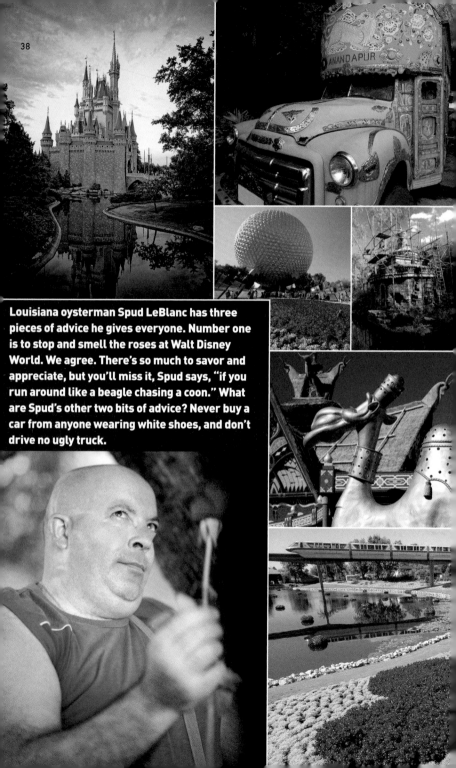

Louisiana oysterman Spud LeBlanc has three pieces of advice he gives everyone. Number one is to stop and smell the roses at Walt Disney World. We agree. There's so much to savor and appreciate, but you'll miss it, Spud says, "if you run around like a beagle chasing a coon." What are Spud's other two bits of advice? Never buy a car from anyone wearing white shoes, and don't drive no ugly truck.

Reader Questions We Can Answer

Is Goofy a dog?

Answer: Well, he has ears like a dog and a canine snout, but he walks upright, talks, and is as socially well adjusted as most people. Plus, we've never seen him sniff TOO MUCH INFORMATION!!

⁴⁰ SPECIAL TIPS FOR SPECIAL PEOPLE

Walt Disney World for Singles

Walt Disney World is great for singles. It is a safe, clean, and low-pressure environment. If you're looking for a place to relax without being hit on, Disney World is perfect. Bars, lounges, and nightclubs are the most laid-back and friendly you're likely to find anywhere. In many, you can hang out and not even be asked to buy a drink (or asked to let someone buy a drink for you). Parking lots are well lit and constantly patrolled. For women alone, safety and comfort are unsurpassed.

There's also no need to while away the evening hours alone in your hotel room. Between the BoardWalk and Downtown Disney, nightlife options abound. If you drink more than you should and are a Disney resort guest, Disney buses will return you safely to your hotel.

▶ **UNOFFICIAL TIP** Virtually every type of entertainment performed fully clothed is available at an amazingly reasonable price at a Disney nightspot.

Walt Disney World for Couples

Weddings and Honeymoons

Disney's intimate wedding (for a maximum of 18 guests, plus the bride and groom) includes a cake and Champagne toast for the couple and four guests, a personalized wedding Web site, a Disney wedding certificate, a photographer, an Annual Pass for the bride and groom, and a wedding album. Packages require a four-night stay at a Disney-owned and -operated resort; some ceremony locations have a limit of ten guests. The cost of this wedding package starts at about $4,500, and also includes a musician, cake, bouquet, limousine ride, and wedding coordinator. If you invite more than 18 guests, you must buy one of Disney's customized wedding packages, which start at $10,000 (Monday through Thursday) and $15,000 (Friday, Saturday, or Sunday), not including taxes and gratuities. If you're short on friends, you can rent Disney characters—there's even a volume discount!

Romantic Getaways

Disney World is a favorite getaway for couples, but not all Disney hotels are equally romantic. Some are too family-oriented; others swarm with convention-goers. For romantic (though expensive) lodging, we recommend Animal Kingdom Lodge and Villas, Bay Lake Tower at the Contemporary Resort, the Polynesian Resort, Wilderness Lodge and Villas, the Grand Floridian, BoardWalk Inn and Villas, and the Yacht Club and Beach Club resorts. The Alligator Bayou section at Port Orleans Riverside, a moderate Disney resort, also has secluded rooms.

© Jeff Bergman

Quiet, Romantic Places To Eat

Quiet, romantic restaurants with good food are rare in the theme parks. Only a handful of locations satisfy both requirements: the Coral Reef, the terrace at the Rose & Crown, the corner booths at The Hollywood Brown Derby, and the upstairs tables at Bistro de Paris. Waterfront dining is available at Portobello and Fulton's Crab House at Downtown Disney, and Narcoossee's at the Grand Floridian Resort.

The California Grill, atop the Contemporary Resort, has the best view at Walt Disney World. If window tables aren't available, ask to be served in the adjoining lounge. Victoria & Albert's at the Grand Floridian is the World's showcase gourmet restaurant; expect to pay big bucks there. Other good choices for couples include Shula's Steakhouse at the Dolphin, Jiko at the Animal Kingdom Lodge, and the Flying Fish Cafe at the BoardWalk.

Eating later in the evening and choosing among the restaurants we've mentioned will improve your chances for quiet, intimate dining, but children—well behaved or otherwise— are everywhere at Walt Disney World, and you won't escape them.

"Breaker 5, breaker 5, this is the Red Rattlesnake.
We got ourselves a convoy!"

Walt Disney World for Seniors

Most seniors we interview enjoy Disney World much more when they tour with folks their own age. If, however, you're considering going to Disney World with your grandchildren, we recommend an orientation visit without them first. If you know first-hand what to expect, it's much easier to establish limits, maintain control, and set a comfortable pace when you visit with the youngsters.

Because seniors are a varied and willing lot, there aren't any attractions we would suggest they avoid. For seniors, as with other Disney visitors, personal taste is more important than age. We hate to see mature visitors pass up an exceptional attraction such as Splash Mountain because younger visitors call it a thrill ride. Splash Mountain, a full-blown adventure, gets its appeal more from music and visual effects than the thrill of the ride. Because you must choose among attractions that might interest you, we provide facts to help you make informed decisions.

Getting Around

Many seniors like to walk, but a seven-hour visit to one of the theme parks normally includes four to eight miles on foot. If you aren't up for that much hiking, let a more athletic member of your party push you in a rented wheelchair. The theme parks also offer fun-to-drive electric carts (convenience vehicles). You can rent a cart at the Magic Kingdom in the morning, return it, go to Epcot, present your deposit slip, and get another cart at no additional charge.

Senior Lodging

If you can afford it, stay in Walt Disney World. If you're concerned about the quality of your accommodations or the availability of transportation, staying inside the Disney complex will ease your mind. The rooms are some of the nicest in the Orlando area and are always clean and well maintained. Plus, transportation is always available to any destination in Disney World at no additional cost. Disney hotels reserve rooms closer to restaurants and transportation for guests of any age who can't tolerate much walking. They also provide golf carts to pick up guests and deliver them to their rooms. Cart service can vary dramatically depending on the time of day and the number of guests requesting service. At check-in time (around 3 p.m.), for example, the wait for a ride can be as long as 40 minutes.

The Contemporary Resort and the adjacent Bay Lake Tower are good choices for seniors who want to be on the monorail system. So are the Grand Floridian and Polynesian resorts, though they cover many acres, necessitating a lot of walking. For a restful, rustic feeling, choose the Wilderness Lodge and Villas. If you want a kitchen and the comforts of home, book Old Key West Resort, the Beach Club Villas, Animal Kingdom Villas, or BoardWalk Villas. If you enjoy watching birds and animals, try Animal Kingdom Lodge and Villas. Try Saratoga Springs for golf.

RVers will find Disney's Fort Wilderness Campground pleasant. Several KOA

campgrounds are also within 20 minutes of Disney World. None offer the wilderness setting or amenities that Disney does, but they cost less.

Senior Dining

Eat breakfast at your hotel restaurant, or save money by having juice and rolls in your room. Follow with an early dinner and be out of the restaurants and ready for evening touring and fireworks long before the main crowd begins to think about dinner. We

44 recommend fitting dining and rest times into the day. Plan lunch as your break in the day. Sit back, relax, and enjoy. Then return to your hotel for a nap or a swim.

▶ **UNOFFICIAL TIP** Make your Advance Reservations for dining before noon to avoid the lunch crowds.

Walt Disney World for Disabled Guests

Valuable information for trip planning is available at **disneyworld.com.** At Walt Disney World, each of the major theme parks offers a free booklet describing disabled services and facilities at that park. The Disney people are somewhat resistant to mailing you the theme-park booklets in advance, but if you are polite and persistent, they can usually be persuaded. The same information can be found on the Web site; click on "Guests with Disabilities" on the home page, at bottom right. Or get a booklet at wheelchair-rental locations in the parks. For specific requests, including specialized accommodations at the resort hotels or on the Disney Transportation System, call ☎ 407-939-7807 (voice) or 407-939-7670 (TTY). When the recorded menu comes up, press "1" on your phone. Calls to this number should be strictly limited to questions and requests regarding disabled services and accommodations. Other questions should be addressed to ☎ 407-824-4321.

Visitors With Special Needs

COMPLETELY OR PARTIALLY NONAMBULATORY GUESTS may easily rent wheelchairs. Most rides, shows, attractions, restrooms, and restaurants in the World accommodate the nonambulatory disabled. If you're in a theme park and need assistance, go to Guest Relations. A limited number of electric carts (motorized convenience vehicles) are available for rent. Easy and fun to drive, they give nonambulatory guests a tremendous degree of freedom and mobility.

Close-in parking is available for disabled visitors at all Disney lots. Request directions when you pay your parking fee. All monorails and most rides, shows, restrooms, and restaurants accommodate wheelchairs.

An information booklet for disabled guests is available at wheelchair-rental locations in each park. Theme-park maps issued to each guest on admission are symbol-coded to show nonambulatory guests which attractions accommodate wheelchairs.

Even if an attraction doesn't accommodate wheelchairs, nonambulatory guests still may ride if they can transfer from their wheelchair to the ride's vehicle. Disney staff, however, aren't trained or permitted to assist in transfers. Guests must be able to board the ride unassisted or have a member of their party assist them. Either way, members of the nonambulatory guest's party will be permitted to go along on the ride.

Because waiting areas of most attractions won't accommodate wheelchairs, nonambulatory guests and their party should request boarding instructions from a Disney attendant as soon as they arrive at an attraction. Almost always, the entire group will be allowed to board without a lengthy wait.

VISITORS WITH DIETARY RESTRICTIONS can be assisted at Guest Relations in the theme parks. For Walt Disney World restaurants outside the theme parks, call the restaurant a day in advance for assistance.

SIGHT-AND/OR HEARING-IMPAIRED GUESTS Guest Relations at the theme parks provides complimentary tape cassettes and portable tape players to assist sight-impaired guests ($25 refundable deposit required). At the same locations, TDDs are available for hearing-impaired guests. In addition to TDDs, many pay phones in the major parks are equipped with amplifying headsets. See your Disney map for locations.

Braille guide maps are available from Guest Relations at all theme parks. Closed captioning is provided on some rides, while many theater attractions provide reflective captioning. A sign-language interpreter performs at some live-theater presentations; for show information, call ☎ 407-824-4321 (voice) or 407-939-8255 (TTY).

NONAPPARENT DISABILITIES We receive many letters from readers whose traveling companion or child requires special assistance, but who, unlike an individual on crutches or in a wheelchair, is not visibly disabled. Some conditions—autism, for example—make it very difficult or even impossible to wait in lines for more than a few minutes, or in queues surrounded by a large number of people.

If you or someone in your touring party has a nonapparent disability, one of the first things to do is obtain a letter from the disabled party's primary physician that explains the specific condition and any special needs the condition implies. The doctor's letter should be explicit enough to fully convey the nature of the condition to the Disney cast member reading the letter. Bring your doctor's note to the Guest Relations window at any Disney theme park and ask for a Guest Assistance Card. This is a special pass designed to allow the disabled individual and his or her touring companions to wait in a separate, uncrowded area, apart from the regular queues at most attractions. One card is good for all four parks, so you do not need to obtain separate cards at each park. You should also pick up a copy of each park's *Guidebook for Guests with Disabilities* (also available online at **disneyworld.com**).

▶ **UNOFFICIAL TIP** If you encounter a guest member who is unfamiliar with the Guest Assistance Card, just ask for a manager and explain your situation.

GETTING THERE
Directions

Motorists can reach any Walt Disney World destination via World Drive off US 192, via Epcot Drive off Interstate 4, or from FL 429 (see map on p. iv).

WARNING! I-4 is an east–west highway but takes a north–south slant through the Orlando-Kissimmee area. This directional change complicates getting oriented in and around Disney World. Logic suggests that highways branching off I-4 should run north and south, but most run east and west here.

FROM I-10
Take I-10 east across Florida to I-75 southbound. Exit onto Florida's Turnpike. Take FL 429 (toll) southbound off the Turnpike. Exit FL 429 at the Hartzog Road/Walt Disney World interchange in the direction of Walt Disney World. Follow the signs to your Disney destination. This is a revised routing based on the 2007 opening of a western entrance to Walt Disney World. It's much faster than continuing on the Turnpike to I-4 to reach Walt Disney World. Also use these directions to reach hotels along US 192–Irlo Bronson Memorial Highway.

FROM I-75 SOUTHBOUND
Exit I-75 southbound onto the Florida Turnpike. Continue south, exiting on FL 429 (toll)

46 southbound. Exit at the Hartzog Road/Walt Disney World interchange in the direction of Walt Disney World. Follow the signs to your Disney destination. As with the previous route, we've revised this one based on the 2007 opening of a western entrance to Walt Disney World. It's much faster than continuing on the Turnpike to I-4 to reach Walt Disney World. Also use these directions to reach hotels along US 192–Irlo Bronson Memorial Highway.

FROM THE ORLANDO INTERNATIONAL AIRPORT

There are two routes from the airport to Walt Disney World. Both take almost exactly the same amount of time to drive except during rush-hour traffic, when Route One via FL 417 is far less congested than Route Two via the Beachline Expressway. Also, Route One eliminates the need to drive on I-4, which is always horribly congested. Both FL 417 and the Beachline Expressway are toll roads, so make sure you have about three dollars' worth of quarters before leaving the airport. Route One: Leaving the airport, go southwest on the Central Florida Greenway (FL 417), a toll road. Take Exit 6 toward FL 535. FL 536 will cross over I-4 and become Epcot Drive. From here, follow the signs to your destination. Route Two: Take FL 528 (Beachline Expressway, a toll road) west for about 12 miles to the intersection with I-4. Go west on I-4 to Exit 67, marked Epcot/Downtown Disney, and follow the signs.

FROM MIAMI, FORT LAUDERDALE, AND SOUTHEASTERN FLORIDA

Head north on Florida's Turnpike to I-4 westbound. Take Exit 67, marked as Epcot/Downtown Disney, and follow the signs.

FROM TAMPA AND SOUTHWESTERN FLORIDA

Take I-75 northbound to I-4. Go east on I-4, take Exit 64 onto US 192 westbound, and follow the signs.

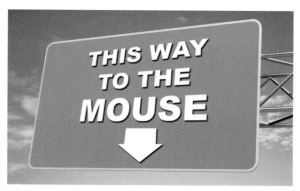

Walt Disney World Exits off I-4

Going east to west (in the direction of Orlando to Tampa), four I-4 exits serve Walt Disney World.

Exit 68 (FL 535/Lake Buena Vista) primarily serves the Downtown Disney Resort Area and Downtown Disney, including the Downtown Disney Marketplace and Disney's West Side. This exit puts you on roads with lots of traffic signals. Avoid it unless you're headed to one of the preceding destinations.

Exit 67 (Epcot/Downtown Disney) delivers you to a four-lane expressway into the heart of Disney World. It's the fastest and most convenient way for westbound travelers to access almost all Disney destinations except Animal Kingdom and ESPN Wide World of Sports.

Exit 65 (Osceola Parkway) is the best exit for westbound travelers to access Animal Kingdom, Animal Kingdom Lodge, Pop Century Resort, All-Star Resorts, and ESPN Wide World of Sports.

Exit 64 (US 192/Magic Kingdom) is the best route for eastbound travelers to all Disney World destinations. For westbound travelers, it's the best exit for accessing the Animal Kingdom and ESPN Wide World of Sports.

Exit 62 (Disney World/Celebration) is the first Disney exit you'll encounter if you're headed eastbound. This four-lane, controlled-access highway connects to the so-called main gate of Walt Disney World.

Transportation To Walt Disney World From The Airport

If you arrive in Orlando by plane, there are four basic options for getting to Walt Disney World:

1. TAXI Taxis carry four to eight passengers (depending on the type of vehicle). Rates vary according to distance. If your hotel is in Walt Disney World, your fare will be about $50, not including tip. For the US 192 Maingate area, your fare will be about $48. If you go to International Drive or downtown Orlando, expect to pay about $30.

2. SHUTTLE SERVICE Mears Motor Transportation Service (☎ 407-423-5566; **mearstransportation.com**) operates from Orlando International Airport. Although this is the shuttle service that will provide your transportation if airport transfers are included in your vacation package, you do not have to be on a package to avail yourself of their services. In practice, the shuttles collect passengers until they fill a van (or sometimes a bus). Once the vehicle is full or close to full, it's dispatched. Mears charges per-person rates (children under age 3 ride free). Both one-way and round-trip services are available. Round trips to the World run about $33 for adults and $26 for children.

3. TOWN-CAR SERVICE Similar to taxi service, a town-car service will transport you directly from Orlando International Airport to your hotel. Instead of hailing a car outside the airport, however, the town-car driver will usually be waiting for you in the baggage claim area of your airline. Town-car companies we've had a good experience with include Tiffany Towncar Service (☎ 888-838-2161 or 407-370-2196; **tiffanytowncars.com**) and Quicksilver Tours & Transportation (☎ 888-GO-TO-WDW or 407-299-1434; **quicksilver-tours.com**). Round trips to the World run about $110 to $120.

RENTAL CARS Rental cars are readily available for both short- and long-term rentals. Most rental companies allow you to drop a rental car at certain hotels or at one of their subsidiary locations in the Walt Disney World general area if you do not want the car for your entire stay. Likewise, you can pick up a car at any time during your stay at the same hotels and locations without trekking back to the airport. A list of discount codes for rental cars also can be found at **mousesavers.com**. With a little effort, you can often get a great deal.

48   Readers planning to stay in the World frequently ask if they will need a car. If your plans don't include restaurants, attractions, or other destinations outside of Disney World, the answer is a very qualified no. However, consider the following:

Plan to Rent a Car:
1. If your hotel is outside Walt Disney World;
2. If your hotel is in Walt Disney World and you want
   to dine someplace other than the theme parks and your
   own hotel;
3. If you plan to return to your hotel for naps or swimming during the day;
4. If you plan to visit other area theme parks or water parks (including Disney's).

▶ **UNOFFICIAL TIP** Sign up for your car-rental company's frequent-renter program before your trip. Most programs are free and let you skip long waits in line to receive your car.

DISNEY'S MAGICAL EXPRESS

Disney's Magical Express is a free bus service that runs between the Orlando International Airport and most Walt Disney World hotels. All guests staying at a Disney-owned and -operated resort are eligible to use the service, even if the stay was booked independent of the Disney Travel Company. (Guests staying at the Swan, Dolphin, and Shades of Green are ineligible for Disney's Magical Express, as these hotels are independently owned.) In addition to transportation, Magical Express provides free luggage-delivery service between your airline and Disney hotel, except for flights arriving after 10 p.m., when you'll need to pick up your suitcases from baggage claim.

You should receive special Magical Express luggage tags about two weeks prior to your departure date. Put a tag on any piece of luggage you plan to check with the airline. When you arrive at the airport, check the bags as you normally would. If you're traveling within the United States, you'll arrive in Orlando and follow the Magical Express signs to your bus; your luggage should be waiting in your hotel room when you check in. (International travelers must retrieve their bags to go through customs. After passing through customs, you'll also head for a bus. Your bags are returned to baggage claim and Disney takes over from there.) Behind the scenes, Disney baggage handlers work with your airline to retrieve suitcases marked with those special tags. All tagged luggage is sent to an airport warehouse, where it's sorted by destination and then loaded onto a truck for delivery. At the resort, the luggage is matched to your reservation. If your room is ready, then the luggage is delivered there; otherwise it's held by the bellhops until you can check in.

In practice the logistical challenge of matching totes and tourists is proving to be a bit more than Disney bargained for, with lost and delayed baggage marring the service's reputation.

HOW TO TRAVEL AROUND THE WORLD

Transportation Trade-Offs For Guests Lodging Outside Walt Disney World

Disney day guests (those not staying inside Disney World) can use the monorail system, the bus system, and the boat system. If, for example, you go to Disney's Hollywood Studios in the morning, and then decide to go to Epcot for lunch, you can take a bus directly there. The most important advice we can give day guests is to park their cars in the lot of the theme park (or other Disney destination) where they plan to finish their day. This is critical if you stay at a park until closing time.

All You Need To Know About Driving To The Theme Parks

1. POSITIONING OF THE PARKING LOTS The Animal Kingdom, Disney's Hollywood Studios, and Epcot parking lots are adjacent to the park entrance. The Magic Kingdom parking lot is adjacent to the Transportation and Ticket Center (TTC). From the TTC you can take a ferry or monorail to the Magic Kingdom entrance.

2. PAYING TO PARK Disney resort guests and Annual Pass holders park free. All others pay. If you pay to park, keep your receipt. If you move your car during the day to another theme park, you will not have to pay again if you show your receipt.

3. FINDING YOUR CAR WHEN IT'S TIME TO DEPART The theme-park parking lots are huge. Jot down the section and row where you park. If you are driving a rental car, jot down the license number (you wouldn't believe how many white rental cars there are).

4. GETTING FROM YOUR CAR TO THE PARK ENTRANCE Each parking lot provides trams to transport you to the park entrance or, in the case of the Magic Kingdom, to the TTC. If you arrive early in the morning, you may find that it is faster to walk to the entrance (or to the TTC) than to take the tram.

5. GETTING TO ANIMAL KINGDOM FOR PARK OPENING If you're staying on property and are planning to be at this theme park when it opens, take a Disney bus from your resort instead of driving. Animal Kingdom's parking lot frequently opens 15 minutes before the park itself—which doesn't leave you enough time to park, hop on a tram, and pass through security before park opening.

6. HOW MUCH TIME TO ALLOT FOR PARKING AND GETTING TO THE PARK ENTRANCE For Epcot and Animal Kingdom, it takes 10 to 15 minutes to pay, park, and walk or ride to the park entrance. At Disney's Hollywood Studios, allow 8 to 12 minutes; at the Magic Kingdom, it's 15 minutes to get to the TTC and another 20 to 30 to reach the park entrance via the monorail or the ferry. Allot another 10 to 20 minutes if you didn't buy your park admission in advance.

7. COMMUTING FROM PARK TO PARK You can commute to the other theme parks via a Disney bus, or to and from the Magic Kingdom and Epcot by monorail. You can also, of course, commute via your own car. Using Disney transportation or your own car, allow 45 to 60 minutes entrance-to-entrance one-way.

8. LEAVING THE PARK AT THE END OF THE DAY If you stay at a park until closing, expect the parking lot trams, monorails, and ferries to be mobbed. If the wait for the parking-lot tram is unacceptable, you can either walk to your car, or walk to the first tram stop on the route and wait there until a tram arrives. When some people get off, you can get on and continue to your appropriate stop.

9. DINNER AND A QUICK EXIT One way to beat closing crowds at the Magic Kingdom is to arrange an Advance Reservation for dinner at one of the restaurants at the Contemporary Resort. When you leave the Magic Kingdom to go to dinner, move your car from the TTC lot to the Contemporary Resort. After dinner, either walk (eight minutes) or take the monorail back to the Magic Kingdom. When the park closes and everyone else is fighting their way onto the monorail or ferry, you can stroll leisurely back to the Contemporary, pick up your car, and be on your way. You can pull the same trick at Epcot by arranging an Advance Reservation at one of the Epcot resorts. After IllumiNations when the park closes, simply exit the park by the International Gateway and walk back to the resort where your car is parked.

10. SCORING A GREAT PARKING PLACE Anytime you arrive at a park after noon, there will be some empty spots up front vacated by early arriving guests who have already departed.

Taking a Shuttle Bus from Your Out-of-the-World Hotel

Many independent hotels and motels near Walt Disney World provide trams and buses. They're fairly carefree, depositing you near theme-park entrances and saving you parking fees. The rub is that they might not get you there as early as you desire (a critical point if you take our touring advice) or be available when you wish to return to your lodging. Also, some shuttles go directly to Disney World, while others stop at additional area lodgings. Each service is a bit different; check the particulars before you make reservations.

If you're depending on shuttles, you'll want to leave the park at least 45 minutes before closing. If you stay until closing and lack the energy to hassle with the shuttle, take a cab. Cab stands are near the Bus Information buildings at the Animal Kingdom, Epcot, Disney's Hollywood Studios, and the TTC. If no cabs are on hand, staff at Bus Information will call one for you.

The Disney Transportation System 51

In the most basic terms, the Disney Transportation System is a hub-and-spoke system. Hubs include the TTC, Downtown Disney, and all four major theme parks (from two hours before official opening time to two to three hours after closing). Although there are some exceptions, there is direct service from Disney resorts to the major theme parks and to Downtown Disney, and from park to park. If you want to go from resort to resort or most anywhere else, you will have to transfer at one of the hubs.

If a hotel offers boat or monorail service, its bus service will be limited, meaning you'll have to transfer at a hub for many Disney World destinations. If you're staying at a Magic Kingdom resort served by the monorail (Polynesian, Contemporary–Bay Lake Tower, or Grand Floridian), you'll be able to commute efficiently to the Magic Kingdom via monorail. If you want to visit Epcot, you must take the monorail to the TTC and transfer to the Epcot monorail. (Guests at the Polynesian can eliminate the transfer by walking five to ten minutes to the TTC and catching the direct monorail to Epcot.)

Walt Disney World Bus Service

Disney buses have an illuminated panel above the windshield that flashes the bus's destination. Also, theme parks have designated waiting areas for each Disney destination. To catch the bus to the Caribbean Beach Resort from Disney's Hollywood Studios, for example, go to the bus stop and wait in the area marked TO THE CARIBBEAN BEACH RESORT. At the resorts, go to any bus stop and wait for the bus displaying your destination on the illuminated panel. Directions to Disney destinations are available when you check in or at your hotel's Guest Relations desk. Guest Relations also can answer questions about the transportation system.

Buses begin service to the theme parks at about 7 a.m. on days when the parks' official opening time is at 9 a.m. Generally, buses run every 20 minutes. Buses to all four parks deliver you to the park entrance. Until one hour before the park opens (before 8 a.m.

52   in this example), buses to the Magic Kingdom deliver you to the TTC, where you transfer to the monorail or ferry to complete your commute. Buses take you directly to the Magic Kingdom starting one hour before the park's stated opening.

To be on hand for the real opening time (when official opening is at 9 a.m.), catch direct buses to Epcot, the Animal Kingdom, and Disney's Hollywood Studios between 7:30 and 8 a.m. Catch direct buses to the Magic Kingdom between 8 and 8:15 a.m. If you must transfer to reach your park, leave 15 to 20 minutes earlier. On days when official opening is at 7 or 8 a.m., move up your departure time accordingly.

For your return bus trip in the evening, leave the park 40 minutes to an hour before closing to avoid the rush. If you're caught in the mass exodus, you may be inconvenienced, but you won't be stranded.

Walt Disney World Monorail Service

Picture the monorail system as three loops. Loop A is an express route that runs counterclockwise connecting the Magic Kingdom with the Transportation and Ticket Center (TTC). Loop B runs clockwise alongside Loop A, making all stops, with service to (in this order) the TTC, Polynesian Resort, the Grand Floridian Resort & Spa, Magic Kingdom, Contemporary Resort, and back to the TTC. The long Loop C dips southeast like a tail, connecting the TTC with Epcot. The hub for all three loops is the TTC (where you usually park to visit the Magic Kingdom). The monorail system serving Magic Kingdom resorts normally starts operation an hour and a half before official opening. If you're staying at a Magic Kingdom resort and you wish to be among the first in the Magic Kingdom at official opening (usually 9 a.m.), board the monorail at the times indicated below.

From the Contemporary Resort–Bay Lake Tower	7:45–8:00 a.m.
From the Polynesian Resort	7:50–8:05 a.m.
From the Grand Floridian Beach Resort	8:00–8:10 a.m.

If you're a day guest, you'll be allowed on the monorail at the TTC between 8:15 and 8:30 a.m. on a day when official opening is 9 a.m. If you want to board earlier, walk from the TTC to the Polynesian Resort and board there. The monorail loop connecting Epcot and the TTC begins operating at 7:30 a.m. on days when Epcot's official opening is 9 a.m. To be at Epcot when the park opens, catch the Epcot monorail at the TTC by 8:05 a.m.

▶ **UNOFFICIAL TIP** Monorails usually operate for two hours after the parks close. If a train is too crowded or you need transportation after the monorails have stopped running, catch a bus.

Walt Disney World Boat Service

Boat service connects Disney's Hollywood Studios with Epcot, stopping at the Swan and Dolphin Resorts, Boardwalk Inn and Villas, Yacht Club Resort, and Beach Club Resort and Villas en route. There is a resort launch service to the Magic Kingdom from the Polynesian, Contemporary and Bay Lake, Grand Floridian, and Wilderness Lodge Resorts as well as from the Fort Wilderness Campground. For day guests ferries serve as an alternative to the monorail from the TTC (Magic Kingdom parking lot) to the Magic Kingdom.

CREDIT CARDS AND MONEY

American Express, Diners Club, Discover, Japan Credit Bureau, MasterCard, and Visa are accepted throughout Walt Disney World.

A LICENSE TO PRINT MONEY

One of Disney's more sublime ploys for separating you from your money is the printing and issuing of Disney Dollars. Available throughout Disney World in denominations of $1, $5, $10, and $50, each emblazoned with a Disney character, the colorful cash can be used for purchases in Disney World, Disneyland, and Disney Stores nationwide. Disney Dollars can also be exchanged one-for-one with U.S. currency, but only while you're in Disney World. Also, you need your sales receipt to exchange for U.S. dollars. Disney money is sometimes a perk (for which you're charged dollar-for-dollar) in Walt Disney Travel Company packages. What Disney hopes of course is that you'll take a pocketful of Disney bucks home and forget where you put them. Calculate the margin on that!

54 PROBLEMS AND HOW TO SOLVE THEM

CAR TROUBLE Security will help if you lock the keys in your parked car or find the battery dead. For more serious problems, the closest repair facility is AAA Car Care Center near the Magic Kingdom lot (☎ 407-824-0976). The nearest off-World repair center is Maingate Citgo (on US 192 west of Interstate 4; ☎ 407-396-2721). Disney security can help you find it. Farther away but highly recommended by one of our Orlando-area researchers is Riker's Automotive & Tire (5700 Central Florida Parkway, near SeaWorld; ☎ 407-238-9800; **rikersauto.com**). Says our source: "They do great work and are the only car place that has never tried to get extra money out of me 'cause I'm a woman and know nothing about cars. I love this place!"

GASOLINE There are three filling stations on Disney property. One station is adjacent to the AAA Car Care Center on the exit road from the TTC (Magic Kingdom) parking lot. It's also convenient to the Shades of Green, Grand Floridian, and Polynesian resorts. Most centrally located is the station at the corner of Buena Vista Drive and Epcot Resorts Boulevard, near the BoardWalk Inn. A third station, also on Buena Vista Drive, is across from the former Pleasure Island site in Downtown Disney.

LOST AND FOUND If you lose (or find) something in the Magic Kingdom, go to City Hall. At Epcot, Lost and Found is in the Entrance Plaza. At Disney's Hollywood Studios, it's at Hollywood Boulevard Guest Relations, and at Animal Kingdom, it's at Guest Relations at the main entrance. If you discover your loss after you have left the park(s), call ☎ 407-824-4245 (for all parks). Ask to be transferred to the specific park's Lost and Found if you're still at the park(s) and discover something is missing.

RAIN Weather bad? Go to the parks anyway. The crowds are lighter on rainy days, and most of the attractions and waiting areas are under cover. Showers, especially during the warmer months, usually don't last very long. Ponchos cost about $7;

umbrellas, about $13. All ponchos sold at Disney World are made of clear plastic, so picking out somebody in your party on a rainy day can be tricky. Walmart sells an inexpensive green poncho that will make your family emerald beacons in a plastic-covered sea of humanity.

▶ **UNOFFICIAL TIP** Rain gear is one of the few bargains at the parks. It isn't always displayed in shops; you have to ask for it.

Medical Matters

RELIEF FOR A HEADACHE Aspirin and other sundries are sold at the Emporium on Main Street in the Magic Kingdom (they're kept behind the counter; you must ask), at retail shops in Epcot's Future World and World Showcase, and in Disney's Hollywood Studios and the Animal Kingdom.

ILLNESSES REQUIRING MEDICAL ATTENTION A Centra Care walk-in clinic is at 12500 South Apopka–Vineland Road (☎ 407-934-CARE). It's open from 8 a.m. to midnight weekdays and 8 a.m. to 8 p.m. weekends. Centra Care also operates a 24-hour physician house-call service and runs a free shuttle (☎ 407-938-0650). Buena Vista Urgent Care (8216 World Center Drive, Suite D; ☎ 407-465-1110) comes highly recommended by *Unofficial Guide* readers.

EastCoast Medical Network (☎ 407-648-5252) has board-certified physicians available 24/7 for house calls to your hotel room. They offer in-room X-rays and IV therapy service as well as same-day dental and specialist appointments. They also rent medical equipment. Insurance receipts, insurance billing, and foreign-language interpretation are provided. Walk-in clinics are also available. You also can inquire about transportation arrangements to the clinics.

DOCS (Doctors on Call Service; ☎ 407-399-DOCS; **doctorsoncallservice.com**) offers 24-hour house-call service. All DOCS physicians are certified by the American Board of Medical Specialties.

PRESCRIPTION MEDICINE Two nearby pharmacies are Walgreens Lake Buena Vista (☎ 407-238-0600) and Winn-Dixie Pharmacy Lake Buena Vista (☎ 407-465-8606). Turner Drugs (☎ 407-828-8125) charges $5 to deliver a filled prescription to your hotel's front desk. The service is available to Disney and non-Disney hotels in Turner Drugs' area. The delivery fee will be charged to your hotel account.

DENTAL EMERGENCIES Call Celebration Dental Group (☎ 407-566-2222).

SERVICES

MESSAGES Messages left at City Hall in the Magic Kingdom, Guest Relations at Epcot, Hollywood Boulevard Guest Relations at Disney's Hollywood Studios, or Guest Relations at the Animal Kingdom can be retrieved at any of the four park facilities.

LOCKERS AND PACKAGE PICK-UP Lockers are available on the ground floor of the Main Street railroad station in the Magic Kingdom, to the right of Spaceship Earth

56   in Epcot, and on the east and west ends of the TTC. At Disney's Hollywood Studios, lockers are to the right of the entrance on Hollywood Boulevard at Oscar's Classical Car Souvenirs. At Animal Kingdom, lockers are inside the main entrance to the left. Lockers are $5 a day plus a $2 deposit.

    Package Pick-Up is available at each major theme park. Ask the salesperson to send your purchases to Package Pick-Up. When you leave the park, they'll be waiting for you. Epcot has two exits, thus two Package Pick-Ups; specify main entrance or International Gateway. If you're staying at a Disney resort, you can also have packages delivered to your hotel's gift shop. If you're leaving within 24 hours, however, take them with you or use the in-park pick-up location.

CAMERAS AND FILM Camera centers at the major parks sell disposable cameras for about $12 ($19 with flash). Film is available throughout the World. Developing is available at most Disney hotel gift shops. You can also have images from your digital camera's memory card burned to a CD while you're in the parks. The cost is around $13 for 120 images and around $6.50 for an additional 120 images. Prints are around 75¢ each. You'll need to leave your digital media with Disney while they create the CD, which typically takes around two to five hours, so make sure you've got extra media on hand.

▶**UNOFFICIAL TIP** Disney no longer offers film developing at the theme parks.

GROCERY STORES Located in the Crossroads Shopping Center, across FL 535 from the Disney World entrance, Gooding's Supermarket is a large grocery. While its location makes it undeniably convenient, its gourmet selections (cheese, wine, and such) aren't nearly as extensive as they used to be, and if you're just looking for staples, you'll find the prices higher than the Tower of Terror, and just as frightening. For down-to-earth prices and a better selection, try Publix at the intersection of International Drive and US 192, or Winn-Dixie on Apopka–Vineland Road about a mile north of Crossroads Shopping Center.

    If you don't have a car or you don't want to take the time to go to the supermarket, GardenGrocer (**gardengrocer.com**) will shop for you and deliver your groceries. For orders of $200 or more, there's no delivery charge; for orders less than $200, the delivery charge is $12; a minimum order of $40 is required. Prices for individual items are pretty much the same as you'd pay at the supermarket. You can also order online at the Gooding's Web site (**goodings .com**); a $50 minimum order is required, and a $20 service charge applies.

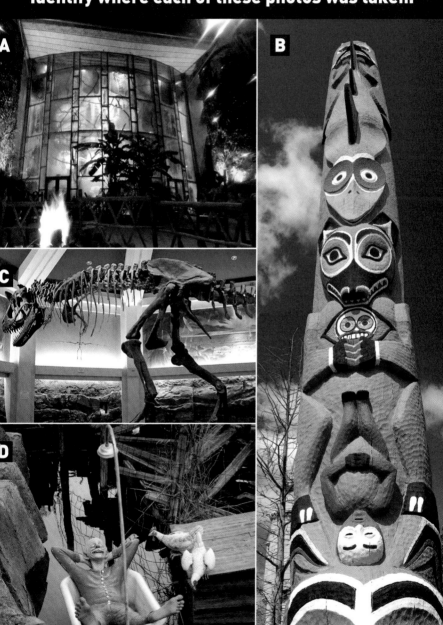

Where in the World?
Identify where each of these photos was taken.

A

B

C

D

A: Animal Kingdom Lodge; B: Canada in Epcot's World Showcase; C: Dinosaur in Animal Kingdom's DinoLand U.S.A. D: Big Thunder Mountain Railroad in Magic Kingdom's Frontierland.

PART 2

WALT DISNEY WORLD RESORTS

CHOOSING A WALT DISNEY WORLD HOTEL

Staying at a Walt Disney World hotel means that you're surrounded by Disney's immersive detail and magic throughout your trip. If you've always wanted to stay at a national park lodge of the American West, for example, Disney's got the Wilderness Lodge Resort, complete with a five-story log-cabin lobby, a pool fed by a model mountain stream, and a working miniature Old Faithful geyser that erupts on the hour, plus restaurants that serve everything from family-style camping fare to trendy Northwest cuisine. And that's just at one hotel! Disney World has more than 20 other such elaborately planned properties, each designed for a different theme and budget.

Regarding cost, the first thing to consider when choosing a Disney hotel is its resort classification. Disney's least-expensive hotels are its **value resorts**, including the All-Star and Pop Century properties. These resorts offer the smallest rooms and fewest amenities. All buildings are essentially three- or four-story rectangles with open-air hallways (that is, your hotel-room door opens directly to the outdoors) and include a mall-style food court. Giant icons, such as 40-foot dogs from *101 Dalmations*, provide the theming at the value resorts.

A step up in cost, architecture, and amenities are Disney's **moderate resorts**, including the Port Orleans properties, and Caribbean Beach and Coronado Springs resorts. Theming at these resorts is much more developed than at the value resorts. Caribbean Beach, for example, has verdant green landscaping, tree-canopied walkways, and a laid-back island feel. Moderate resorts also feature larger rooms, more functional dressing areas, and storage space, as well as more dining options.

Disney's **deluxe resorts** are its top-of-the-line hotels, with the largest rooms, most amenities and recreation options, and best restaurant choices. Most deluxe resorts are located either within walking distance of one of the theme parks or offer direct monorail or boat service to one park's entrance. Besides transportation options, deluxe resorts also offer the most theming of any Disney properties, from the 19th-century Victorian gingerbread architectural ornamentation of the Grand Floridian to the African safari–themed Animal Kingdom Lodge, complete with wildlife roaming a savanna outside your window.

Besides these three main categories, Disney also offers **deluxe villa** resorts, including suites. These are studio, one-, two- and three-bedroom accommodations, some with full kitchens. Many deluxe villa resorts, such as the Beach Club Villas, are attached to one of Disney's deluxe resorts. Regardless, deluxe villa rooms equal or surpass those found at the deluxe resorts.

Finally, there's the Fort Wilderness Resort and Campground, which offers both campsites (tent and RV) and fully-equipped cabins, in an expansive wooded setting. No less themed than any of the other resorts, Fort Wilderness offers everything from campfire sing-alongs to boating and horseback riding.

Amenities and Recreation Disney resorts offer a staggering variety of amenities and recreational opportunities. All provide elaborate swimming pools, themed shops, restaurants or food courts, bars or lounges, and access to five Disney golf courses. The more you pay for your lodging, the more amenities and opportunities are at your disposal.

Making Reservations

DISNEY RESORTS	☎ 407-W-Disney or disneyworld.com
DOLPHIN RESORT	☎ 407-934-4000 or swandolphin.com
SWAN RESORT	☎ 407-934-3000 or swandolphin.com
SHADES OF GREEN	☎ 407-824-3400 or shadesofgreen.org

60 POP CENTURY RESORT

Opened in 2004, Pop Century is Disney's newest and, in our opinion, best value resort. Its basic design is similar to that found in the All-Star Resorts, with motel-style rectangular buildings decorated by large, colorful icons that represent various decades of late 20th-century American culture. Giant yo-yos, eight-track tapes, and Big Wheels will help you identify which building you're in. Swimming pools shaped like bowling pins, computers, and flower petals sit between the buildings.

Rooms at Pop Century are virtually identical to those at the other value resorts (we think the bedspreads and wall photos are the only differences). Pop Century's check-in desk, food court, laundry facilities, and bus stops are far better, however, at handling large crowds than the All-Star Resorts. That makes Pop Century easier on families visiting during crowded times of the year. Various catchphrases—"awesome," "peace, love, and happiness"—plastered around the resort provide endless amuse-ment for grade-school kids and, after hearing, "Like, you said that? Seriously?" from them, a lesson in irony for us parents.

↕ STRENGTHS	WEAKNESSES ↕
- Super kid-friendly theme	- Small guest rooms
- Low (for Disney) rates	- No full-service dining
- Large swimming pools	- Large, confusing layout
- Pleasant setting along Bonnet Creek	- No character meals
- Food court	- Limited recreation options
- Convenient self-parking	
- Fast check-in	

When you explain what an eight-track was to your kids, don't do so by referring to cassettes or records.

Pop Century has perhaps the best set of pools of any Disney value resort.

ALL-STAR RESORTS

Disney's version of a budget resort features three distinct themes executed in the same hyperbolic style. Spread over a vast expanse, the resorts comprise 30 three-story motel-style guest-room buildings. Although the three resorts are neighbors, each has its own lobby, food court, and registration area. The All-Star Sports Resort features huge sports icons: bright football helmets, tennis rackets, and baseball bats—all taller than the buildings they adorn. Similarly, the All-Star Music Resort features 40-foot guitars, maracas, and saxophones, while kids will get a kick out of seeing giant replicas of Herbie the Love Bug and four-story tongue-wagging Dalmatians at the All-Star Movies Resort. Lobbies of all are loud (in both decibels and brightness) and cartoonish, with checkerboard walls and photographs of famous athletes, musicians, or film stars. Each resort has two main pools; Music's are shaped like musical instruments (a Piano Pool and a guitar-shaped Calypso Pool), and one of Movies' is star-shaped.

All six pools feature plastic replicas of Disney characters, some shooting water pistols. Because of the decor, All-Star Sports is a popular resort for cheerleading and athletic teams participating at

↑ STRENGTHS

- Super kid-friendly theme
- Low (for Disney) rates
- Large swimming pools
- Convenient self-parking
- Close to McDonald's

WEAKNESSES ↓

- Remote location from rest of WDW
- Small guest rooms (except for suites at Music Resort)
- No full-service dining
- Large, confusing layout
- Congested bus-loading areas
- No character meals
- Limited recreation options

the ESPN Wide World of Sports complex. If you're looking for a quieter-than-average value resort, ask when booking about any group events that might be happening during your stay. Also, Sports is the first of the three All-Star Resorts visited on Disney's bus line, so guests here spend slightly less time in transit than at the other resorts.

Rooms at the All-Star Resorts are small—around 260 square feet—and feature two full beds or one king-size bed, a TV, desk and chairs, and a dresser. There's very little counter space, and the bathroom is small enough that you've got to have your mind made up before going in. Standard rooms are virtually identical at all three resorts; just look at whether the bedspread has movie props, footballs, or drums to tell which one you're at. However, All-Star Music does have 182 suites (two formerly separate rooms connected by a doorway), which provide around 520 square feet of space for larger families.

Pools at all of the value resorts are large enough to handle big crowds.

A standard All-Star Music Resort room

... and bathroom.

All of the value resorts have themed, mall-style food courts.

64 CARIBBEAN BEACH RESORT

Opened in 1988, Caribbean Beach was Disney's first moderate resort. More than 20 years later, the building's bright colors, island-style theming, and lush landscaping are its strong points. Wandering the grounds, for example, you'll find tucked-away benches surrounded by tropical plants and faux cannon defenses to protect the resort from invaders. The scenery at night is among Disney World's most romantic. The check-in desk and food courts, however, are a long walk from many of the rooms, so you may want to have a car while staying here.

Besides its standard tropical theme, Caribbean Beach's rooms are decorated in the style of two recent Disney films: *Finding Nemo* and *Pirates of the Caribbean*. Nemo rooms feature Nemo and Dory bedspreads and wall borders, while Pirates rooms have ship-shaped beds, carpet that looks like a wood deck, skull-draped curtains for the dressing area, and a profile of the *Flying Dutchman* etched into the shower wall. We're not entirely sure that we want our wives reminded of Johnny Depp all that much, but it's a total (total!) coincidence that these rooms are completely sold out every time we visit.

↑ STRENGTHS	WEAKNESSES ↓
- Attractive Caribbean theme - Children's play area - Convenient self-parking - Walking, jogging, biking - Lakefront setting	- Large, confusing layout - Long lines to check in - Lackluster on-site dining - No easily accessible off-site dining - No character meals - Extreme distance of many guest rooms from dining and services - Occasionally poor bus service

CORONADO SPRINGS RESORT

Coronado Springs Resort, near Animal Kingdom, is Disney's only midpriced convention property. Inspired by northern Mexico and the American Southwest, the resort is divided into three separately themed areas. The two- and three-story ranchos call to mind southwest cattle ranches, while the two- and three-story cabanas are modeled after Mexican beach resorts. The multistoried casitas embody elements of Spanish architecture found in Mexico's great cities. The landscaping is a bit less verdant than at other resorts, to better reflect the southwestern theme. All buildings surround a 15-acre lake, and there are three small pools, as well as one large swimming complex with a reproduction of a Mayan steppe pyramid with a waterfall cascading down its side.

Rooms here are decorated with sunset colors and feature hand-painted Mexican wall hangings. Lighting, especially over the work areas, is above average for Disney's moderate resorts, and Coronado's rooms rated highest in the *Unofficial Guide*'s battery of tests.

Coronado Springs offers one full-service restaurant as well as Disney World's most interesting food court, Pepper Market.

↑ STRENGTHS	WEAKNESSES ↓
- Nice guest rooms - Good view from waterside guest rooms - Food court - Themed swimming area with waterslides - Lakefront setting - Fitness center - Business center - Convenient self-parking	- Insufficient on-site dining - Extreme distance of many guest rooms from dining and services - Low-flow showerheads make rinsing off take longer

© Disney

66

PORT ORLEANS RIVERSIDE

Readers consistently rank Port Orleans Riverside as one of Disney's best resorts in any category, and it's not hard to see why. Themed after Mississippi River communities in postwar Louisiana, the property includes buildings styled as three-story mansions with towering columns and red brick paths, as well as more rustic two-story bayou-style buildings. Port Orleans guests enjoy incredibly detailed landscaping throughout the resort, with realistic miniature "swamps" carefully placed between the walkways of the bayou-style buildings, elaborate fountains and lawns adorning the "mansions," and a rotating waterwheel at the food court.

Regardless of whether you're in a mansion or a bayou shack, rooms at Port Orleans Riverside look the same on the inside and are comparable to the other Disney moderate resorts. The food court at Riverside is large enough to handle crowds well, and the swimming pools get top marks from readers.

 STRENGTHS

- Creative swimming areas
- Nice guest rooms
- Beautiful landscaping and grounds
- Pleasant setting along Bonnet Creek
- Food courts
- Convenient self-parking
- Children's play areas
- Varied recreational offerings
- Boat service to Downtown Disney

WEAKNESSES

- Large, confusing layout
- Extreme distance of many guest rooms from dining and services
- Insufficient on-site dining
- No easily accessible off-site dining
- No character meals
- Congested bus-loading areas

PORT ORLEANS FRENCH QUARTER

↑ STRENGTHS

- Creative swimming areas
- Especially nice guest rooms
- Beautiful landscaping and grounds
- Pleasant setting along Bonnet Creek
- Food courts
- Convenient self-parking
- Children's play areas
- Varied recreational offerings
- Boat service to Downtown Disney

WEAKNESSES ↓

- Large, confusing layout
- Extreme distance of many guest rooms from dining and services
- Insufficient on-site dining
- No easily accessible off-site dining
- No character meals
- Congested bus-loading areas

Easily the most romantic and intimate of Disney's moderate resorts, Port Orleans French Quarter is a perennial favorite of *Unofficial Guide* readers. Designed like a sanitized version of New Orleans, French Quarter is about half the size of the other moderate resorts. Features include colorful buildings, snug walkways, and a waterfront that practically begs you to walk alongside it at sunset—drink in one hand, sweetie in the other, and the kids off somewhere nearby not getting into too much trouble.

Rooms at French Quarter are about the same size as those at other moderate resorts. If you're worried about the counter space available with two separate sinks, a shelf runs along the back of both. The food court is relatively small and works best for breakfast and snacks, and the pool complex is great for small children.

© Disney

68

ANIMAL KINGDOM LODGE AND VILLAS

Disney's Animal Kingdom Lodge combines African tribal architecture with the exotic, rugged style of grand East African national park lodges. Your entrance into the lodge's main-building (Jambo House), five-story lobby, featuring a thatched roof and native art and artifacts, will definitely make an impression. So too will the lodge's restaurants—Boma's buffet and Jiko's fine dining—which readers consistently rank among the best in Walt Disney World.

The Animal Kingdom Lodge's swimming complex is among the best in Walt Disney World, too, with a zero-entry pool for small children and enough space for everyone. The lodge's rooms feature hand-carved furnishings and colorful soft goods. Most rooms have balconies, and those that face the savanna offer the opportunity to see wildlife grazing throughout the day. At night, the lodge offers campfire storytelling and night-vision goggles to better see the nocturnal animals.

Kidani Village, sister resort to Animal Kingdom Lodge, has similar design, theming, and artwork, albeit on a smaller scale. Kidani rooms are decorated in lighter tones but feature hand-carved furniture and balconies similar to those in Jambo House.

 STRENGTHS

- Exotic theme
- Uniquely appointed guest rooms
- Most rooms have private balconies
- Views of savanna and animals from guest rooms
- Themed swimming area
- Excellent on-site dining, including a buffet
- On-site nature programs and storytelling
- Health and fitness center
- On-site child-care center
- Proximity to non-Disney restaurants on US 192

WEAKNESSES

- Remote location

Rooms at Jambo House feature hand-carved woods and colorful fabrics.

The lobby of the Animal Kingdom Lodge—Jambo House.

Sanaa is Kidani Village's sit-down restaurant.

70

YACHT CLUB AND BEACH CLUB RESORTS AND VILLAS

The two best features of the Yacht and Beach Club resorts are their location right next to Epcot (especially World Showcase's restaurants) and Stormalong Bay, easily the best swimming pool complex of any Walt Disney World resort. Both Yacht and Beach Club properties feature similar nautical theming, and except for the color scheme, you'd be hard-pressed to say which was which.

Rooms at both resorts have two double beds or one king bed, a nice desk area for working, and lots of storage space. Some rooms have balconies. Dressing areas feature plenty of space for getting prepped in the mornings, and the bath features good lighting.

The Beach Club Villas offer studio, one-bedroom, and two-bedroom accommodations. Situated on the Epcot side of the resort, the villas' lack of a lake view is made up for by its surroundings, which are quiet enough to make you forget that you're next to a theme park.

⬆ STRENGTHS

- Nautical, New England theme
- Attractive guest rooms
- Good on-site dining
- Children's programs, character meals
- Excellent selection of nearby off-site dining
- Boat service to Epcot and Disney's Hollywood Studios
- Ten-minute walk to rear entrance of Epcot
- Ten-minute walk to BoardWalk
- 15-minute walk to Disney's Hollywood Studios
- Best resort swimming complex at WDW
- Health and fitness center
- Convenient self-parking
- View from waterside guest rooms
- On-site child-care facility

WEAKNESSES ⬇

- No transportation to Epcot's main entrance, except by taxi
- No convenient counter-service food
- Poor room-to-hall soundproofing

© Disney

The Yacht and Beach Clubs share Stormalong Bay, Disney's best resort swimming complex.

CONTEMPORARY RESORT AND BAY LAKE TOWER

It's no coincidence that for the opening of the Magic Kingdom in 1971, Disney designed its monorail to run right through the middle of the Contemporary Resort. The Contemporary was Disney's statement that a new era of design was underway at its Florida property, extending Disney's theming and entertainment architecture beyond the parks and into its entire urban landscape.

While the sleek angles and concrete-and-glass exterior might not be for everyone, rooms at the Contemporary are the nicest on Disney property. Most feature two queen beds (a room with a king-size bed is also available), a glass desk, sofa, and balcony. Wood accents and splashes of color are dotted throughout. Bathrooms have a clever pocket door, which slides into the wall, rather than swinging, to provide additional space. Most tower rooms have views of either the Magic Kingdom or Bay Lake.

Opened in 2009, Bay Lake Tower is a 16-story, 295-unit resort that features studio, one-, two-, and three-bedroom villas, some with spectacular views of the Magic Kingdom. Laid out in a semicircle, Bay Lake Tower is connected to the Contemporary Resort by an elevated, covered walkway and shares monorail service with the Contemporary. Bay Lake Tower has a fabulous pool and pool bar, but shares dining and recreational activities with the Contemporary.

↑ STRENGTHS

- On Magic Kingdom monorail and decor in public areas
- Ten-minute walk to Magic Kingdom
- Interesting A-frame architecture
- Nicest guest rooms at WDW
- Great views of the Magic Kingdom or Bay Lake
- Children's programs, character meals
- Excellent children's pool
- Marina
- Recreational options, including super games arcade
- Restaurant selection via monorail
- On-site child-care facility

WEAKNESSES ↓

- Sterility of theme

Contemporary Resort pool

The Contemporary features the nicest rooms on Disney property.

Bay Lake Tower

Bay Lake Tower pool

POLYNESIAN RESORT

Disney's Polynesian Resort would be the place we'd retire to if we ever hit the lottery. With its tropical landscaping, well-appointed rooms, and good on-site restaurants, it's one of the few Walt Disney World resorts where you could skip the parks entirely and be perfectly content just exploring the grounds. Everything about the Poly (as it's known to its fans) is designed to relax, from the exotic plants that greet you at the entrance to the white-sand beach complete with hammocks and lounge chairs.

Rooms at the Poly are among the nicest in Walt Disney World, with hand-carved, textured surfaces throughout, as well as flat-panel televisions, built-in closets, and plenty of storage. Bathrooms are among the best designed of any Disney resort, with lots of counter space and larger-than-average showers.

The Polynesian's South Pacific theme runs throughout the grounds, including its tropical lobby and extending to its volcano-topped main pool (a separate "quiet pool")

↑ STRENGTHS

- Relaxed and casual ambience
- Ferry service to the Magic Kingdom
- Romantic atmosphere
- Exotic theme that children love
- On Magic Kingdom monorail
- Epcot monorail within walking distance
- Transportation and Ticket Center adjoins resort
- Newly redecorated rooms among nicest at WDW
- Child care, children's programs, and character meals
- Excellent swimming complex
- Recreational options

WEAKNESSES ↓

- Overly large and confusing layout
- Walkways exposed to rain
- Noise from nearby motor speedway
- Front-desk inefficiency

is available in the middle of the resort). The main pool offers a zero-entry end for smaller kids to splash and play. At night, the Poly's pool and beach offer excellent views of the Magic Kingdom's fireworks display.

The Poly's white-sand beach.

Watching fireworks from the Polynesian's main pool.

WILDERNESS LODGE & VILLAS

Now that Adirondack-Yellowstone style is trendy again, you might want to stay at the Ralph Lauren–rustic Wilderness Lodge, with its breathtaking eight-story atrium, 90-foot stone fireplace, interior waterfalls, totem poles, and on-the-hour geyser. Everywhere you look are carved animals, and for puzzle lovers, more hidden Mickeys per square foot than you can stand.

Rooms at the Wilderness Lodge are furnished in modern Mission style, crossed with Sundance-catalog cowhides, leather, and quilts; most have two queen-size beds, but some have one queen and bunk beds. Its Pacific Northwest–style restaurant, Artist Point, is not only good but also lovely and specializes in Pacific Northwest cuisine (of the planked-salmon variety, not pan-Asian).

 STRENGTHS

- Magnificently rendered theme
- The favorite resort of children
- Romantic setting/architecture
- Good on-site dining
- Great views from guest rooms
- Extensive recreational options
- Elaborate swimming complex
- Health and fitness center
- Child-care facility on-site

WEAKNESSES ↓

- No character meals
- Smallest rooms of any deluxe resort
- Must take boat or bus to get to off-site dining options

78

GRAND FLORIDIAN RESORT

Disney's flagship hotel is inspired by Florida's grand Victorian seaside resorts from the turn of the last century. The Grand Floridian integrates verandas, intricate latticework, dormers, and turrets beneath a red-shingle roof to capture the most memorable elements of 19th-century ocean-resort architecture. A five-story domed lobby encircled by enameled balustrades and overhung by crystal chandeliers establishes the resort's understated opulence.

Rooms at the Grand Floridian are luxurious yet warm and inviting, with wood trim and fabrics in beachy tones. The typical room has an armoire, marble-topped sinks, and a ceiling fan, plus two queen beds, a daybed, reading chair, and table with side chairs. All rooms have been recently refurbished, and many include a balcony.

The Grand Floridian's pools are among the largest in Walt Disney World. The beachfront pool contains a waterslide perfect for little ones, plus a waterfall, while the courtyard pool offers more quiet for adults. In addition to swimming, the Grand Floridian offers a white-sand beach, tennis courts, fitness center, jogging trail, and watercraft options for Seven Seas Lagoon.

 STRENGTHS

- On Magic Kingdom monorail
- Ferry service to Magic Kingdom
- Excellent guest rooms
- Children's programs, character meals
- Excellent children's pools
- Beach
- Recreation options
- Restaurant selection via monorail
- On-site child-care facility

WEAKNESSES

- Somewhat formal
- Cavernous, impersonal lobby
- Overly large physical layout
- Only one on-site restaurant suitable for younger children
- Children don't get theme
- Imposing, rather formal public areas

The Grand Floridian's pools are among the best in Walt Disney World.

BOARDWALK INN AND VILLAS RESORT

Disney's BoardWalk Inn is a detailed replica of an early-20th-century Atlantic coast boardwalk, complete with shopping, restaurants, and bakeries along a wide wooden walkway. Both the boardwalk and the resort's entrance are lighted like a landing strip at night, but you'll find the lobby more subdued, with a dignified decor grounded in weathered pastel blues, greens, and pinks. The BoardWalk's pool has an amusement-park theme that includes a great waterslide for families.

Rooms at the BoardWalk Inn are well-appointed and decorated in yellow-and-white striped wallpaper and green curtains. Rooms typically have two queen beds, a sleeper sofa, desk and chair, and ceiling fans. Most rooms also have balconies, and the views are better than at most other resorts. The bath and dressing areas have plenty of room for families, although the lighting here and in the room is a bit dark. The BoardWalk Villas, connected to the inn, are decorated in warmer colors and feature one- and two-bedroom villas in addition to the one-room studios.

↑ STRENGTHS

- Lively seaside and amusement-pier theme
- Newly refurbished guest rooms
- Ten-minute walk to Epcot's rear entrance
- 15-minute walk to Disney's Hollywood Studios
- Boat service to Disney's Hollywood Studios and Epcot
- Well-themed swimming complex
- Three-minute walk to BoardWalk midway and nightlife
- Good selection of off-site dining within walking distance
- Health and fitness center
- Good views from waterside guest rooms

WEAKNESSES ↓

- No restaurants within easy walking distance suitable for young children
- No restaurants in hotel
- Limited children's activities and no character meals
- No transportation to Epcot's main entrance
- Distance of guest self-parking

SARATOGA SPRINGS RESORT & SPA AND TREEHOUSE VILLAS

Saratoga Springs Resort & Spa is themed, Disney says, after an upstate New York Victorian lakeside retreat from the 1880s. And if the average New York Victorian lakeside retreat of the 1880s had about 18 gargantuan four-story pastel-color buildings situated around a massive lake, plus a pool complex, spa, state-of-the-art fitness center, on-site dining, and a golf course, then Disney's got themselves one heck of a history book! Or, it could be a sign that they need to stop paying the marketing guys by the adjective.

 STRENGTHS

- Extremely nice studio rooms and villas
- Lushly landscaped setting
- Best fitness center at Walt Disney World
- Convenient self-parking
- Close to Downtown Disney
- Best spa at Walt Disney World
- Golf on property
- Hiking, jogging, and water recreation
- Excellent themed swimming complex

WEAKNESSES

- Traffic congestion at resort's southeast exit
- Small living areas in villas
- Distance of some accommodations from dining and services
- No character meals
- Most distant of all Disney resorts from the theme parks
- Theme and atmosphere not very kid-friendly

That said, Saratoga Springs's layout and architecture combine to hide the fact that the resort is fairly large. Most guest buildings are situated close to the water, and their size is the perfect scale to complement the lake. Taller buildings would have made it look like a pond, while smaller buildings would have made the resort seem too spread out. Walking trails around the grounds guide you both around the buildings and the water, with excellent views from almost any angle.

Rooms at Saratoga Springs are a little more upscale and masculine than in other Disney resorts. Chairs, sofas, and tables are quite substantial, perhaps a little too large for the rooms they inhabit. The overall effect, however, is sophisticated and restful. A total of 840 studio, one-, two-, and three-bedroom villas are available. Dining and bus transportation aren't the resort's strong points, so we suggest having access to a car.

Opened in 2009, Treehouse Villas is a complex of 60 villas situated between Old Key West and the Grandstand section of

Saratoga Springs proper. True to their name, the villas stand on stilts ten feet off the ground and are surrounded by densely wooded landscape. Each villa is an eight-sided structure with three bedrooms and two bathrooms in approximately 1,074 square feet—about the same size or slightly smaller than two-bedroom villas elsewhere. The treehouses have an open floor plan, however, that makes up for the smaller size.

The interior of each villa is decorated with natural materials, such as stone floors, granite countertops, and stained-wood furniture. Bathrooms are tiled and have excellent space and storage. One bedroom has bunk beds for small children, while the master bedroom and second bedroom have queen beds. A sleeper sofa and chairs in the living room means the treehouses can sleep nine if needed. Smaller families will love the extra space (ours did), as well as the layout and amenities.

OLD KEY WEST RESORT

Old Key West is a large aggregation of two- to three-story buildings modeled after Caribbean residences and guesthouses of the Florida Keys. Set around a golf course and along Bonnet Creek, buildings are arranged in small, neighborhood-style clusters.

As the original Disney Deluxe Villa (i.e., time-share) property, Old Key West has some of the roomiest accommodations in Walt Disney World. The one- and two-bedroom villas include a laundry room and a full kitchen, as well as a master bathroom big enough to hold a small party. All villas are tastefully decorated with wicker and upholstered furniture in light-colored schemes. Finally, each villa has a private balcony that overlooks either a private courtyard, garden, or water view.

Amenities at Old Key West include a full-service restaurant, modest fitness center, marina, and sundries shop. Each cluster of buildings has a quiet pool, and a larger pool is at the community hall with a waterslide in the shape of a giant sandcastle. Transportation from Old Key West is sometimes a challenge, so we recommend having access to a car.

↑ STRENGTHS

- Extremely nice studios and villas
- Full kitchens in villas
- Quiet, lushly landscaped setting
- Convenient self-parking
- Small, private swimming pools
- Recreation options
- Boat service to Downtown Disney

WEAKNESSES ↓

- Large, confusing layout
- Substandard bus service
- Limited on-site dining
- No easily accessible off-site dining
- Extreme distance of many accommodations from dining and services
- No character meals

© J. David Adams

BOYS WILL BE BOYS MALE-BONDING RESORT

Expand your capacity for connecting and sharing with other men at this rustic resort operated by an all-male staff. Enjoy manly activities and rituals designed to increase your sensitivity and open you up emotionally. Facilities are first-class. The Wad-O-Meat Restaurant features whole animals roasted on spits and eaten with the hands, and Bronco Bob's Bar offers 832 different kinds of beer. The sweat lodge can accommodate 72 average-size men or 55 fat guys, and men are allowed to swim in the pool without showering first. Activities include group drumming, chest beating, ritual hugging, hog calling, vine swinging, squirrel skinning, marshmallow roasting, and Twister.

↑ STRENGTHS

- No women allowed
- No children allowed
- Men not required to lower toilet seats
- Crying not seen as a sign of weakness

WEAKNESSES ↓

- No women allowed
- No one to pick out your clothes
- Some men refuse to leave
- Some men transferred to Weight Watchers or Betty Ford

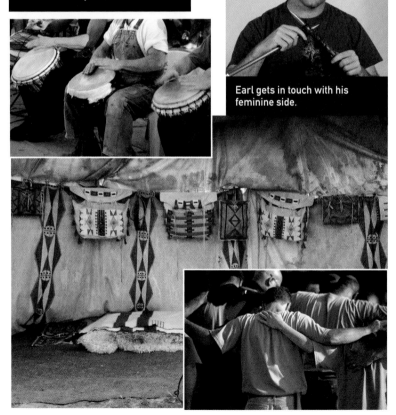

Earl gets in touch with his feminine side.

SHADES OF GREEN

Shades of Green is a resort within Walt Disney World, but is owned and operated by the U.S. Armed Forces. Available only to U.S. military personnel (including members of the National Guard and reserves, retired military, and employees of the U.S. Public Health Service and the Department of Defense), Shades of Green is the equivalent of Disney's deluxe resorts, at generally lower prices.

While Shades of Green doesn't have a major theme, the buildings and lobby interior have the rustic look and exposed wood beams of a mountain resort. Several pools are available within the resort, and Shades of Green is surrounded by Disney golf courses open to all guests.

Rooms at Shades of Green are large and well appointed, with light-oak furniture, soft hues, and the occasional bright accent. There's not a kernel of theming to be found here—no Aztec wallpaper or jaunty sailboat curtains—but for many folks that's a welcome relief. Most rooms have a private balcony.

 STRENGTHS

- Large guest rooms
- Informality
- Quiet setting
- Views of golf course from guest rooms
- Convenient self-parking
- Swimming complex, fitness center
- Video arcade
- Game room with pool tables
- Ice-cream shop

WEAKNESSES

- No interesting theme
- Limited on-site dining
- Limited bus service

THE SWAN AND THE DOLPHIN

It takes a special kind of architect to say ". . . and at the top of the hotels, we're going to have giant fish from outer space. Wait . . . giant swans! OK, a couple of each." Beyond the odd icons, however, are some of the nicest rooms available in Walt Disney World.

Although the hotels are on Disney property—right next to the Yacht Club and BoardWalk Inn resorts—they're owned by Sheraton (Dolphin) and Westin (Swan). Perhaps because they're owned by hotel companies, rooms at these resorts tend to be a cut above most comparable Disney resorts, with better beds and soft goods and a little less theming and ambience. Like Disney's deluxe resorts, the Swan and Dolphin are huge properties, with multiple restaurants and pools, and enough recreation options to keep you busy all day.

Rooms at the Swan and Dolphin are tastefully decorated in mostly neutral tones with accents of color. Besides the bedding, most rooms feature excellent desk space and lighting, which is especially useful for business travelers. Bathrooms and dressing areas are on the smaller side, but are functional.

 STRENGTHS

- Extremely nice guest rooms
- Good on-site and nearby dining
- Health and fitness center; many recreation options
- Boat service to Disney's Hollywood Studios and Epcot
- Excellent beach, swimming complex
- Best WDW resort for business travelers
- On-site child-care facilities and character meals
- View from guest rooms
- Ten-minute walk to BoardWalk nightlife
- Participates in Extra Magic Hours program

WEAKNESSES

- Confusing layout
- No transportation to Epcot's main entrance
- Distant self-parking, daily fee
- Resorts do not qualify for Disney's Magical Express service

FORT WILDERNESS RESORT AND CAMPGROUND

If camping and cabin life are your thing, you've found a home at Fort Wilderness. With campsites that accommodate single-person tents up to bus-size RVs, and separate cabins that sleep six adults, Fort Wilderness is Disney's largest resort. It's also Disney's most diverse, with recreation options that include boating, biking, swimming, horseback riding, a petting zoo, and walking trails, plus an outdoor movie theater and campfire sing-alongs at night.

Fort Wilderness's cabins are considered moderate rooms in Disney's resort categorization, but they've got a full refrigerator, oven, and microwave, plus an outdoor charcoal grill. A Murphy bed swings down in the living room and is comfortable enough for adults to use. The cabins also have one decent-sized bathroom and another separate bedroom that sleeps four. Restaurant options include the popular Trails End buffet (occasionally featuring an ahead-of-its-time doughnut sampler) and the *Hoop-Dee-Doo Revue* musical dinner show.

STRENGTHS

- Informality
- Children's play areas
- Best recreation options at WDW
- Special day and evening programs
- Campsite amenities
- Shower and toilet facilities
- Hoop-Dee-Doo Revue musical show
- Convenient self-parking
- Off-site dining via boat at Magic Kingdom

WEAKNESSES

- Isolated location
- Complicated bus service
- Confusing campground layout
- Lack of privacy
- Very limited on-site dining options
- Limited automobile traffic
- Crowding at beaches and pools
- Small baths in cabins
- Extreme distance to store and restaurant facilities from many campsites

© Disney

SEVEN DWARVES CAVERN RESORT

If you're a late sleeper, you'll love this resort—it's all underground where that irksome morning sun can't bother you. And wives, listen to this! If you've ever wanted to stick your husband's golf clubs where the sun don't shine, it doesn't get any darker than the 7-D Cavern Resort. The temperature is maintained at a brisk 55 degrees, so you never have to worry about roasting under the duvet. Happily, the pool, while 100 feet below ground, is heated—and is even graced by a life-size statue of Snow White in her bathing costume. Finally, getting to the action is a snap on the Doc and Dopey Mine Train that extends beneath all four theme parks, and unlike other Disney mine trains, it never runs away. One note of caution: You'll see canaries in cages located in tunnels throughout the resort. If the canary is happy and singing, don't disturb it. If the canary is dead or seems a little under the weather, report it to the first cast member you encounter. Private canaries for your room are available to rent.

↑ STRENGTHS ⁝

- Quiet
- Seclusion
- Transportation to the parks
- Kids love the cavern theme
- Milk and perishables stay cold without renting a mini-fridge

WEAKNESSES ↓

- Dripping stalactites
- An occasional mole in the guest rooms
- Easy for children to become lost (drop bread crumbs or pebbles)
- Chiseled rock furniture

PART 3

WALT DISNEY WORLD WITH KIDS

ABOUT FAMILY VACATIONS

It has been suggested that the phrase *family vacation* is a bit of an oxymoron because you can never take a vacation from the responsibilities of parenting if your children are traveling with you. Though you leave work and normal routine far behind, your children require as much attention, if not more, when traveling as they do at home.

Parenting on the road is an art. It requires imagination and organization. Think about it: You have to do all the usual stuff (feed, dress, bathe, supervise, teach, comfort, discipline, put to bed, and so on) in an atmosphere where your children are hyperstimulated, without the familiarity of place and the resources you take for granted while at home. Although it's not impossible—and can even be fun—parenting on the road is not something you want to learn on the fly, particularly at Walt Disney World.

The point we want to drive home is that preparation, or the lack thereof, can make or break your Walt Disney World vacation. Believe us, you don't want to leave the success of your expensive Disney vacation to chance. But don't confuse chance with good luck. Chance is what happens when you fail to prepare; good luck is when preparation meets opportunity.

Broadly speaking, you need to prepare yourself and your children mentally, emotionally, physically, organizationally, and logistically. You also need a basic understanding of the theme parks and a well-considered plan for how to go about seeing them.

Mental and Emotional Preparation

Mental preparation begins with realistic expectations about your Disney vacation and consideration of what each adult and child in your party most wants and needs from his or her Walt Disney World experience. Getting in touch with this aspect of planning requires a lot of introspection and good, open family communication.

1. **Division of Labor** Talk about what you and your partner need and what you expect to happen on the vacation. This discussion alone can preempt some unpleasant surprises mid-trip. If you are a two-parent (or two-adult) family, do you have a clear understanding of how the parenting workload is to be distributed?

2. **Togetherness** Another dimension to consider is how much togetherness seems appropriate to you. For some parents, a vacation represents a rare opportunity to really connect with their children, to talk, exchange ideas, and get reacquainted. For others, a vacation affords the time to get a little distance, to enjoy a round of golf while the kids are enjoying the theme park. The point here is to think about your and your children's preferences and needs concerning your time together.

3. **Lighten Up** Prepare yourself mentally to be a little less compulsive on vacation about correcting small behavioral deviations and pounding home the lessons of life. So what if Matt eats hamburgers for breakfast, lunch, and dinner every day? You can make him eat peas and broccoli when you get home. Roll with the little stuff.

4. **Something for Everyone** If you travel with an infant, toddler, or any child who requires a lot of special attention, make sure that you have some energy and time remaining for the rest of your brood. In the course of your planning, invite each child to name something special to do or see at Disney World with Mom or Dad alone.

5. **Whose Idea Was This, Anyway?** The discord that many vacationing families experience arises from the kids being on a completely different wavelength from Mom and Dad. Parents and grandparents are often worse than children when it comes to conjuring fantasy scenarios of what a Walt Disney World vacation will be like. It can be many things, but believe us when we tell you that there's a lot more to it than just riding Dumbo and seeing Mickey.

90   6. Know Thyself and Nothing to Excess   This good advice was made available to ancient Greeks courtesy of the oracle of Apollo at Delphi, who gave us permission to pass it along to you. First, concerning the "know thyself" part, we want you to do some serious thinking about what you want in a vacation. We also want you to entertain the notion that having fun and deriving pleasure from your vacation may be very different indeed from exhausting yourself trying to do and see as much as possible. Plan on seeing the theme parks in bite-size chunks with plenty of sleeping, swimming, napping, and relaxing in between.

7. Routines that Travel   If you observe certain routines at home—for example, reading a book before bed or having a bath first thing in the morning—try to incorporate these familiar activities into your vacation schedule. They will provide your children with a sense of security and normalcy. Maintaining a normal routine is especially important with toddlers.

Physical Preparation

You'll find that some physical conditioning, coupled with a realistic sense of the toll that Disney World takes on your body, will preclude falling apart in the middle of your vacation. As one of our readers put it, "If you pay attention to eat, heat, feet, and sleep, you'll be OK."

Build Naps and Rest into Your Itinerary   The theme parks are huge; don't try to see everything in one day. Tour early in the morning and return to your hotel around 11:30 a.m. for lunch, a swim, and a nap. Even during off-season, when crowds are smaller and temperatures more pleasant, the size of the major theme parks will exhaust most children under age 8 by lunchtime. Return to the park in late afternoon or early evening and continue touring. When it comes to naps, this mom does not mince words:

One last thing for parents of small kids—take the book's advice. Get out of the park, and take the nap, take the nap, TAKE THE NAP! Never in my life have I seen so many parents screaming at, ridiculing, or slapping their kids. (What a vacation!) Disney [parks are] overwhelming for kids and adults.

A mom from Rochester, New York, was equally adamant:

[You] absolutely must rest during the day. Kids went from 8 a.m. to 9 p.m. in the park. Kids did great that day, but we were all completely worthless the next day. Definitely must pace yourself. Don't ever try to do two full days of park sightseeing in a row.

▶ UNOFFICIAL TIP Naps and relief from the frenetic pace of the theme parks, even during the off-season, are indispensable. If you plan to return to your hotel at midday and would like your room made up, let housekeeping know.

Build Endurance   Though most children are active, their normal play usually doesn't condition them for the exertion required to tour a Disney theme park. We recommend starting a program of family walks four to six weeks before your trip to get in shape. Aim for being able to walk at least six miles without falling apart. A Pennsylvania mom tells how she got her first grader in shape:

We had our 6-year-old begin walking with us a bit every day one month before leaving—when we arrived, her little legs could carry her, and she had a lot of stamina.

A father of two had this to say:

My wife walked with my son to school every day when it was nice. His stamina was outstanding.

Other Recommendations for Making the Dream Come True

When planning a Disney World vacation with young children, consider the following:

AGE Although the color and festivity of Disney World excite all children, and specific attractions delight toddlers and preschoolers, Disney entertainment is generally oriented to older children and adults. Children should be a fairly mature 7 years old to appreciate the Magic Kingdom and the Animal Kingdom, and a year or two older to get much out of Epcot or Disney's Hollywood Studios.

▶ **UNOFFICIAL TIP** When considering a trip to Walt Disney World, think about whether your kids are old enough to enjoy what can be a very fun, but taxing, trip.

TIME OF YEAR TO VISIT Avoid the hot, crowded summer months, especially if you have preschoolers. Go in October, November (except Thanksgiving), early December, January, February, or May. If you have children of varied ages and they're good students, take the older ones out of school and visit during the cooler, less congested off-season. Arrange special assignments relating to the educational aspects of Disney World. If your children can't afford to miss school, take your vacation as soon as the school year ends in late May or early June. Alternatively, try late August before school starts.

WHERE TO STAY The time and hassle involved in commuting to and from the theme parks will be lessened if you stay in a hotel close to the theme parks. We should point out that this doesn't necessarily mean you have to lodge at a hotel in Walt Disney World. Because Walt Disney World is so geographically dispersed, many off-property hotels are actually closer to the theme parks than some Disney resorts. Regardless of whether you stay in or out of the World, it's imperative that you take young children out of the parks each day for a few hours of rest. Neglecting to relax is the best way we know to get the whole family in a snit and ruin the day (or the vacation).

If you have young children, you must plan ahead. Make sure your hotel is within  20 minutes of the theme parks. It's true that you can revive somewhat by retreating to a Disney hotel for lunch or by finding a quiet restaurant in the theme parks, but there's no substitute for returning to the familiarity and comfort of your own hotel. Regardless of what you have heard, children too large to sleep in a stroller won't relax unless you take them back to your hotel. If it takes renting a car to make returning to your hotel practicable, rent the car.

If you are traveling with children age 12 and younger and want to stay in the World, we recommend the Polynesian, Grand Floridian, or Wilderness Lodge and Villas resorts (in that order), if they fit your budget. All three are connected to the Magic Kingdom and Epcot (with transfer) by monorail. For less expensive rooms, try the Port Orleans Resort. Bargain accommodations are available at the All-Star and

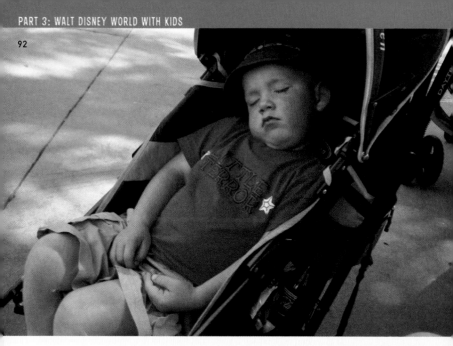

Pop Century resorts. Fully equipped log cabins at Fort Wilderness Campground are also good economy lodging.

BE IN TOUCH WITH YOUR FEELINGS When you or your children get tired and irritable, call a time-out and regroup. Trust your instincts. What would feel best? Another ride, an ice-cream break, or going back to the room for a nap? The way to protect your considerable investment in your Disney vacation is to stay happy and have a good time. You don't have to meet a quota for experiencing attractions. Do what you want.

SETTING LIMITS AND MAKING PLANS Avoid arguments and disappointment by establishing guidelines for each day, and get everybody committed. Include the following:

1. Wake-up time and breakfast plans
2. When to depart for the park
3. What to take with you
4. A policy for splitting the group or for staying together
5. What to do if the group gets separated or someone is lost
6. How long you intend to tour in the morning and what you want to see, including plans in the event an attraction is closed or too crowded
7. A policy on what you can afford for snacks
8. A time for returning to the hotel to rest
9. When you will return to the park and how late you will stay
10. Dinner plans
11. A policy for buying souvenirs, including who pays: Mom and Dad or the kids
12. Bedtimes

WHAT KIDS WANT According to research by Yesawich, Pepperdine, Brown, and Russell, the chart below shows what kids want and don't want when taking a vacation. Kids have a lot in common about what they want, less so concerning what they don't want. The "don't want" entries in the chart are the four most common responses.

WHAT DO KIDS WANT?

To go swimming/have pool time	80%
To eat in restaurants	78%
To stay at a hotel or resort	76%
To visit a theme park	76%
To stay up late	73%

WHAT DO KIDS **NOT** WANT?

To get up early	52%
To ride in a car	36%
To play golf	34%
To go to a museum	31%

BE FLEXIBLE Any day at Walt Disney World includes some surprises; be prepared to adjust your plan. Listen to your intuition.

LEAST COMMON DENOMINATORS Somebody is going to run out of steam first, and when he or she does, the whole family will be affected. Sometimes a snack break will revive the flagging member. Sometimes, however, it's better to just return to your hotel. Pushing the tired or discontented beyond their capacity will spoil the day for them—and you. Accept that energy levels vary and be prepared to respond to members of your group who poop out.

AVOID MELTDOWNS
(At least the unpleasant kind)

Deal with fatigue and behavioral problems early before they get out of hand. Both children and adults have meltdowns every day at Walt Disney World, and once you or junior launch a stem-winder, it's tough to regain your vacation equilibrium. Don't push too hard or pressure kids to ride attractions that frighten them. If you sense that your group is getting testy, stop for a break or head back to the hotel for a swim and a nap. Choose your battles wisely. Avoid arguments and confrontations over insignificant issues.

▶ UNOFFICIAL TIP Just because they're on vacation doesn't mean that you should let the kids monopolize your trip—maintain some of your everyday rules, and you'll all have a better time together.

Stop, listen (really), comfort

Freeze the action when things start to get out of hand.
Remember that your kids are tired and overstimulated.
Now's the time to be the adult; you throwing a big fat fit
will only make matters worse. Instead, try to listen, calm,
and comfort.

Good meltdowns

Sometimes a good meltdown will prevent a bad one.

Other Stuff to Think About

OVERHEATING, SUNBURN, AND DEHYDRATION These are the most common problems of younger children at Disney World. Carry and use sunscreen. Be sure to put sunscreen on children in strollers, and make sure that arms and legs are shaded by

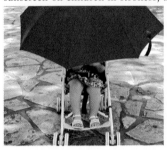

the stroller's canopy. To avoid overheating, rest regularly in the shade or in an air-conditioned restaurant or show. Plastic squeeze bottles with caps are sold in all major parks for about $3. Refill these or another type of water bottle regularly to avoid dehydration.

▶**UNOFFICIAL TIP** Teaching your kids to tell you clearly what they want or need will help make the trip more enjoyable for everyone.

▶**UNOFFICIAL TIP** We recommend renting a stroller for children age 6 and younger and carrying plastic bottles of water.

BLISTERS AND SORE FEET Guests of all ages should wear comfortable, well-broken-in shoes and a pair of socks designed specifically for hiking (we've had great success with SmartWool socks). If you or your children are susceptible to blisters, bring precut moleskin bandages, available at most drugstores. When you feel a hot spot, stop, air out your foot, and place a moleskin bandage over the area before a blister forms. Young children may not tell you about a developing blister until

it's too late, so inspect the feet of preschoolers two or more times a day. Johnson & Johnson makes bandages especially for blisters. These can be used after a blister has formed or as a substitute for moleskin when you feel a hot spot.

FIRST AID Each major theme park has a first-aid center. In the Magic Kingdom, it's at the end of Main Street to your left, between Casey's Corner and The Crystal Palace. At Epcot, it's on the World Showcase side of Odyssey Center. At Disney's Hollywood Studios, it's in the Guest Relations building inside the main entrance. At Animal Kingdom, it's in Discovery Island, on your left just before you cross the bridge to Africa. If you or your children have a medical problem, go to a first-aid center. The staff in these facilities are friendlier than the personnel in most doctor's offices and are accustomed to treating everything from paper cuts to allergic reactions.

CHILDREN ON MEDICATION Some parents of hyperactive children on medication discontinue or decrease the child's dosage at the end of the school year. If you have such a child, be aware that Disney World might overstimulate him or her. Consult your physician before altering your child's medication regimen.

SUNGLASSES If you want your younger children to wear sunglasses, put a strap or string on the frames, so the glasses will stay on during rides and can hang from the child's neck while indoors.

THINGS YOU FORGOT OR THINGS YOU RAN OUT OF Rain gear, diapers, diaper pins, formula, film, painkillers, topical sunburn treatments, and other sundries are sold at all major theme parks and at Typhoon Lagoon, Blizzard Beach, and Downtown Disney. Rain gear is a bargain, but most other items are high. Ask for goods you don't see displayed.

INFANTS AND TODDLERS AT THE THEME PARKS The major parks have centralized facilities for infant and toddler care. Everything necessary for changing diapers, preparing formulas, and warming bottles and food is available. Supplies are for sale (two diapers plus ointment are $3.50, for example), and there are rockers and special chairs for nursing mothers. At the Magic Kingdom, the Baby Center is next to The Crystal Palace at the end of Main Street. At Epcot, Baby Services is near the Odyssey Center, to the right of Test Track in Future World. At Disney's Hollywood Studios, Baby Care is in the Guest Relations building to the left of the entrance. At Animal Kingdom, Baby Changing/Nursing is in Discovery Island in the park's center. Dads are welcome at the centers and can use most services. In addition, many men's restrooms in the major parks have changing tables.

Infants and toddlers are allowed to experience any attraction that doesn't have minimum-height or age restrictions. If you think you might try nursing during a theater attraction, be advised that most shows run about 17 to 20 minutes. Exceptions are *The Hall of Presidents* at the Magic Kingdom and *The American Adventure* at Epcot, which run 23 and 29 minutes, respectively.

UNIFORMS We recommend springing for vacation uniforms. Buy for each child several sets of jeans (or shorts) and T-shirts, all matching, and all the same. For a one-week trip, for example, get each child three pairs of khaki shorts, three light-yellow T-shirts, and three pairs of SmartWool or CoolMax hiking socks. What's the point? First, you don't have to play fashion designer, coordinating a week's worth of stylish combos. Each morning the kids put on their uniform. It's simple, it saves time, and there are no decisions to make or arguments about what to wear. Second, uniforms make your children easier to spot and keep together in the theme parks. Third, the uniforms give your family, as well as the vacation itself, some added identity. We think the family on the left have incredible uniforms. Don't you agree?

LABELS A great idea, especially for younger children, is to attach labels with your family name, hometown, the name of your hotel, the dates of your stay, and your cell phone number inside their shirts.

STROLLERS

The good news is that strollers are available for a modest rental fee at all four theme parks. If you rent a stroller at the Magic Kingdom and decide to go to Epcot, the Animal Kingdom, or Disney's Hollywood Studios, turn in your Magic Kingdom stroller and present your receipt at the next park. You'll be issued another stroller without additional charge.

Both single strollers and double strollers are available. Obtain strollers at the Magic Kingdom entrance, to the left of Epcot's entrance plaza and at Epcot's International Gateway, and at Oscar's Super Service just inside the entrance of Disney's Hollywood Studios. At Animal Kingdom, strollers are located to the right just inside the entrance. Rental at all parks is fast and efficient, and returning the stroller is a breeze. You can ditch your rental stroller anywhere in the park when you're ready to leave.

When you enter a show or board a ride, you must park your stroller, usually in an open, unprotected area. If it rains before you return, you'll need a cloth, towel, or diaper to dry it. Strollers are a must for infants and toddlers, but we have observed many sharp parents renting strollers for somewhat older children (up to 6 or so years old). The stroller prevents parents from having to carry children when they sag and provides a convenient place to carry water and snacks.

If you go to your hotel for a break and intend to return to the park, leave your rental stroller by an attraction near the park entrance, marking it with something personal like a bandanna. When you return, you'll know in an instant which stroller is yours.

Be aware that rental strollers are too large for all infants and many toddlers. It's permissible to bring your own stroller. Remember, however, that only collapsible strollers are allowed on monorails, parking-lot trams, and buses.

▶ **UNOFFICIAL TIP** Orlando Stroller Rentals (☎ 800-281-0884; **www.orlandostroller rentals.com**) offers folding strollers of higher quality than Disney's all-plastic models. OSR will drop your stroller off at your hotel before you arrive and pick it up when you're done.

STROLLER WARS

Sometimes strollers disappear while you're enjoying an attraction. Disney cast members often rearrange strollers parked at the entrance to a ride or show in an effort to tidy up or clear a pedestrian path. If your stroller isn't exactly where it was left, you'll probably find it a few feet away. Sometimes, however, strollers are actually ripped off. Disney will replace a ripped-off stroller at no charge, but who wants the hassle? We recommend taking protective measures to ward off overly zealous cast members and stroller crooks. Sometimes just putting a personal item such as a bandanna on the stroller handle will suffice. Other times you might need to make a stronger statement.

How to keep your stroller from being stolen

DISNEY, KIDS, AND SCARY STUFF

Monsters and special effects at Disney's Hollywood Studios are more real and sinister than those in the other parks. If your child has difficulty coping with the witch in Snow White's Adventures, think twice about exposing him to machine-gun battles, earthquakes, and the creature from *Alien* at the Hollywood Studios. Preschoolers should start with Dumbo and work up to the Jungle Cruise in late morning, after being revved up and before getting hungry, thirsty, or tired. Pirates of the Caribbean is out for preschoolers. You get the idea.

THE FRIGHT FACTOR

While each youngster is different, following are seven attraction elements that alone or combined could push a child's buttons and indicate that a certain attraction isn't age appropriate for that child:

1. NAME OF ATTRACTION Young children will naturally be apprehensive about something called The Haunted Mansion or Tower of Terror.

2. VISUAL IMPACT OF ATTRACTION FROM OUTSIDE Splash Mountain, the Tower of Terror, and Big Thunder Mountain Railroad look scary enough to give adults second thoughts, and they terrify many young children.

3. VISUAL IMPACT OF THE INDOOR-QUEUING AREA Pirates of the Caribbean's caves and dungeons and The Haunted Mansion's "stretch rooms" can frighten children.

4. INTENSITY OF ATTRACTION Some attractions are overwhelming, inundating the senses with sights, sounds, movement, and even smell. Epcot's *Honey, I Shrunk the Audience*, for example, combines loud sounds, lasers, lights, and 3-D cinematography to create a total sensory experience. For some preschoolers, this is two or three senses too many.

© Disney

5. VISUAL IMPACT OF THE ATTRACTION Sights in various attractions range from falling boulders to lurking buzzards, from grazing dinosaurs to waltzing ghosts. What one child calmly absorbs may scare the bejeepers out of another child the same age.

6. DARK Many Disney World attractions operate indoors in the dark. For some children, this triggers fear. A child who gets frightened on one dark ride (Snow White's Scary Adventures, for example) may be unwilling to try other indoor rides.

7. THE TACTILE EXPERIENCE OF THE RIDE Some rides are wild enough to cause motion sickness, wrench backs, and discombobulate guests of any age.

As a footnote to the preceding, be aware that gaining the courage and confidence in regard to the attractions is not necessarily an upwardly linear process. A dad from Maryland explains:

> **As a 4-year-old, my daughter absolutely adored The Haunted Mansion. At 5 she was scared to death of it! At 6 she was fine again. Just because a child loves a ride at one age does not mean that he or she will love it on the next trip. The terror curve can go in either direction. (And then back again.)**

104 SMALL-CHILD FRIGHT-POTENTIAL CHART

This is a quick reference to identify attractions to be wary of, and why. The chart represents a generalization, and all kids are different. It relates specifically to kids ages 3 to 7. On average, children at the younger end of the range are more likely to be frightened than children in their sixth or seventh year.

Magic Kingdom

MAIN STREET, U.S.A.

Main Street Vehicles Not frightening in any respect.

Walt Disney World Railroad Not frightening in any respect.

ADVENTURELAND

Enchanted Tiki Room A thunderstorm, loud volume, and simulated explosions frighten some preschoolers.

Jungle Cruise Moderately intense, some macabre sights. A good test attraction for little ones.

Pirates of the Caribbean Slightly intimidating queuing area; intense boat ride with gruesome (though humorous) sights and a short, unexpected flume slide.

Magic Carpets of Aladdin Much like Dumbo. A favorite of young children.

Swiss Family Treehouse May not be suitable for kids afraid of heights.

FRONTIERLAND

Big Thunder Mountain Railroad Visually intimidating from outside, with moderately intense visual effects. Wild enough to frighten adults. Switching-off option (see p. 107).

Country Bear Jamboree Not frightening in any respect.

Frontierland Shootin' Arcade Not frightening in any respect.

Splash Mountain Visually intimidating from outside, with moderately intense visual effects. Ride is somewhat hair-raising for all ages. Switching-off option (see p. 107).

Tom Sawyer Island Some very young children are intimidated by dark tunnels that can be easily avoided.

LIBERTY SQUARE

The Hall of Presidents Not frightening, but boring for young ones.

The Haunted Mansion Name raises anxiety, as do sounds and sights of waiting area. Intense attraction with humorously presented macabre sights. Ride itself is gentle.

Liberty Belle Riverboat Not frightening in any respect.

FANTASYLAND

Cinderella's Golden Carrousel Not frightening in any respect.

Dumbo the Flying Elephant A tame midway ride; great favorite of most young children.

It's a Small World Not frightening in any respect.

Mad Tea Party Midway-type ride can induce motion sickness in all ages.

The Many Adventures of Winnie the Pooh Frightens a small percentage of preschoolers.

Peter Pan's Flight Not frightening in any respect.

Snow White's Scary Adventures Moderately intense spook-house-genre attraction with some grim characters. Absolutely terrifies many preschoolers.

MICKEY'S TOONTOWN FAIR

All attractions except roller coaster Not frightening in any respect.

Goofy's Barnstormer (children's coaster) May frighten some preschoolers.

TOMORROWLAND

Astro Orbiter Visually intimidating from the waiting area, but the ride is relatively tame.

Buzz Lightyear's Space Ranger Spin Dark ride with cartoonlike aliens may frighten some preschoolers.

Monsters, Inc. Laugh Floor May frighten a small number of preschoolers.

Space Mountain Very intense roller coaster in the dark; the Magic Kingdom's wildest ride and a scary roller coaster by any standard. Switching-off option (see p. 107).

Stitch's Great Escape! Very intense. May frighten children age 9 and younger. Switching-off option (see p. 107).

Tomorrowland Speedway Noise of waiting area slightly intimidates preschoolers; otherwise, not frightening.

Tomorrowland Transit Authority Not frightening in any respect.

Walt Disney's Carousel of Progress Not frightening in any respect.

Epcot

FUTURE WORLD

Honey, I Shrunk the Audience Extremely intense visual effects and loudness frighten many young children.

Innoventions East and West Not frightening in any respect.

Journey into Imagination with Figment Loud noises and unexpected flashing lights startle younger children.

The Land—*Circle of Life* Theater Not frightening in any respect.

The Land—Living with the Land Not frightening in any respect.

The Land—Soarin' May frighten children age 7 and younger. Really a very mellow ride.

Mission: Space Extremely intense space-simulation ride that has been known to frighten guests of all ages. Preshow may also frighten some children. Switching-off option (see p. 107).

The Seas—The Seas with Nemo & Friends Very sweet but may frighten some toddlers.

The Seas—Sea Base Alpha Exhibits Not frightening in any respect.

The Seas—*Turtle Talk with Crush* Not frightening in any respect.

Spaceship Earth Dark, imposing presentation intimidates a few preschoolers.

Test Track Intense thrill ride may frighten any age. Switching-off option (see p. 107).

Universe of Energy Dinosaur segment frightens some preschoolers; visually intense, with some intimidating effects.

WORLD SHOWCASE

The American Adventure Not frightening in any respect.

Canada—*O Canada!* Not frightening in any respect, but audience must stand.

China—*Reflections of China* Not frightening in any respect.

France—*Impressions de France* Not frightening in any respect.

Germany Not frightening in any respect.

Italy Not frightening in any respect.

Japan Not frightening in any respect.

Mexico—Gran Fiesta Tour Not frightening in any respect.

Morocco Not frightening in any respect.

Norway—Maelstrom Visually intense in parts. A few preschoolers are frightened by the 20-foot plunge at the end.

United Kingdom Not frightening in any respect.

Disney's Hollywood Studios

American Idol Experience At times, the singing may frighten anyone.

Backstage Walking Tours Not frightening in any respect.

Fantasmic! Terrifies some preschoolers.

The Great Movie Ride Intense in parts; some visually intimidating sights. Frightens many preschoolers.

Honey, I Shrunk the Kids Movie Set Adventure Not scary (though oversized).

Indiana Jones Epic Stunt Spectacular Intense show with powerful special effects, but young children generally handle it well.

Jim Henson's Muppet-Vision 3-D Intense and loud, but not frightening.

Lights! Motors! Action! Extreme Stunt Show Intense with loud noises and explosions, but not threatening in any way.

The Magic of Disney Animation Not frightening in any respect.

Playhouse Disney—Live on Stage! Not frightening in any respect.

Rock 'n' Roller Coaster The wildest coaster at Walt Disney World. May frighten guests of any age. Switching-off option (see p. 107).

Sounds Dangerous Noises in the dark scare children as old as 8.

Star Tours Extremely intense visually for all ages. Switching-off option (see p. 107).

Studios Backlot Tour Nonintimidating except for Catastrophe Canyon, where an earthquake and flash flood are simulated.

Toy Story Mania! Dark ride may frighten some preschoolers.

The Twilight Zone Tower of Terror Visually intimidating to young children; contains intense and realistic special effects. The plummeting elevator at the ride's end frightens many adults as well as kids. Switching-off option (see p. 107).

Voyage of the Little Mermaid Not frightening in any respect.

Walt Disney: One Man's Dream Not frightening in any respect.

Animal Kingdom

The Boneyard Not frightening in any respect.

Dinosaur High-tech thrill ride rattles riders of all ages. Switching-off option (see p. 107).

Expedition Everest Frightening to guests of all ages.

Festival of the Lion King Not frightening in any respect, but a bit loud.

Finding Nemo: The Musical Not frightening in any respect, but loud.

Flights of Wonder Swooping birds alarm a few small children.

It's Tough to Be a Bug! Very intense and loud with special effects that startle viewers of all ages and potentially terrify young children.

Kali River Rapids Potentially frightening and certainly wet for all ages. Switching-off option (see p. 107).

Kilimanjaro Safaris A "collapsing" bridge and proximity of real animals make a few young children anxious.

Maharaja Jungle Trek Some children may balk at the bat exhibit.

The Oasis Not frightening in any respect.

Pangani Forest Exploration Trail Not frightening in any respect.

Primeval Whirl A beginner roller coaster. Most children age 7 and older take it in stride.

Rafiki's Planet Watch Not frightening in any respect.

TriceraTop Spin A midway-type ride that will frighten only a small percentage of younger children.

Wildlife Express Train Not frightening in any respect.

If you have a plucky child who doesn't meet the minimum-height requirement for her favorite attraction, bump her up a couple of feet with a big hair-do.

SWITCHING OFF (AKA THE BABY SWAP)

Several attractions have minimum-height and/or age requirements. Some couples with children too small or too young forgo these attractions, while others take turns to ride. Missing some of Disney's best rides is an unnecessary sacrifice, and waiting in line twice for the same ride is a tremendous waste of time. Instead, take advantage of the switching-off option, also called "the baby swap."

To switch off, there must be at least two adults. Everybody waits in line together, adults and children. When you reach an attendant (called a "greeter"), let him or her know that you want to switch off. The greeter will allow everyone, including the young children, to enter the attraction. When you reach the loading area, one adult rides while the other stays with the kids. Then the riding adult disembarks and takes charge of the children while the other adult rides. A third adult in the party can ride twice, once with each of the switching-off adults, so that the switching-off adults don't have to experience the attraction alone.

Most rides with age and height minimums load and unload in the same area, facilitating switching off. An exception is Space Mountain, where the first adult at the end of the ride must also inform the unloading attendant that he or she is switching off. The attendant will admit the first adult to an internal stairway that goes back to the loading area.

THE DISNEY CHARACTERS

The large and friendly costumed versions of Mickey, Minnie, Donald, Goofy, and others—known as Disney characters—provide a link between Disney animated films and the theme parks. To people emotionally invested, the characters in Disney films are as real as next-door neighbors, never mind that they're drawings on plastic. In recent years, theme-park personifications of the characters also have become real to us. It's not a person in a mouse costume; it's Mickey himself. Similarly, meeting Goofy or Snow White is an encounter with a celebrity, a memory to be treasured.

While Disney animated-film characters number in the hundreds, only about 250 have been brought to life in costume. Of these, fewer than a fifth are "greeters" (characters who mix with patrons); the others perform in shows or parades. Originally confined to the Magic Kingdom, characters are now found in all major theme parks and Disney hotels.

Character Watching

Watching characters has become a pastime. Families once were content to meet a character occasionally. They now pursue them relentlessly, armed with autograph books and cameras. Because some characters are only rarely seen, character watching has become character collecting. (To cash in on character collecting, Disney sells autograph books throughout the World.) Mickey, Minnie, and Goofy are a snap to bag; they seem to be everywhere. But some characters, like Tinker Bell and Jiminy Cricket, seldom come out, and quite a few appear only in parades or stage shows. Other characters appear only in a location consistent with their starring role. Cinderella, predictably, reigns at Cinderella Castle in Fantasyland, while Br'er Fox and Br'er Bear frolic in Frontierland near Splash Mountain.

Preparing Your Children To Meet The Characters

Almost all characters are quite large, and several, like Br'er Bear, are huge! Small children don't expect this, and preschoolers especially can be intimidated. Discuss the characters with your children before you go.

On first encounter, don't thrust your child at the character. Allow the little one to deal with this big thing from whatever distance feels safe. If two adults are present, one should stay near the youngster while the other approaches the character and demonstrates that it's safe and friendly. Some kids warm to the characters immediately; some never do. Most take a little time and several encounters. There are two kinds of characters: furs,or those whose costumes include face-covering headpieces (including animal characters and such humanlike characters as Captain Hook), and face characters, those for whom no mask or headpiece is necessary. These include Mary Poppins, Ariel, Jasmine, Aladdin, Cinderella, Belle, Snow White, Esmeralda, and Prince Charming.

Only face characters speak. Because cast members couldn't possibly imitate the furs' distinctive cinema voices, Disney has determined that it's more effective to keep such characters silent. Lack of speech notwithstanding, headpiece characters are warm and responsive, and they communicate effectively with gestures. Tell children in advance that these characters don't talk. Some character costumes are cumbersome and give cast members very poor visibility. (Eyeholes frequently are in the mouth of the costume or even on the neck or chest.) Children who approach the character from the back or side may not be noticed, even if the child touches the character. It's possible in this situation for the character to accidentally step on the child or knock him down. A child should approach a character from the front, but occasionally not even this works. Duck characters (Donald, Daisy, Uncle Scrooge), for example, have to peer around their bills. If a character appears to be ignoring your child, pick up your child and hold her in front of the character until the character responds. It's OK for your

110

The Unofficial Guide authors go undercover to collect wait times in Adventureland.

© Jennifer Lazzaro

child to touch, pat, or hug the character. Understanding the unpredictability of children, the character will keep his feet still, particularly refraining from moving backward or sideways. Most characters will pose for pictures or sign autographs. Costumes make it difficult for characters to wield a normal pen. If your child collects autographs, carry a pen the width of a Magic Marker.

The Big Hurt

Many children expect to meet Mickey the minute they enter the park and are disappointed if they don't. If your children can't enjoy things until they see Mickey, ask a cast member where to find him.

If the cast member doesn't know, he or she can phone to find out.

▶ **UNOFFICIAL TIP** Don't underestimate your child's excitement at meeting the Disney characters—but also be aware that very small children may find the large costumed characters a little frightening.

You can see Disney characters in live shows at all the theme parks and in parades at the Magic Kingdom and Disney's Hollywood Studios. Consult your daily entertainment schedule for times. If you want to meet the characters, get autographs, and take photos, consult the park map or the handout *Times Guide* sometimes provided to supplement the park map. If there is a particular character you're itching to meet, ask any cast member to call the character hotline for you. The hotline will tell you (via the cast member) if the character is out and about, and if so, where to find it.

AT THE MAGIC KINGDOM Characters are encountered more frequently here than anywhere else in Walt Disney World. There almost always will be a character next to City Hall on Main Street and usually one or more in Town Square or near the

railroad station. Characters appear in all the lands but are generally more plentiful 111
in Fantasyland and Mickey's Toontown Fair. At Mickey's Toontown Fair, you can
meet the Big M privately in his Judge's Tent. Characters actually work shifts at the
Toontown Hall of Fame next to Mickey's Country House. Here, you can line up to
meet different assortments of characters. Each assortment has its own greeting area
and, of course, its own line. In Fantasyland, Cinderella regularly greets diners at Cinderella's Royal Table in the castle, and Ariel holds court in her own grotto. Nearby,
check out the Fantasyland Character Festival by the lagoon opposite Dumbo. Also
look for characters in the central hub, by Splash Mountain in Frontierland, and by
Walt Disney's *Carousel of Progress* in Tomorrowland.

Characters are featured in afternoon and evening parades and also play a
major role in Castle Forecourt shows (at the entrance to the castle on the central
hub side). Find performance times for shows and parades in the park's daily entertainment schedule (*Times Guide*). Sometimes characters stay to greet the audience
after shows.

▶ **UNOFFICIAL TIP** If it's rainy at the Magic Kingdom, look for characters on the
veranda of Tony's Town Square or in the Town Square Exposition Hall next to Tony's
Restaurant.

AT EPCOT Today, characters are plentiful at Epcot and usually appear in their normal garb. In Future World, one or more characters—including Mickey, Minnie,
Pluto, Goofy, and Chip 'n' Dale—can be found from opening until early evening
at the Epcot Character Spot in Innoventions West (waits of an hour or more are not
uncommon). In the World Showcase, most pavilions host a character or two. Donald
struts his stuff in Mexico, while Mulan and Mushu greet guests in China. Princess
Aurora, Belle, and the Beast hang out in France, and Snow White and Dopey are
regulars in Germany, as are Jasmine, Aladdin, and the Genie in Morocco. Pooh and
friends, Alice in Wonderland, and Mary Poppins appear in the United Kingdom, and
the Brother Bear characters lurk around Canada. In addition, character shows are
performed daily at the America Gardens Theatre in World Showcase. Check the daily
entertainment schedule (*Times Guide*) for times.

Krissy's secret? Dab on
some almond extract
perfume and act like a nut.

AT DISNEY'S HOLLYWOOD STUDIOS Characters are likely to turn up anywhere at the Studios but are most frequently found inside and outside the Animation Building, along Mickey Avenue (leading to the sound stages), at Al's Toy Barn, at Star Tours, and on the Streets of America. The main meet-and-greet area, however, is at the giant sorcerer's hat at the end of Hollywood Boulevard, where up to four characters hold court from 9 a.m. until about 1 p.m. Characters are also prominent in shows, with *Voyage of the Little Mermaid* running almost continuously and an abbreviated version of *Beauty and the Beast* performed several times daily at the Theater of the Stars. Check the daily entertainment schedule (*Times Guide*) for showtimes at Crossroads of the World.

AT ANIMAL KINGDOM Camp Minnie-Mickey in the Animal Kingdom is a special location designed specifically for meeting characters. Meet Mickey, Minnie, Goofy, and Donald on designated character-greeting trails. Elsewhere in the park, Pooh, Eeyore, Tigger, and Piglet appear at the river landing opposite Flame Tree Barbecue, and you might encounter a character or two at Rafiki's Planet Watch. Also at Camp Minnie-Mickey are two stage shows featuring characters from *The Lion King*.

▶**UNOFFICIAL TIP** To find out where any character is or will be appearing, call ☎ 407-824-2222.

Please instruct your children not to abduct the characters.

Which is the real Disney superhero?

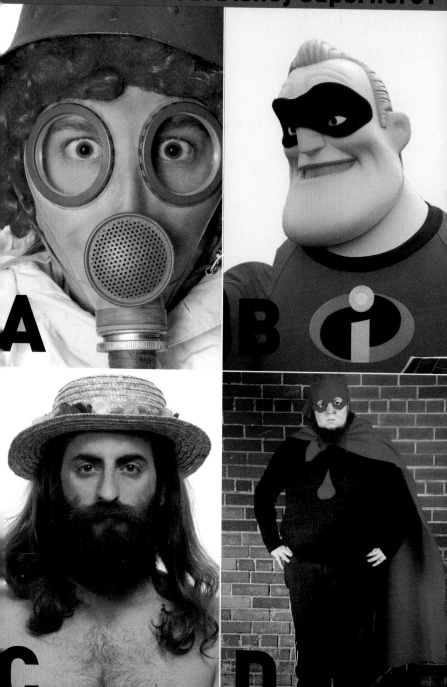

A

B

C

D

¹¹⁴ CHARACTER DINING

Fraternizing with characters has become so popular that Disney offers character breakfasts, brunches, and dinners where families can dine in the presence of Mickey, Minnie, Goofy, and other costumed versions of animated celebrities. Besides grabbing customers from Denny's and Hardee's, character meals provide a familiar, controlled setting in which young children can warm gradually to characters; several characters attend all meals. Adult prices apply to persons age 10 or older, children's prices to ages 3 to 9; little ones under age 3 eat free. For additional information on character dining, call ☎ 407-939-3463 (WDW-DINE).

Because character dining is very popular, we recommend arranging Advance Reservations as far in advance as possible by calling ☎ 407-939-3463 (WDW-DINE). The Disney dining reservations system makes Advance Reservations for character meals up to 180 days prior to the day you wish to dine. Breakfast and lunch at Cinderella's Royal Table are without a doubt the hottest ticket at Disney World. Reconfirm all character-meal Advance Reservations three weeks or so before you leave home by calling ☎ 407-WDW-DINE. Keep in mind that an Advance Reservation is not a reservation per se, only a commitment to seat you ahead of walk-in patrons at the scheduled date and time. A reserved table won't await you, but you will be seated ahead of patrons who failed to call ahead. Even with Advance Reservations, expect to wait at least 10 to 30 minutes to be seated.

How to Choose a Character Meal

We receive a lot of mail asking for advice about character meals. Some meals are better than others, sometimes much better. Here's what we look for when we evaluate character meals:

1. THE CHARACTERS The various meals offer a diverse assortment of Disney characters. Selecting a meal that features your children's special favorites is a good first step. Check the Character-meal Hit Parade chart that follows to see which characters are assigned to each meal.

2. ATTENTION FROM THE CHARACTERS In all character meals, the characters circulate among the guests hugging children, posing for pictures, and signing autographs. How much time a character spends with you and your children will depend primarily on the ratio of characters to guests. The more characters and fewer guests the better. Because many character meals never fill to capacity, the character-to-guest ratios found in our Character-meal Hit Parade chart have been adjusted to reflect an average attendance as opposed to a sell-out crowd. Even so, there's quite a range.

3. THE SETTING Some character meals are staged in exotic settings, while for others, moving the venue to

an elementary-school cafeteria would be an improvement. In our chart we rate the setting of each character meal with the familiar scale of zero to five stars. Two restaurants, Cinderella's Royal Table in the Magic Kingdom and the Garden Grill Restaurant in the Land Pavilion at Epcot, deserve special mention. Cinderella's Royal Table is situated on the first and second floors of Cinderella Castle in Fantasyland, offering guests a look at the inside of the castle. The Garden Grill is a revolving restaurant that overlooks several scenes from the Living with the Land boat-ride attraction.

© Disney

4. THE FOOD Although some food served at character meals is quite good, most is average—in other words, palatable but nothing to get excited about. In terms of variety, consistency, and quality, restaurants generally do a better job with breakfast than with lunch or dinner (if served). Some restaurants offer a buffet, while others opt for one-skillet, family-style service, in which all the hot items on the bill of fare are served from the same pot or skillet. To help you sort it out, we rate the food at each character meal in our chart using the tried-and-true five-star scale.

5. THE PROGRAM Some larger restaurants stage modest performances where the characters dance, head up a parade or conga line around the room, or lead songs and cheers. For some guests, these productions lend a celebratory air to the proceedings; for others, they turn what was already pandemonium into absolute chaos. In either event, the antics consume time that the characters could be spending with families at their table.

6. NOISE If you want to eat in peace, character meals are a bad choice. That having been said, some are much noisier than others. Once again, our chart gives you some idea of what to expect.

7. WHICH MEAL? Although character breakfasts seem to be the most popular, character lunches and dinners are usually more practical because they do not interfere with your early-morning touring. During hot weather especially, a character lunch at midday can be heavenly.

8. COST Breakfasts run $19 to $36 for adults and $15 to $23 for kids ages 3 to 9. For character lunches, expect to pay $21 to $36 for adults and $15 to $24 for kids. Dinners are $27 to $60 for adults and $18 to $26 for children. Cinderella's Royal Table may be even more. Little ones age 2 and younger eat free.

9. FRIENDS For some venues, Disney has stopped specifying the characters scheduled for a particular character meal. Instead, they tell you that it's a certain character "and friends." For example, "Pooh and friends," meaning Eeyore, Piglet, and Tigger, or some combination thereof, or "Mickey and friends" with some assortment chosen among Minnie, Goofy, Pluto, Donald, Daisy, Chip, and Dale. Most combos are pretty self-evident, but others, such as "Mary Poppins and friends," are unclear, but don't expect Dick Van Dyke.

10. THE BUM'S RUSH Most character meals are leisurely affairs, and you can usually stay as long as you want. An exception is Cinderella's Royal Table. Because Cindy's is in such high demand, the restaurant does everything short of pre-chewing your food to move you through.

CHARACTER-MEAL HIT PARADE

1. CINDERELLA'S ROYAL TABLE

LOCATION:	Magic Kingdom
MEALS SERVED:	Breakfast/Lunch/Dinner
CHARACTERS:	Cinderella, Snow White, Belle, Jasmine, Aladdin, The Fairy Godmother (dinner)
SERVED:	Daily
SETTING:	★★★★★
TYPE OF SERVICE:	Family-style at breakfast (all you care to eat); Set menu at lunch and dinner
FOOD VARIETY AND QUALITY:	★★★
NOISE LEVEL:	Quiet
CHARACTER-TO-GUEST RATIO:	1:26

2. AKERSHUS ROYAL BANQUET HALL

LOCATION:	Epcot
MEALS SERVED:	Breakfast/Lunch/Dinner
CHARACTERS:	4–6 characters chosen from Belle, Mulan, Snow White, Sleeping Beauty, Esmeralda, Mary Poppins, Jasmine, Pocahontas
SERVED:	Daily
SETTING:	★★★★
TYPE OF SERVICE:	Family-style (all you care to eat) and menu
FOOD VARIETY AND QUALITY:	★★★½
NOISE LEVEL:	Quiet
CHARACTER-TO-GUEST RATIO:	1:54

3. CHEF MICKEY'S

LOCATION:	Contemporary
MEALS SERVED:	Breakfast/Dinner
CHARACTERS:	Breakfast: Minnie, Mickey, Chip, Pluto, Goofy; Dinner: Mickey, Pluto, Chip, Dale, Goofy
SERVED:	Daily
SETTING:	★★★
TYPE OF SERVICE:	Buffet
FOOD VARIETY AND QUALITY:	★★★
NOISE LEVEL:	Loud
CHARACTER-TO-GUEST RATIO:	1:56

4. THE CRYSTAL PALACE

LOCATION:	Magic Kingdom
MEALS SERVED:	Breakfast/Lunch/Dinner
CHARACTERS:	Breakfast: Pooh, Tigger, Eeore, Piglet; Dinner: Pooh, Tigger, Eeore
SERVED:	Daily
SETTING:	★★★
TYPE OF SERVICE:	Buffet
FOOD VARIETY AND QUALITY:	★★½ (breakfast); ★★★1/2 (dinner)
NOISE LEVEL:	Very loud
CHARACTER-TO-GUEST RATIO:	1:67 (breakfast); 1:89 (dinner)

5. 1900 PARK FARE

LOCATION:	Grand Floridian
MEALS SERVED:	Breakfast/Dinner
CHARACTERS:	Breakfast: Mary Poppins, Alice In Wonderland, The Mad Hatter, and Friends; Dinner: Cinderella, Prince Charming, and Friends
SERVED:	Daily
SETTING:	★★★
TYPE OF SERVICE:	Buffet
FOOD VARIETY AND QUALITY:	★★★
NOISE LEVEL:	Moderate
CHARACTER-TO-GUEST RATIO:	1:54 (breakfast); 1:44 (dinner)

6. THE GARDEN GRILL RESTAURANT

LOCATION:	Epcot
MEALS SERVED:	Lunch/Dinner
CHARACTERS:	Chip 'n' Dale
SERVED:	Daily
SETTING:	★★★★½
TYPE OF SERVICE:	Family-style (all you care to eat)
FOOD VARIETY AND QUALITY:	★★½
NOISE LEVEL:	Very quiet
CHARACTER-TO-GUEST RATIO:	1:46

7. RESTAURANTOSAURUS

LOCATION:	Animal Kingdom
MEALS SERVED:	Breakfast
CHARACTERS:	Mickey, Donald, Pluto, Goofy
SERVED:	Daily
SETTING:	★★★
TYPE OF SERVICE:	Buffet
FOOD VARIETY AND QUALITY:	★★★
NOISE LEVEL:	Very loud
CHARACTER-TO-GUEST RATIO:	1:112

8. CAPE MAY CAFE

LOCATION:	Beach Club
MEALS SERVED:	Breakfast
CHARACTERS:	Goofy, Pluto, Minnie, Donald
SERVED:	Daily
SETTING:	★★★
TYPE OF SERVICE:	Buffet (all you care to eat)
FOOD VARIETY AND QUALITY:	★★½
NOISE LEVEL:	Moderate
CHARACTER-TO-GUEST RATIO:	1:67

9. 'OHANA

LOCATION:	Polynesian Resort
MEALS SERVED:	Breakfast
CHARACTERS:	Mickey, Pluto, Lilo, Stitch
SERVED:	Daily
SETTING:	★★
TYPE OF SERVICE:	Family-style
FOOD VARIETY AND QUALITY:	★★½
NOISE LEVEL:	Moderate
CHARACTER-TO-GUEST RATIO:	1:57

10. HOLLYWOOD & VINE

LOCATION:	Disney's Hollywood Studios
MEALS SERVED:	Breakfast/Lunch
CHARACTERS:	Jojo, Goliath, June, Leo
SERVED:	Daily
SETTING:	★★½
TYPE OF SERVICE:	Buffet
FOOD VARIETY AND QUALITY:	★★★
NOISE LEVEL:	Moderate
CHARACTER-TO-GUEST RATIO:	1:71

11. GARDEN GROVE

LOCATION:	Swan
MEALS SERVED:	Breakfast/Dinner
CHARACTERS:	Breakfast: Goofy and Pluto; Dinner: Goofy and Pluto or Rafiki and Timon
SERVED:	Saturday And Sunday (breakfast); daily (dinner)
SETTING:	★★★
TYPE OF SERVICE:	Buffet/Menu
FOOD VARIETY AND QUALITY:	★★★½
NOISE LEVEL:	Moderate
CHARACTER-TO-GUEST RATIO:	1:198

BABYSITTING

CHILD-CARE CENTERS Child care isn't available inside the theme parks, but three Magic Kingdom resorts connected by monorail or boat (Polynesian, Grand Floridian, and Wilderness Lodge and Villas), four Epcot resorts (the Yacht Club and Beach Club resorts, the Swan, and the Dolphin), and Animal Kingdom Lodge, along with the Hilton at Walt Disney World, have child-care centers for potty-trained children older than age 3. Services vary, but children generally can be left between 4:30 p.m. and midnight. Milk and cookies and blankets and pillows are provided at all centers, and dinner is provided at most. Play is supervised but not organized, and toys, videos, and games are plentiful. Guests at any Disney resort or campground may use the services.

The most elaborate of the child-care centers (variously called "clubs" or "camps") is Never Land Club at the Polynesian Resort. The rate for children ages 4 to 12 is $11 per hour, per child. All the clubs accept reservations (some six months in advance!) with a credit-card guarantee. Call the club directly, or reserve through Disney central reservations at ☎ 407-WDW-DINE. Most clubs require a 24-hour cancellation notice and levy a hefty penalty of two hours' time or $22 per call for no-shows. A limited number of walk-ins are usually accepted on a first-come, first-served basis.

IN-ROOM BABYSITTING There are three companies that provide in-room sitting in Walt Disney World and surrounding tourist areas, including the International Drive–Orange County Convention Center area, the Universal-Orlando area, and the Lake Buena Vista area. They are **Kid's Nite Out** (☎ 407-828-0920; **kidsniteout.com**), **All About Kids** (☎ 407-812-9300; **all-about-kids.com**), and **Fairy Godmothers** (☎ 407-277-3724 or 407-275-7326). Kid's Nite Out also serves hotels in the greater Orlando area, including downtown. All three provide sitters older than 18 years of age who are insured, bonded, and trained in CPR. Some sitters have more advanced medical/first-aid training and/or education credentials. All sitters are screened, reference-checked, and police-checked. In addition to caring for your children in your guest room, the sitters will, if you direct (and pay), take your children to the theme parks or other venues of your choice. Many of the sitters arrive loaded with reading books, coloring books, and games. All three services offer bilingual sitters.

Warning: This is not a Disney character. If you grab her limbs, pull at her clothes, or hug her without permission, she will put you in time-out.

Time-out is 20 minutes. Guilt is forever.

PART 4

DINING IN WALT DISNEY WORLD

DISNEY DINING 101

ADVANCE RESERVATIONS When you call Advance Reservations, your name and essential information are taken as if you were making an honest to goodness reservation. The Disney representative then says you have Advance Reservations for your restaurant of choice on the date and time you've requested and usually explains that this means you will be seated ahead of walk-ins—that is, those without Advance Reservations. Advance Reservations are recommended for all full-service restaurants except those in the Downtown Disney Resort Area, which are operated independently of the Walt Disney Company. Advance Reservations are required for character buffets and recommended for all other buffets and family-style restaurants. The restaurants accept American Express, Diners Club, Japan Credit Bureau, MasterCard, and Visa, among others.

DRESS Dress is informal at most theme-park restaurants, but a business-casual dress code applies at Disney's Signature (read: upscale) restaurants, which means khakis, dress slacks, jeans, or dress shorts with a collared shirt for men and jeans, dresses, skirts, or dress shorts with a blouse or sweater for women. A full listing of the Signature restaurants is available at the Walt Disney World Web site (go to **tinyurl.com/signaturedining**).

▶**UNOFFICIAL TIP** The only restaurant that requires jackets for men and dressy clothes for women is Victoria & Albert's at the Grand Floridian Resort.

SMOKING Walt Disney World restaurants adopted a nonsmoking policy several years ago, after Florida voters passed an amendment to the state's constitution that prohibits smoking in restaurant lounges. (Freestanding bars—those that get less than 10% of their revenues from food sales—are exempt from the ban.)

Where to park your butts. Barstools at the Rainforest Cafe at Downtown Disney Marketplace.

122

WALT DISNEY WORLD RESTAURANT CATEGORIES

In general, food and beverage offerings at Walt Disney World are defined by service, price, and convenience:

FULL-SERVICE RESTAURANTS Full-service restaurants are in all Disney resorts (except the All-Star complex, Port Orleans French Quarter, and Pop Century) and all major theme parks, Downtown Disney Marketplace, and Disney's West Side.

Catch a flick at the Sci-Fi Dine-In Theater at Disney's Hollywood Studios' Backlot.

BUFFETS AND FAMILY-STYLE RES-TAURANTS Many buffets have Disney characters in attendance, and most have a separate children's menu featuring hot dogs, burgers, chicken nuggets, pizza, macaroni and cheese, and spaghetti and meatballs. In addition to the buffets, several restaurants serve a family-style, all-you-can-eat, fixed-price meal.

If you want to eat a lot but don't feel like standing in yet another line, consider one of the all-you-can-eat family-style restaurants. These feature platters of food brought to your table in courses by a server. You can sample everything on the menu and eat as much as you like. You can even go back to a favorite appetizer after you finish the main course.

Where the Jurassic set come to eat and be eaten: T-REX at Downtown Disney Marketplace.

FOOD COURTS Featuring a collection of counter-service eateries under one roof,

© Disney

Coral Reef at The Seas in Epcot.

food courts can be found at all Disney theme parks and at the moderate (Coronado Springs, Caribbean Beach, and Port Orleans) and value (All-Star and Pop Century) Disney resorts.

COUNTER SERVICE Counter-service fast food is available in all theme parks and at Downtown Disney Marketplace, Pleasure Island, Disney's BoardWalk, and Disney's West Side. The food compares in quality to McDonald's, Captain D's, or Taco Bell but is more expensive, though it's often served in larger portions.

FAST CASUAL Somewhere between burgers and formal dining are the establishments in Disney's "fast-casual" category. Initially launched with three restaurants (the Tomorrowland Terrace Noodle Station in the Magic Kingdom, Sunshine Seasons Food Fair in Epcot, and Backlot Express at Disney's Hollywood Studios), fast-casual restaurants feature menu choices that are a cut above what you'd normally see at a typical counter-service location. The three initial locations all feature Asian or Mediterranean cuisine, something previously lacking inside the parks. Entrees cost about $2 more on average than traditional counter-service options, but the variety and quality make them worth the price.

VENDOR FOOD Vendors abound at the theme parks, Downtown Disney Marketplace, Disney's West Side, and Disney's BoardWalk. Offerings include popcorn, ice-cream bars, churros (Mexican pastries), soft drinks, bottled water, and (in theme parks) fresh fruit. Prices include tax, and payment must be in cash.

Sunshine Seasons Food Fair at The Land in Epcot.

124 MAGIC YOUR WAY DINING PLANS

Disney offers dining plans to accompany its Magic Your Way ticket system. They're available to all Disney-resort guests except those staying at the Swan, the Dolphin, the hotels of the Downtown Disney Resort Area, and Shades of Green, none of which are Disney-owned or -operated. Guests must also purchase a Magic Your Way package, have Annual Passes, or be members of the Disney Vacation Club (DVC) to participate in the plan. Except for DVC members, a three-night minimum stay is typically also required. Overall cost is determined by the number of nights you stay at a Disney resort.

Magic Your Way Plus Dining Plan This dining plan provides, for each member of your group, for each night of your stay, one counter-service meal, one full-service meal, and one snack at participating Disney dining locations and restaurants, including room service at some Disney resorts (type "Disney dining plan locations 2010" into your favorite Internet search engine to find sites with the entire list). For guests age 10 and up, the price (which varies seasonally) is $42 to $47 per night; for guests ages 3 to 9, the price is $12 to $13 per night, tax included. Children younger than age 3 eat free from an adult's plate.

The counter-service meal includes a main course (sandwich, dinner salad, pizza, or the like), dessert, and nonalcoholic drink, or a complete combo meal (a main course and a side dish—think burger and fries), dessert, and nonalcoholic drink, including tax. The full-service sit-down meal includes a main course, dessert, a nonalcoholic drink, and tax. If you're dining at a buffet, the full-service meal includes the buffet, a nonalcoholic drink, and tax. The snack includes items normally sold from carts or small stands throughout the parks and resorts: ice cream, popcorn, soft drinks, fruit, chips, apple juice, and the like.

For instance, if you're staying for three nights, each member of your party will be credited with three counter-service meals, three full-service meals, and three snacks. All those meals will be put into an individual meal account for each person in your group. Meals in your account can be used on any combination of days, so you're not required to eat every meal every day. Thus, you can skip a full-service meal one day and have two on another day.

Disney's top-of-the-line restaurants (dubbed Disney Signature restaurants in the plan), along with all the dinner shows, count as two full-service meals. If you dine at one of these locations, two full-service meals will be deducted from your account for each person dining.

In addition to the preceding, the dining plan comes with several other important rules:

- Everyone staying in the same resort room must participate in the plan.
- Children ages 3 to 9 must order from the kids' menu, if one is available. This rule is occasionally not enforced at Disney's counter-service restaurants, enabling older children to order from the regular (adult) menu.
- In-room minibars and refillable mugs are not included in the plan.
- A full-service meal can be breakfast, lunch, or dinner. The greatest savings occur when you use your full-service meal allocations for dinner.
- The meal plan expires at midnight on the day you check out of the Disney resort. Unused meals are nonrefundable.
- The dining plan is occasionally unavailable when using certain room-only discounts.

Quick Service Dining Plan This plan includes meals, snacks, and nonalcoholic drinks at most counter-service eateries in Walt Disney World. The cost is $32 per day for guests age 10 and up, $10 per day for kids ages 3 to 9. The plan includes two counter-service meals and two snacks per day, plus one refillable drink mug per person, per package (eligible for refills only at counter-service locations only in your Disney resort), and 30 minutes of play at a Disney-resort arcade. The economics of the plan are difficult to justify unless you're drinking gallons of soda or coffee to offset Disney's inflated prices.

Magic Your Way Deluxe Dining Plan This dining option offers a choice of full-service or counter-service meals for three meals a day at any participating restaurant. In addition to the three meals a day, the plan also includes two snacks per day and a refillable drink mug. The Deluxe Plan costs $72 for adults and $21 for children for each night of your stay.

In addition to food, all plans include deal sweeteners such as a free round of miniature golf, a certificate for a five- by ten-inch print from Disney's PhotoPass, a sort of two-for-one certificate for the use of Sea Raycers watercraft, a commemorative luggage tag, and such.

Disney ceaselessly tinkers with the dining plans' rules, meal definitions, and participating restaurants. For example, it's possible (though not documented) to exchange a sit-down-meal credit for a counter-service meal, although doing this even once can negate any savings you get from using a plan in the first place.

Things to Consider When Evaluating the Plus Dining Plan

If you prefer to always eat at counter-service restaurants, you'll be better off with the Quick Service plan. Other poor candidates for the Plus Plan include finicky eaters, light eaters, families who can't agree on restaurants, and those who can't get reservations at their first- or second-choice sit-down restaurants.

Our research indicates that the plan saves the typical family around $1 per person per day, assuming the family uses every meal credit. But skipping a single full-service meal during a visit of five or fewer days can mean the difference between saving and losing money. In our experience, having a scheduled sit-down meal for every day of a weeklong vacation can be mentally exhausting, especially for kids and teens. One option might be to schedule a meal at a Disney Signature restaurant, which requires two full-service credits, and have no scheduled sit-down meal on another night.

Book your restaurants as soon as possible. Then decide whether the dining plan makes economic sense.

For an in-depth discussion of the various plans, including number crunching (and even algebra!), visit **TouringPlans.com** (click "Dining" on the home page, then "Disney Dining Plan").

Pesky Technicalities and Administrative Problems

Readers report experiencing a host of problems with both understanding and using the Disney Dining Plan. Confused guests lead to longer lines at some counter-service locations. Some servers may not know what is included as a snack or what composes a meal, leading to frustration. The menu choices for kids age 9 and under are very limited but often include mac and cheese and chicken nuggets. Substitution is often not an option.

Readers also report difficulties in keeping their accounts straight. Check receipts after every purchase to make sure your credits are deducted correctly.

A mom from Radford, Virginia, suggests eating a late lunch instead of dinner because the amount of food served is the same. She also recommends using the snacks as breakfast once in the parks.

▶ **UNOFFICIAL TIP** If you're interested in trying a theme-park full-service restaurant, be aware that the restaurants continue to serve after the park's official closing time. Incidentally, don't worry if you're depending on Disney transportation: Buses, boats, and monorails run two to three hours after the parks close.

GETTING A LEG UP AT WALT DISNEY WORLD

Fast food in the theme parks covers all the major food groups: cow, pig, turkey, and pizza. Vendors —offering such delights as fresh fruit, popcorn, ice cream, churros, giant smoked turkey legs (you can hardly taste the steroids), and our personal favorite, sticky beavers—abound at the parks. Of the vendor specialties, the smoked turkey legs are the most popular. At any time of day you can enjoy neo-Neanderthals lustily gnawing away on Butterball femurs. The legs are tasty, filling, and affordable. Did we mention messy? No? Well, these big boys are juicy to the max. When you bury your face in one expect to come up dripping. Though prodigious numbers of legs are consumed daily, demand reaches its zenith on the Fourth of July. While normal Americans are eating pig, guzzling beer, and playing with gunpowder, Disney theme-park guests are getting down with turkey legs. If you want to partake in this ritual, we recommend a bib and a pocketful of moist towelettes.

Orlando Convention & Visitors Bureau (right)

¹²⁸ ETHNIC DINING AT WALT DISNEY WORLD

One of the best things about a Walt Disney World vacation is the opportunity to try exotic ethnic foods from around the world (the *real* world!). From Chinese braised chicken lips (Moo Goo Gai Pucker) to deep-fried cod buttocks (Deep-Fried Cod Buttocks) to the fabled gaucho treat of cow meat with hide on (Woolly Bully), a veritable feast awaits you at breathtakingly exorbitant prices. If you're not familiar with some of the menu items, so what? Try them anyway—what's the worst that can happen? Here we've pictured authentic spaghetti carbonara from a recipe created in the little Italian village of Annerire il Polmone.

There are many different kinds of brats in Germany. Be careful which one you wish for.

Bratwurst

Brat Worst

WALT DISNEY WORLD RESTAURANTS: RATED AND RANKED

OVERALL RATING The overall rating represents the entire dining experience: style, service, and ambience, in addition to taste, presentation, and quality of food. Five stars is the highest rating and indicates that the restaurant offers the best of everything. Four-star restaurants are above average, and three-star restaurants offer good, though not necessarily memorable, meals. Two-star restaurants serve mediocre fare, and one-star restaurants are below average. Our star ratings don't correspond to ratings awarded by AAA, Mobil, Zagat, or other restaurant reviewers.

COST The next rating tells how much a complete meal will cost. The cost quoted includes a main dish with vegetable or side dish, and a choice of soup or salad. Appetizers, desserts, drinks, and tips aren't included. We've rated the cost as inexpensive, moderate, or expensive.

Inexpensive	**$15 or less per person**
Moderate person *(Yeah, we know. Since when is $28 a head "moderate"? Welcome to Walt Disney World.)*	**$15–$28 per**
Expensive	**More than $28 per person**

QUALITY RATING The food quality is rated on a scale of one to five stars, five being the best rating attainable. The quality rating is based expressly on the taste, freshness of ingredients, preparation, presentation, and creativity of food served. There is no consideration of price in this rating.

VALUE RATING If, on the other hand, you are looking for both quality and value, then you should check the value rating, expressed as stars.

★★★★★ Exceptional value, a real bargain
★★★★ Good value
★★★ Fair value, you get exactly what you pay for
★★ Somewhat overpriced
★ Significantly overpriced

READERS' RESTAURANT-SURVEY RESPONSES For each Disney World restaurant profiled, we include the results of last year's reader-survey responses. Results are expressed as a percentage of responding readers who liked the restaurant well enough to eat there again (thumbs up 👍), as opposed to the percentage of responding readers who had a bad experience and wouldn't go back (thumbs down 👎).

CUISINE	LOCATION	OVERALL RATING
AFRICAN		
Jiko	Animal Kingdom Lodge	★★★★ ½
Boma	Animal Kingdom Lodge	★★★★
Tusker House	Animal Kingdom	★½
AMERICAN		
California Grill	Contemporary	★★★★½
The Hollywood Brown Derby	DHS	★★★★
Artist Point	Wilderness Lodge	★★★½
Cape May Cafe	Beach Club	★★★½
Captain's Grille	Yacht Club	★★★
Cinderella's Royal Table	Magic Kingdom	★★★
The Crystal Palace	Magic Kingdom	★★★
50's Prime Time Cafe	DHS	★★★
The Garden Grill	Epcot	★★★
House of Blues	West Side	★★★
Liberty Tree Tavern	Magic Kingdom	★★★
Trail's End	Fort Wilderness Resort	★★★
T-REX	Downtown Disney	★★★
The Wave	Contemporary	★★★
Whispering Canyon Cafe	Wilderness Lodge	★★★
Boatwrights	Port Orleans	★★½
Chef Mickey's	Contemporary	★★½
ESPN Club	BoardWalk	★★½
Hollywood & Vine	DHS	★★½
1900 Park Fare	Grand Floridian	★★½
Rainforest Cafe	Downtown Disney and Animal Kingdom	★★½
Big River Grille	BoardWalk	★★
Olivia's Cafe	Old Key West	★★
Plaza Restaurant	Magic Kingdom	★★
Sci-Fi Dine-In	DHS	★★
Turf Club Bar & Grill	Saratoga Springs	★★
Wolfgang Puck Cafe	West Side	★★
Tusker House	Animal Kingdom	★½
BUFFET		
Boma	Animal Kingdom Lodge	★★★★
Akershus	Epcot	★★★½
Biergarten	Epcot	★★★½
Cape May Cafe	Beach Club	★★★½
The Crystal Palace	Magic Kingdom	★★★
Trail's End	Fort Wilderness Resort	★★★
Chef Mickey's	Contemporary	★★½
Hollywood & Vine	DHS	★★½
1900 Park Fare	Grand Floridian	★★½
Tusker House	Animal Kingdom	★½
CHINESE		
Nine Dragons	Epcot	★★★
ENGLISH		
Rose & Crown	Epcot	★★★
FRENCH		
Bistro de Paris	Epcot	★★★
Les Chefs de France	Epcot	★★★

CUISINE	LOCATION	OVERALL RATING
GERMAN		
Biergarten	Epcot	★★★½
GOURMET		
Victoria & Albert's	Grand Floridian	★★★★
INDIAN/AFRICAN		
Sanaa	Animal Kingdom Lodge	★★★★
IRISH		
Raglan Road Irish Pub	Downtown Disney	★★★★
ITALIAN		
Il Mulino	Swan	★★★
Portobello	Downtown Disney	★★★
Mama Melrose's	DHS	★★½
Tony's Town Square Restaurant	Magic Kingdom	★★½
Tutto Italia	Epcot	★★½
JAPANESE		
Kimonos	Swan	★★★★
Teppan Edo	Epcot	★★★½
Tokyo Dining	Epcot	★★★
MEDITERRANEAN		
Cítricos	Grand Floridian	★★★½
MEXICAN		
San Angel Inn	Epcot	★★★
MOROCCAN		
Restaurant Marrakesh	Epcot	★★
NORWEGIAN		
Akershus	Epcot	★★★½
POLYNESIAN/PAN-ASIAN		
'Ohana	Polynesian	★★★
Kona Cafe	Polynesian	★★★
Yak & Yeti	Animal Kingdom	★★★
SEAFOOD		
Flying Fish Cafe	BoardWalk	★★★★
Artist Point	Wilderness Lodge	★★★½
Narcoossee's	Grand Floridian	★★★½
bluezoo	Dolphin	★★★
Cap'n Jack's	Downtown Disney	★★½
Coral Reef	Epcot	★★½
Fulton's Crab House	Downtown Disney	★★½
Shutters	Caribbean Beach	★★
STEAK		
Shula's Steak House	Dolphin	★★★★
Le Cellier Steakhouse	Epcot	★★★½
Yachtsman Steakhouse	Yacht Club	★★★
Shutters	Caribbean Beach	★★

132 FULL-SERVICE RESTAURANT PROFILES

Akershus Royal Banquet Hall ★★★½

NORWEGIAN/BUFFET   EXPENSIVE   QUALITY ★★★   VALUE ★★★
READER-SURVEY RESPONSES 81% 👍 19% 👎   DISNEY DINING PLAN Yes

Norway, World Showcase, Epcot; 407-939-3463
Reservations Required; credit card required to reserve at breakfast and lunch. **Dining Plan credits** 1 per person, per meal. **When to go** Anytime. **Cost range** Breakfast $29 (child $18), lunch $31 (child $19), dinner $36 (child $20). **Service** ★★★★. **Character breakfast** 8:30–10:30 a.m. **Character lunch** Daily, 11:20 a.m.–2:55 p.m. **Character dinner** Daily, 4:20–8:30 p.m.
Home to Princess Storybook Meals for breakfast, lunch, and dinner—the characters are the focus rather than the food. Modeled on a 14th-century fortress, Akershus offers all-you-can-eat *koldtbord* (cold buffet), braised pork shank, mustard-glazed salmon, and traditional *kjott-kake* (ground-beef-and-lamb patty).

Artist Point ★★★½

AMERICAN   EXPENSIVE   QUALITY ★★★★   VALUE ★★★
READER-SURVEY RESPONSES 88% 👍 12% 👎   DISNEY DINING PLAN Yes

Wilderness Lodge and Villas; 407-824-3200
Reservations Recommended. **Dining Plan credits** 2 per person, per meal. **When to go** Anytime. **Cost range** $20–$43 (child $6–$11). **Service** ★★★★. **Dinner** Daily, 5:30–9:30 p.m.
Enjoy roasted cedar-plank salmon, buffalo short rib, braised Penn Cove mussels, smoky Portobello soup, or berry cobbler in the cavernous Pacific Northwest–decorated dining room with a view of wildflowers, the lake, a waterfall, and even an erupting geyser.

Biergarten ★★★½

GERMAN   EXPENSIVE   QUALITY ★★★   VALUE ★★★★
READER-SURVEY RESPONSES 89% 👍 11% 👎   DISNEY DINING PLAN Yes

Germany, World Showcase, Epcot; 407-939-3463
Reservations Recommended. **Dining Plan credits** 1 per person, per meal. **When to go** Lunch or dinner. **Cost range** Lunch $20 (child $11), dinner $29 (child $14). **Service** ★★★★.
Lunch Daily, noon–3:45 p.m. **Dinner** Daily, 4 p.m.–park closing.
Graze at a hefty German buffet that includes schnitzel, a variety of wursts, spaetzle, roast chicken, and sauerbraten (dinner only). You'll be seated with other guests, but the lively 25-minute dinner show (one every hour) and noisy dining room are part of the fun.

Big River Grille & Brewing Works ★★

AMERICAN   MODERATE   QUALITY ★★   VALUE ★★
READER-SURVEY RESPONSES 64% 👍 36% 👎   DISNEY DINING PLAN Yes

Disney's BoardWalk; 407-560-0253
Reservations Not accepted. **Dining Plan credits** 1 per person, per meal. **When to go** Anytime. **Cost range** $15–$29 (child $5). **Service** ★★★. **Lunch and dinner** Daily, 11:30 a.m.–11 p.m.
This is the place for handcrafted beers. A good choice for late-night diners, it serves hazelnut-crusted mahimahi and flame-grilled meat loaf with gravy. Outside seating, weather permitting.

Bistro de Paris ★★★

FRENCH   EXPENSIVE   QUALITY ★★★½   VALUE ★★
READER-SURVEY RESPONSES 77% 👍 23% 👎   DISNEY DINING PLAN Yes

France, World Showcase, Epcot; 407-939-3463
Reservations Recommended. **Dining Plan credits** 1 per person, per meal. **When to go** Late dinner. **Cost range** $32–$43. **Service** ★★★★. **Dinner** Daily, 5:30–8:30 p.m.
For a quiet dinner and conversation, this is the spot. Request a table at the windows to view World Showcase Lagoon. Start with a mussel-and-saffron soup with aioli toast and end with the crème brûlée—try Maine lobster, beef tenderloin, or rack of lamb for your entree.

bluezoo ★★★

SEAFOOD   EXPENSIVE   QUALITY ★★★   VALUE ★★
READER-SURVEY RESPONSES 50% 👍 50% 👎   DISNEY DINING PLAN No

Walt Disney World Dolphin; 407-934-1111

Reservations Required. **When to go** Anytime. **Cost range** $28–$60 (child $10–$16). **Service** ★★★★. **Dinner** Daily, 5–11 p.m.
In a dreamy setting designed by noted architect Jeffrey Beers, the menu features sashimi-grade tuna steak and tenderloin of beef filet, but you can make a meal of the simple bowl of clam chowder with salt-cured bacon and the roasted-beet salad with greens, goat cheese, and candied walnuts.

Boatwrights Dining Hall ★★½

AMERICAN/CAJUN   MODERATE   QUALITY ★★★   VALUE ★★
READER-SURVEY RESPONSES 74% 👍 26% 👎   DISNEY DINING PLAN Yes

Port Orleans Resort Riverside; 407-939-3463
Reservations Recommended for dinner. **Dining Plan credits** 1 per person, per meal. **When to go** Early evening. **Cost range** Dinner $16.50–$27 (child $7.50). **Service** ★★★. **Dinner** Daily, 5–10 p.m.
Diners sit in a large, noisy room beneath a riverboat under construction. The basic fare with a Cajun flair is pretty homogenized. The only table-service restaurant in the Port Orleans Resort, it gets busy and there can be waits. Try the jambalaya with chicken and andouille sausage.

Boma ★★★★

AFRICAN   EXPENSIVE   QUALITY ★★★★   VALUE ★★★★½
READER-SURVEY RESPONSES 91% 👍 9% 👎   DISNEY DINING PLAN Yes

Animal Kingdom Lodge; 407-938-3000
Reservations Mandatory. **Dining Plan credits** 1 per person, per meal. **When to go** Anytime. **Cost range** Breakfast $17 (child $10), dinner $31 (child $15). **Service** ★★★★. **Breakfast** Daily, 7:30–11 a.m. **Dinner** Daily, 4:30–10 p.m.
A number of food stations encourage diners to roam about and graze on the watermelon-rind salad, Moroccan seafood salad, roasted meats, Durban spiced roasted chicken, or vegetable skewers.

California Grill ★★★★½

AMERICAN   EXPENSIVE   QUALITY ★★★★½   VALUE ★★★
READER-SURVEY RESPONSES 92% 👍 8% 👎   DISNEY DINING PLAN Yes

Contemporary Resort; 407-939-3463
Reservations Recommended. **Dining Plan credits** 2 per person, per meal. **When to go** During evening fireworks. **Cost range** $22–$44 (child $7–$11). **Service** ★★★★★. **Dinner** Daily, 5:30–10 p.m. **Lounge** Daily, 5 p.m.–10 p.m.
The award-winning California Grill, on the 15ᵗʰ floor, offers one of the best spots for watching the Magic Kingdom fireworks. Try the sushi, oven-fired flatbreads, or grilled pork tenderloin with creamy polenta and Zinfandel glaze. Noise levels make conversation nearly impossible.

© Disney

Cape May Cafe ★★★½

AMERICAN/BUFFET   MODERATE   QUALITY ★★★½   VALUE ★★★★
READER-SURVEY RESPONSES 88% 👍 12% 👎   DISNEY DINING PLAN Yes

Beach Club Resort; 407-934-3358
Reservations Recommended. **Dining Plan credits** 1 per person, per meal. **When to go** Anytime. **Cost range** Breakfast $19 (child $11), dinner $27 (child $13). **Service** ★★★★★. **Breakfast** Daily, 7:30–11 a.m. **Dinner** Daily, 5:30–9:30 p.m.
The buffet features peel-and-eat shrimp, tasty (albeit chewy) clams, mussels, fish of the day, hand-carved prime rib, barbecued ribs, corn on the cob, Caesar salad, and a good dessert bar. The kids' bar includes chicken fingers, hot dogs, fried fish, and mac and cheese. Character breakfast with Goofy, Minnie, and Chip 'n' Dale. It's a convenient place to dine before *IllumiNations*.

134 Cap'n Jack's Restaurant ★★½

SEAFOOD MODERATE QUALITY ★★ VALUE ★★
READER-SURVEY RESPONSES 51% 👍 49% 👎 DISNEY DINING PLAN No

Downtown Disney Marketplace; 407-828-3971
Reservations Not required. **When to go** Anytime. **Cost range** Lunch $10–$19 (child $7.60), dinner $15–$24 (child $7.60). **Service ★★★★★. Lunch and dinner** Daily, 11:30 a.m.–10:30 p.m.
A pier house on the edge of Buena Vista Lagoon that serves clam chowder, crab cakes, baked salmon, and shrimp pasta. For landlubbers, there's roast chicken and beef pot roast. The lagoonside setting offers views of amateur boaters, and the sunsets are pretty here.

Captain's Grille ★★★

AMERICAN MODERATE QUALITY ★★★½ VALUE ★★★
READER-SURVEY RESPONSES 89% 👍 11% 👎 DISNEY DINING PLAN Yes

Yacht Club Resort; 407-939-3463
Reservations Not necessary. **Dining Plan credits** 1 per person, per meal. **When to go** Breakfast or lunch. **Cost range** Breakfast buffet $16 (child $9), lunch $10–$18 (child $7.50), dinner $15–$28. **Service ★★★★★. Breakfast** Daily, 7–11 a.m. **Lunch** Daily, 11:30 a.m.–2 p.m. **Dinner** Daily, 5:30–9:30 p.m.
This large, somewhat noisy dining room features a bright nautical theme. Breakfast features a buffet or an à la carte menu, with such selections as crab-cake Benedict. Lunch includes grilled-chicken and roast-turkey sandwiches. Dinner has prime rib, fish of the day, and roast chicken.

Le Cellier Steakhouse ★★★½

STEAK EXPENSIVE QUALITY ★★★½ VALUE ★★★
READER-SURVEY RESPONSES 88% 👍 12% 👎 DISNEY DINING PLAN Yes

Canada, World Showcase, Epcot; 407-939-3463
Reservations Recommended. **Dining Plan credits** 1 per person, per meal. **When to go** Before 6 p.m. **Cost range** Lunch $12.50–$30, dinner $22–$35 (child $7.50). **Service ★★★★. Lunch** Daily, 11:30 a.m.–3 p.m. **Dinner** Daily, 4–8:50 p.m.
With a wine cellar setting, Le Cellier specializes in Canadian Cheddar cheese soup, steaks, and seared King salmon. Le Cellier is Epcot's most popular restaurant. Make Advance Reservations as far ahead as possible.

Chef Mickey's ★★½

AMERICAN/BUFFET EXPENSIVE QUALITY ★★★ VALUE ★★★
READER-SURVEY RESPONSES 87% 👍 13% 👎 DISNEY DINING PLAN Yes

Contemporary Resort; 407-939-3463
Reservations Required. **Dining Plan credits** 1 per person, per meal. **When to go** Early evening. **Cost range** Breakfast $23 (child $13), dinner $30 (child $15). **Service ★★★★. Breakfast** Daily, 7–11:30 a.m. **Dinner** Daily, 5–9:30 p.m.
An open dining room with the monorail overhead, it's a popular Disney character restaurant with Mickey Mouse (Goofy, Minnie, Donald, and Pluto are on hand, too). It's noisy, busy, and fun for families. Breakfast: French toast, biscuits and gravy. Dinner: oven-roasted prime rib and ham.

Les Chefs de France ★★★

FRENCH EXPENSIVE QUALITY ★★★ VALUE ★★★
READER-SURVEY RESPONSES 79% 👍 21% 👎 DISNEY DINING PLAN Yes

France, World Showcase, Epcot; 407-939-3463
Reservations Recommended. **Dining Plan credits** 1 per person, per meal. **When to go** Anytime. **Cost range** Lunch $12–$20 (child $7–$8), dinner $18–$33 (child $7–$8). **Service ★★★★. Lunch** Daily, noon–3 p.m. **Dinner** Daily, 5–9 p.m.
An animatronic six-inch-tall version of Remy, the rodent star of *Ratatouille,* visits a few times each day. Sample seared tuna with olives and caper sauce, fresh greens, *frites,* and grilled beef tenderloin with a black-pepper sauce. The best deal is the three-course lunch ($20) that includes French onion soup with Gruyère or lobster bisque, *croque monsieur* (toasted ham-and-cheese sandwich) or quiche, and crème brûlée.

© Disney

Cinderella's Royal Table ★★★

AMERICAN   EXPENSIVE   QUALITY ★★★   VALUE ★★
READER-SURVEY RESPONSES 85% 🖒 15% 👎   DISNEY DINING PLAN Yes

Cinderella Castle, Fantasyland, Magic Kingdom; 407-939-3463

Reservations Mandatory; credit card required to reserve; must prepay in full. **Dining Plan credits** 2 per person, per meal. **When to go** Early. **Cost range** Character breakfast, $35 adults, $24 children; character lunch, $38 adults, $25 children; character dinner, $43 adults, $27 children. **Service** ★★★★. **Character breakfast** Daily, 8–10:20 a.m. **Character lunch** Daily, noon–3 p.m. **Character dinner** Daily, 4–8:30 p.m.

A medieval banquet hall on the second floor of Cinderella Castle. All meals are fixed-price character affairs, with the menus changing periodically. Breakfast is standard-issue. Lunch favorites include pasta, salmon, and Major Domo's Favorite Pie (beef in Cabernet sauce, mashed potatoes, and puff pastry). Dinner fare includes roast lamb chops, pan-seared salmon, or prime rib; kids can choose from chicken strips, baked pasta, and a junior-sized Major Domo's Pie. Assorted princesses attend at breakfast and lunch; the Fairy Godmother, along with Suzy and Perla (two of Cinderella's mice), is present at dinner. The cost of the meal includes group photos.

Cítricos ★★★½

MEDITERRANEAN   EXPENSIVE   QUALITY ★★★★½   VALUE ★★★
READER-SURVEY RESPONSES 91% 🖒 9% 👎   DISNEY DINING PLAN Yes

Grand Floridian Resort & Spa; 407-824-4379

Reservations Recommended; credit card required to reserve Chef's Domain. **Dining Plan credits** 2 per person, per meal. **When to go** Anytime. **Cost range** $22–$46 (child $6–$13). **Service** ★★★★★. **Dinner** Daily, 5:30–10 p.m.

This is one of the best-kept dining secrets at Disney World—it's generally easy to get Advance Reservations here. Try the sautéed shrimp with lemon, feta cheese, pasta, tomatoes, and white wine; bone-in rib eye; or braised veal shank. For an extra-special night, reserve the Chef's Domain, a private room for up to 12 guests where the chef creates a special menu.

Coral Reef ★★½

SEAFOOD   EXPENSIVE   QUALITY ★★   VALUE ★★
READER-SURVEY RESPONSES 79% 🖒 21% 👎   DISNEY DINING PLAN Yes

The Seas, Future World, Epcot; 407-939-3463

Reservations Recommended. **Dining Plan credits** 1 per person, per meal. **When to go** Lunch. **Cost range** Lunch $13–$28 (child $7.59), dinner $17–$31 (child $7.59). **Service** ★★★★. **Lunch** Daily, 11:30 a.m.–3:20 p.m. **Dinner** Daily, 4 p.m.–park closing.

Coral Reef offers one of the best theme-park views anywhere: below the water level of the humongous saltwater tank in the Seas Pavilion. Sharks, rays, and even humans swim by. Enjoy creamy lobster soup, blackened catfish with pepper Jack cheese grits, grilled New York strip steak, and Chocolate Wave dessert. Divers in the tank are willing to hold up a WILL YOU MARRY ME? sign for romantic diners.

The Crystal Palace ★★★

AMERICAN/BUFFET   MODERATE   QUALITY ★★★½   VALUE ★★★
READER-SURVEY RESPONSES 91% 🖒 9% 👎   DISNEY DINING PLAN Yes

Main Street, U.S.A., Magic Kingdom; 407-939-3463

Reservations Recommended. **Dining Plan credits** 1 per person, per meal. **When to go** Anytime. **Cost range** Breakfast $19 (child $11), lunch $21 (child $12), dinner $29 (child $14). **Service** ★★★. **Breakfast** Daily, 8–10:30 a.m. **Lunch** Daily, 11:30 a.m.–2:45 p.m. **Dinner** Daily, 3:15 p.m.–park closing.

A turn-of-the-20th-century glass pavilion offers the best dining value in the Magic Kingdom. Menu items change often but have included waffles and pancakes layered with fresh fruit, prime rib, slow-roasted pork, Thai curry mussels, grilled vegetables with balsamic glaze, pasta with wild mushrooms and chicken, shrimp, and an ice-cream-sundae bar. Winnie the Pooh and friends dance about and pose with the kids. Kids get their own buffet with mac and cheese and chicken fingers.

ESPN Club ★★½

AMERICAN/SANDWICHES   MODERATE   QUALITY ★★★   VALUE ★★★
READER-SURVEY RESPONSES 78% 🖒 22% 👎   DISNEY DINING PLAN Yes

Disney's BoardWalk; 407-939-1177

Reservations Not accepted. **Dining Plan credits** 1 per person, per meal. **When to go** Anytime. **Cost range** $10–$15 (child $8). **Service** ★★★. **Hours** Daily, 11:30 a.m.–1 a.m.

A sports bar to the *n*th degree, with basketball-court flooring, sports memorabilia, and of

136   course, lots of televisions. The bar area features sports-trivia video games. Family-friendly and one of the cheapest dining spots on the BoardWalk, offering such fare as Buffalo-style wings, fresh grilled mahimahi on a whole-grain roll, pulled pork with fries, extreme Reuben, and marinated grilled chicken on rosemary focaccia.

50's Prime Time Cafe ★★★

AMERICAN   MODERATE   QUALITY ★★★   VALUE ★★★
READER-SURVEY RESPONSES 83% 👍 17% 👎   DISNEY DINING PLAN Yes

Hollywood Boulevard, Disney's Hollywood Studios; 407-939-3463
Reservations Suggested. **Dining Plan credits** 1 per person, per meal. **When to go** Anytime. **Cost range** Lunch $11.50–$17 (child $8), dinner $12.50–$21 (child $8). **Service** ★★★★★. **Lunch** Daily, 11 a.m.–3:55 p.m.; opens at 10:30 a.m. on Sunday and Wednesday. **Dinner** Daily, 4 p.m.–park closing.
Like eating a meal in your own kitchen, 1950s style. Meat loaf, pot roast, chicken, and other homey fare are served. The peanut butter–and-jelly milk shake is worth every calorie. Diners really get a kick out of the classic comedies playing on black-and-white televisions, as well as the servers who nag you to "take your elbows off the table" or "finish every last bite."

Flying Fish Cafe ★★★★

SEAFOOD   EXPENSIVE   QUALITY ★★★★   VALUE ★★★
READER-SURVEY RESPONSES 96% 👍 4% 👎   DISNEY DINING PLAN Yes

Disney's BoardWalk; 407-939-3463
Reservations Recommended. **Dining Plan credits** 1 per person, per meal. **When to go** Anytime. **Cost range** $26–$42 (child $6–$12). **Service** ★★★★★. **Dinner** Sunday–Thursday, 5:30–10 p.m.; Friday and Saturday, 5:30–10:30 p.m.
A whimsical remembrance of a 1930s Coney Island roller coaster served as the inspiration for the decor and the name. The fare here changes frequently, but you'll always find the potato-wrapped snapper, the restaurant's signature dish; char-crusted New York strip steak; and the Jonah lump crab cakes. Desserts are seasonal, but the house-made sorbets and Valrhona-chocolate galette are divine. You'll often see children in the noisy dining room because of the BoardWalk location. If you can't get a table, check on seating availability at the counter.

Fulton's Crab House ★★½

SEAFOOD   EXPENSIVE   QUALITY ★★★½   VALUE ★★
READER-SURVEY RESPONSES 83% 👍 17% 👎   DISNEY DINING PLAN No

Downtown Disney Marketplace; 407-939-3463
Reservations Accepted. **When to go** Early evening. **Cost range** Lunch $10–$18 (child $6–$20), dinner $21–$52 (child $7–$20). **Service** ★★★★. **Lunch** Daily, 11:30 a.m.–3:30 p.m. **Dinner** Daily, 4–11 p.m.
A large lounge on the first deck is where you'll spend a good deal of time waiting for your table. If you don't get fresh seafood back home, go early, request a table on the deck, order a Seafood Tower ($20 per person), and while away a few hours. Other dishes include stone crab, fresh fish, fresh oysters, Fulton's crab-and-lobster bisque, cioppino (a fish and shellfish stew in a tomato broth), and Alaskan king and Dungeness crab. Waits can be long—more than an hour even on weeknights.

© Disney

The Garden Grill Restaurant ★★★

AMERICAN EXPENSIVE QUALITY ★★★ VALUE ★★★
READER-SURVEY RESPONSES 90% 👍 10% 👎 DISNEY DINING PLAN Yes

The Land, Future World, Epcot; 407-939-3463
Reservations Recommended. **Dining Plan credits** 1 per person, per meal. **When to go** Anytime.
Cost range $29 (child $14). **Service ★★★★**. **Dinner** 4:30–8 p.m.

Tables revolve above scenes of a desert, a rain forest, and a farm from Living with the Land, the
pavilion's ride-through attraction. This is one of the quietest dining spots for getting photos
with Mickey, Chip 'n' Dale, and various other Disney characters. Dishes include marinated
flank steak, turkey with cranberry-orange relish, and fish of the day. Dessert is fruit cobbler.
The kids' menu includes mac and cheese, chicken tenders, potatoes, and vegetables. Salads are
made with produce grown right in The Land's garden downstairs.

Hollywood & Vine ★★½

AMERICAN MODERATE QUALITY ★★★ VALUE ★★★
READER-SURVEY RESPONSES 67% 👍 33% 👎 DISNEY DINING PLAN Yes

Hollywood Boulevard, Disney's Hollywood Studios; 407-939-3463
Reservations Recommended; credit card required to reserve *Fantasmic!* Dinner package. **Dining Plan
credits** 1 per person, per meal. **When to go** Anytime. **Cost range** Breakfast buffet $23 (child $13),
lunch buffet $25 (child $14), dinner buffet $25 (child $13). **Service ★★★★**. **Breakfast and lunch** Character meals; breakfast daily, 8–11:20 a.m.; lunch daily, 11:40 a.m.–2:25 p.m. **Dinner** Daily, 5–9 p.m.

Large Art Deco–style cafeteria, very noisy, with a menu that changes daily. Fare may include
chilled salads, fish of the day, carved and grilled meats, vegetables and pasta, and fresh fruits
and breads. *Playhouse Disney* characters visit at the breakfast and lunch all-you-can-eat buffets.

The Hollywood Brown Derby ★★★★

AMERICAN EXPENSIVE QUALITY ★★★★ VALUE ★★★
READER-SURVEY RESPONSES 78% 👍 22% 👎 DISNEY DINING PLAN Yes

Hollywood Boulevard, Disney's Hollywood Studios; 407-939-3463
Reservations Recommended; credit card required to reserve *Fantasmic!* dinner package. **Dining
Plan credits** 2 per person, per meal. **When to go** Early evening. **Cost range** Lunch $15–$29 (child
$6–$11), dinner $22–$36 (child $6–$11). **Service ★★★★★**. **Lunch** Daily, 11:30 a.m.–3 p.m.
Dinner Daily, 3:30 p.m.–park closing.

A replica of the original Brown Derby restaurant (not the one shaped like a derby) in California, the elegant
dining room has Cobb salad (named for Bob Cobb, the original restaurant's owner), spice-rubbed black
grouper, and grapefruit cake. This is the Studios' top dining experience—service is outstanding, and the
kitchen turns out above-average creations. *And* the dining room is quiet enough for conversation.

House of Blues ★★★

REGIONAL AMERICAN MODERATE QUALITY ★★★½ VALUE ★★★
READER-SURVEY RESPONSES 93% 👍 7% 👎 DISNEY DINING PLAN No

Downtown Disney West Side; 407-934-2623
Reservations Accepted. **When to go** Early evening; Sunday gospel brunch. **Cost range** $11–$28;
brunch $33.50 (child $17.25). **Service ★★★★**. **Brunch** 2 seatings on Sunday, 10:30 a.m. and 1 p.m.
Lunch and dinner Sun.–Tues., 11:30 a.m.–11 p.m.; Wed. and Thurs. 11:30 a.m.–midnight; Fri. and
Sat., 11:30 a.m.–1 a.m.

You'd think it was a ramshackle hut in the bayou if the place weren't bigger than all of Louisiana. If you're planning on taking in one of the acts at the performance space next door, you're
better off going there first so you can get a good seat, then eating afterward. There is often a
live band in the restaurant on weekends as well. Menu features New Orleans–inspired cuisine
such as jambalaya and shrimp po'boys.

Il Mulino ★★★

ITALIAN EXPENSIVE QUALITY ★★★ VALUE ★★
READER-SURVEY RESPONSES 67% 👍 33% 👎 DISNEY DINING PLAN No

Walt Disney World Swan; 407-934-1609
Reservations Accepted. **When to go** Anytime. **Cost range** $16–$45 (child $12–$16).
Service ★★. **Dinner** 5–11 p.m. nightly.

Il Mulino takes an upscale-casual approach to Italian cuisine, with family-style platters for
sharing in the noisy dining room. You can request private dining in one of the smaller rooms.
The cuisine focuses on Italy's Abruzzi region, with hearty pastas and big cuts of meat. Try the
bucatini Amatriciana or the 12-ounce filet of beef with spicy caper-tomato sauce.

138   Jiko—The Cooking Place   ★★★★½

AFRICAN/FUSION   EXPENSIVE   QUALITY ★★★★½   VALUE ★★★½
READER-SURVEY RESPONSES 96% 👍 4% 👎   DISNEY DINING PLAN Yes
Animal Kingdom Lodge and Villas; 407-938-3000
Reservations Mandatory. **Dining Plan credits** 2 per person, per meal. **When to go** Anytime.
Cost range $19–$39 (child $6–$11). **Service** ★★★★★. **Dinner** Daily, 5:30–10 p.m.
Young students from Africa, part of a yearlong cultural-exchange program, greet guests as they
enter Jiko's spacious dining room, inspired by the opening scenes of *The Lion King*. Jiko has
been winning awards and accolades (including AAA's Four Diamond Award) for its interesting
fare—such as Kalamata-olive flatbread; cucumber, tomato, and red-onion salad; and maize-
crusted Pacific halibut—and stellar wine list, one of the largest collections of South African
wines in any North American restaurant, with more than 1,800 bottles.

Kimonos   ★★★★

JAPANESE   MODERATE   QUALITY ★★★★½   VALUE ★★★
READER-SURVEY RESPONSES 90% 👍 10% 👎   DISNEY DINING PLAN No
Walt Disney World Swan; 407-934-1609
Reservations Accepted for parties of 6 or more. **When to go** Anytime. **Cost range** Sushi and rolls
à la carte, $4.75–$16. **Service** ★★★★★. **Dinner** Daily, 5:30 p.m.–midnight; bar opens at 5 p.m.
Although sushi and sashimi are the focus, Kimonos also serves hot appetizers, including
tempura-battered shrimp and vegetables, Kobe beef and duck satays, spicy Thai egg-drop soup,
and miso soup. There are no full entrees here, just good sushi and appetizers. Though dining
continues, Kimonos transitions to a karaoke venue each night about 9 p.m.

Kona Cafe   ★★★

NEW AMERICAN/PAN-ASIAN   MODERATE   QUALITY ★★★   VALUE ★★★★
READER-SURVEY RESPONSES 90% 👍 10% 👎   DISNEY DINING PLAN Yes
Polynesian Resort; 407-939-3463
Reservations Accepted. **Dining Plan credits** 1 per person, per meal. **When to go** Anytime.
Cost range Breakfast $9–$14.50 (child $5), lunch $11.50–$19 (child $8), dinner $17–$28 (child $8).
Service ★★★★. **Breakfast** Daily, 7:30–11:45 a.m. **Lunch** Daily, noon–2:45 p.m. **Dinner** Monday–
Saturday, 5–9:45 p.m.
If you want to escape the Magic Kingdom for a quiet lunch, hop on the monorail or take the
resort launch to the Polynesian to Kona Cafe. Breakfast: Tonga toast (a decadent French toast
layered with bananas). Lunch: Asian noodle bowl, fish tacos, pot stickers, sticky wings. Dinner:
macadamia mahimahi, shrimp and scallops with sushi rice, pan-Asian noodles.

Liberty Tree Tavern   ★★★

AMERICAN   MODERATE   QUALITY ★★★   VALUE ★★★
READER-SURVEY RESPONSES 86% 👍 14% 👎   DISNEY DINING PLAN Yes
Liberty Square, Magic Kingdom; 407-939-3463
Reservations Suggested. **Dining Plan credits** 1 per person, per meal. **When to go** Anytime. **Cost
range** Lunch $6–$19 (child $8), dinner $29 (child $14). **Service** ★★★★★. **Lunch** Daily, 11:30
a.m.–3 p.m. **Dinner** Daily, 4–9 p.m.
For lunch, New England–style pot roast, roast turkey, and sandwiches. Family-style dining at
dinner, with all-you-can-eat turkey, carved beef, and smoked pork loin. Though the Liberty
Tree is the best of the Magic Kingdom's full-service restaurants, it's often overlooked at lunch.
Make Advance Reservations here for about an hour or so before parade time—after you eat,
you can walk right out and watch the parade. Disney terminated character meals at the Liberty
Tree Tavern in 2009 but brought the characters back while the Crystal Palace was being
rehabbed. Whether the characters remain will most likely depend on an improving economy.

Mama Melrose's Ristorante Italiano   ★★½

ITALIAN   MODERATE   QUALITY ★★★   VALUE ★★
READER-SURVEY RESPONSES 79% 👍 21% 👎   DISNEY DINING PLAN Yes
Backlot, Disney's Hollywood Studios; 407-939-3463
Reservations Suggested; credit card required to reserve *Fantasmic!* Dinner package. **Dining
Plan credits** 1 per person, per meal. **When to go** Anytime. **Cost range** Lunch $12–$20 (child
$8), dinner $12–$22 (child $8). **Service** ★★★. **Lunch** Daily, noon–3:30 p.m. **Dinner** Daily,
3:30 p.m.–park closing.
Because of Mama Melrose's out-of-the-way location, you can sometimes just walk in, especially

in the evening. Portions here are fairly large—it's possible to dine cheaply on just an appetizer or two. Try the bruschetta, crispy calamari, toasted Italian bread salad, penne alla vodka, or spicy Italian sausage.

Narcoossee's ★★★½

SEAFOOD EXPENSIVE QUALITY ★★★½ VALUE ★★ READER-SURVEY RESPONSES 95% 👍 5% 👎 DISNEY DINING PLAN Yes

Grand Floridian Resort & Spa; 407-939-3463
Reservations Recommended. **Dining Plan credits** 2 per person, per meal. **When to go** Early evening. **Cost range** $20–$59 (child $6–$13). **Service ★★★★★.** **Dinner** Daily, 5:30–10 p.m.
Narcoossee's is a freestanding octagonal building at the edge of Seven Seas Lagoon with a noisy dining room. It offers a great view of the Magic Kingdom and the boats that dock nearby to pick up and drop off guests after a day

at the park. Try the Maine lobster, grilled salmon, crab cakes, or grilled filet mignon.

Nine Dragons Restaurant ★★★

CHINESE MODERATE QUALITY ★★★ VALUE ★★ READER-SURVEY RESPONSES 71% 👍 29% 👎 DISNEY DINING PLAN Yes

China, World Showcase, Epcot; 407-939-3463
Reservations Recommended. **Dining Plan credits** 1 per person, per meal. **When to go** Lunch or dinner. **Cost range** Lunch $15–$22 (child $8), dinner $16–$26 (child $8). **Service ★★★.** **Lunch** Daily, 11:30 a.m.–4 p.m. **Dinner** Daily, 4:30 p.m.–park closing.
Completely remodeled in 2008, Nine Dragons features a lighter, more contemporary cuisine, such as honey-sesame chicken, pepper shrimp with spinach noodles, and five-spiced fish. Fare is overpriced and compares poorly in quality and variety with many local Chinese restaurants.

1900 Park Fare ★★½

AMERICAN/BUFFET MODERATE QUALITY ★★★ VALUE ★★★ READER-SURVEY RESPONSES 87% 👍 13% 👎 DISNEY DINING PLAN Yes

Grand Floridian Resort & Spa; 407-824-3000
Reservations Strongly recommended but not required. **Dining Plan credits** 1 per person, per meal. **When to go** Breakfast or dinner. **Cost range** Breakfast $21 (child $12), dinner $30 (child $15). **Service ★★★★.** **Breakfast** Daily, 8–11 a.m. **Dinner** Daily, 4:30–8:30 p.m.
This bright, cavernous room is periodically filled with music from an antique band organ. Buffet includes prime rib, salmon, and chicken Marsala. A good choice for character dining, but too bright and loud for adults without children. The prime rib is 1900 Park Fare's major draw at dinner, but go someplace else if you prefer your beef on the rare side of medium.

'Ohana ★★★

POLYNESIAN MODERATE QUALITY ★★★½ VALUE ★★★ READER-SURVEY RESPONSES 87% 👍 13% 👎 DISNEY DINING PLAN Yes

Polynesian Resort; 407-939-3463
Reservations Recommended. **Dining Plan credits** 1 per person, per meal. **When to go** Anytime. **Cost range** Character breakfast $23 (child $13), dinner $31 (child $15). **Service ★★★★.** **Breakfast** Daily, 7:30–11 a.m. **Dinner** Daily, 5–10 p.m.
At any given moment, there may be a Hula-hoop contest or a coconut race, where kids push coconuts around the room with broomsticks. There is no menu. As soon as you're seated, your server will begin to deliver food. Bread and salad are followed by shrimp skewers, honey-glazed chicken wings, and wonton chips. The main course is steak, pork loin, turkey, and sausage, accompanied by stir-fried vegetables placed on a lazy Susan in the center of the table. Strolling singers and characters at breakfast provide entertainment. Sit in the main dining room, where the fire pit is located.

Olivia's Cafe ★★

AMERICAN MODERATE QUALITY ★★½ VALUE ★★ READER-SURVEY RESPONSES 63% 👍 37% 👎 DISNEY DINING PLAN Yes

Old Key West Resort; 407-939-3463 *(continued on next page)*

140 Reservations Recommended. **Dining Plan credits** 1 per person, per meal. **When to go** Lunch. **Cost range**
Breakfast $9–$12 (child $5), lunch $10.50–$17 (child $8), dinner $15–$28 (child $7.50). **Service ★★★★.**
Breakfast Daily, 7:30–10:30 a.m. **Lunch** Daily, 11:30 a.m.–5 p.m. **Dinner** Daily, 5–10 p.m.
This is Disney's idea of Key West: lots of pastels, mosaic-tile floors, tropical trees in the center of
the room, and plentiful nautical gewgaws. There is some outside seating, which looks out over the
waterway. Appetizers include crab cakes, chicken wings, and conch chowder. Entrees include prime
rib, fennel-dusted grouper, and plantain-wrapped mahimahi.

Plaza Restaurant ★★

AMERICAN   MODERATE   QUALITY ★★   VALUE ★★
READER-SURVEY RESPONSES 88% 🖒 12% 🖓   DISNEY DINING PLAN Yes

Main Street, U.S.A., Magic Kingdom; 407-939-3463
Reservations Suggested. **Dining Plan credits** 1 per person, per meal. **When to go** Anytime. **Cost
range** $10.50–$12 (child $8). **Service ★★★★. Hours** 11 a.m.–15 minutes before park closing.
Tucked away on a side street at the end of Main Street, U.S.A., as you head to Tomorrowland, the Plaza
evokes small-town diners across America. You pay top dollar for a tuna-salad sandwich or a burger, but on
a hot Florida day, it's an air-conditioned respite. House specialties include the vegetarian sandwich, club
sandwich, chicken-strawberry salad, and ice-cream desserts such as the Plaza banana split or sundae.

Portobello ★★★

ITALIAN   EXPENSIVE   QUALITY ★★★   VALUE ★★
READER-SURVEY RESPONSES 63% 🖒 37% 🖓   DISNEY DINING PLAN No

Downtown Disney; 407-934-8888
Reservations Recommended. **When to go** Anytime. **Cost range** Lunch $10–$24 (child $5–$13), din-
ner $20–$80 (child $5–$13). **Service ★★★★. Lunch** Daily, 11:30 a.m.–4 p.m. **Dinner** Daily, 4–11 p.m.
Portobello has a new look—a faux-Tuscan–inspired interior—and a new identity: a country
Italian trattoria. Enjoy such dishes as wood-burning-oven pizzas or farfalle pasta with roasted
chicken, snow peas, asparagus, and Parmesan cream sauce.

Raglan Road Irish Pub & Restaurant ★★★★

IRISH   MODERATE   QUALITY ★★★½   VALUE ★★★
READER-SURVEY RESPONSES 79% 🖒 21% 🖓   DISNEY DINING PLAN No

Downtown Disney; 407-938-0300
Reservations Recommended. **When to go** Monday–Saturday after 8 p.m. **Cost range** Lunch
$11.50–$16 (child $6.50–$9), dinner $13.50–$24
(child $6.50–$9). **Service ★★★½. Hours**
11 a.m.–1 or 1:30 a.m. **Dinner** Served until
11 p.m., with pub food available until closing.
Many elements of this pub, including the bar, were
handcrafted from hardwoods in Ireland and sent to
the United States for reassembly. Enjoy oven-roasted
loin of ham with cabbage and mashed potatoes, beer-
battered fish-and-chips, a very froufrou but yummy
shepherd's pie, or chicken-and-wild-mushroom pie.
The must-have appetizer is the Dalkey Duo: batter-
fried cocktail sausages with a mustard dipping sauce.
The real draw here is the Celtic music. A talented
band plays Monday through Saturday. A tasteful
Celtic dancer wanders in and dances on the table to
some of the numbers.

Rainforest Cafe ★★½

AMERICAN   MODERATE   QUALITY ★★   VALUE ★★
READER-SURVEY RESPONSES 72% 🖒 28% 🖓   DISNEY DINING PLAN No

Downtown Disney Marketplace; 407-827-8500
Animal Kingdom; 407-938-9100
Reservations Accepted. **When to go** After lunch crunch, in late afternoon, and before dinner
hour. **Cost range** $11–$40 (child $8). **Service ★★★. Hours** *Downtown Disney Marketplace:*
Sunday–Thursday, 11 a.m.–11 p.m.; Friday and Saturday, 11 a.m.–midnight; *Animal Kingdom:*
Daily, 8:30 a.m.–park closing.
The Downtown Disney version of the national chain sits beneath a giant volcano that can be

seen (and heard) erupting all over the Marketplace. Inside is a huge dining room designed to look like a jungle, complete with audio-animatronic elephants, bats, and monkeys. There is occasional thunder and even some rainfall. The Animal Kingdom version, featuring a huge waterfall, is easier on the eyes externally. Long waits are not worth the wait for Rasta Pasta with grilled chicken and walnut pesto, turkey wraps, crab-cake sandwiches, coconut shrimp, or slow-roasted pork ribs. If you're willing to pay to avoid the long wait, stop by the day before and purchase a Safari Club membership for $15. By presenting your card on the day you want to dine, you'll be seated much faster (and get 10% off entrees). The shopping experience must be the attraction because food preparations are spotty, and waits can be horrendous.

Restaurant Marrakesh ★★

MOROCCAN MODERATE QUALITY ★★½ VALUE ★★
READER-SURVEY RESPONSES 81% 👍 19% 👎 DISNEY DINING PLAN Yes

Morocco, World Showcase, Epcot; 407-939-3463
Reservations Required. **Dining Plan credits** 1 per person, per meal. **When to go** Anytime. **Cost range** Lunch $17–$28 (child $7), dinner $21–$43 (child $7). **Service ★★★★. Lunch** Daily, noon–3:15 p.m. **Dinner** Daily, 3:30 p.m.–park closing.
Marrakesh re-creates a Moroccan palace and serves bastilla (a minced-chicken pie sprinkled with cinnamon sugar), followed by roast lamb. Split an order of couscous. If you're hungry, curious, or both, get one of the combination platters for two. A Moroccan band and belly dancing provide entertainment. This is one of the least busy World Showcase restaurants, so it's usually easy to get a table. Diners at Marrakesh sit at tables instead of on the floor, and eat with utensils rather than with their hands. Picky kids can choose from chicken tenders, pasta, and burgers.

Rose & Crown Dining Room ★★★

ENGLISH MODERATE QUALITY ★★★½ VALUE ★★
READER-SURVEY RESPONSES 82% 👍 18% 👎 DISNEY DINING PLAN Yes

United Kingdom, World Showcase, Epcot; 407-939-3463
Reservations Recommended. **Dining Plan credits** 1 per person, per meal. **When to go** Anytime. **Cost range** Lunch $11–$16 (child $8), dinner $13–$25 (child $8). **Service ★★★★★. Lunch** Daily, noon–3:20 p.m. **Dinner** Daily, 4:30 p.m.–park closing.
The Rose & Crown is both a pub and a dining establishment. The traditional English pub has a large, cozy bar. Fish-and-chips, bangers and mash (sausage and mashed potatoes), and tamarind-glazed pork loin washed down with Bass ale round out the menu. This is a prime spot for viewing *IllumiNations,* so try to get a table on the patio for late evening.

Sanaa ★★★★

INDIAN/AFRICAN EXPENSIVE QUALITY ★★★★ VALUE ★★★★
READER-SURVEY RESPONSES Too new to rate DISNEY DINING PLAN Yes

Animal Kingdom Lodge–Kidani Village; 407-939-3463
Reservations Recommended. **Dining Plan credits** 1 per person, per meal. **When to go** Lunch or dinner. **Cost range** Lunch $14–$19, dinner $18–$28. **Service ★★★★. Lunch** Daily, 11:30 a.m.–4 p.m. **Dinner** Daily, 4:30 p.m.–park closing.
One floor down from the new Kidani Village lobby, Sanaa's dining room is inspired by Africa's outdoor markets with windows that look out on the resort's savanna—giraffes, water buffalo, and other animals wander within yards of you as you dine. A variety of Indian-African creations—such as Indian-style breads (naan, roti, paratha, and paneer paratha) with mango-lime pickle, coriander chutney, and mint-and-onion raita; lamb *kefta;* tandoori chicken; and duck confit with red-curry sauce—are offered.

San Angel Inn ★★★

MEXICAN EXPENSIVE QUALITY ★★ VALUE ★★
READER-SURVEY RESPONSES 72% 👍 28% 👎 DISNEY DINING PLAN Yes

Mexico, World Showcase, Epcot; 407-939-3463
Reservations Recommended. **Dining Plan credits** 1 per person, per meal. **When to go** Anytime. **Cost range** Lunch $15–$24 (child $8), dinner $24–$34 (child $8). **Service ★★★. Lunch** Daily, 11:30 a.m.–4 p.m. **Dinner** Daily, 4:30 p.m.–park closing.
A romantically crafted open-air cantina, the restaurant overlooks both the Gran Fiesta Tour attraction and the bustling plaza of a small Mexican village. *Tacos de pato,* with duck meat, tamarind sauce, and a garnish of avocado, pineapple, and chives; mole poblano, chicken with a sauce made from several kinds of peppers and unsweetened Mexican chocolate; and some interesting regional fish

142 preparations. The menu goes beyond typical Mexican selections, offering special and regional dishes
that are difficult to find in the United States. Mariachi or marimba bands perform in the courtyard.

Sci-Fi Dine-In Theater Restaurant ★★

AMERICAN MODERATE QUALITY ★★½ VALUE ★★
READER-SURVEY RESPONSES 72% ⚬ 28% ⚬ DISNEY DINING PLAN Yes

Backlot, Disney's Hollywood Studios; 407-939-3463
Reservations Recommended. **Dining Plan credits** 1 per person, per meal. **When to go** Anytime.
Cost range Lunch $12–$22 (child $7.50), dinner $12–$23 (child $7.50). **Service ★★★★★**. **Lunch**
Sunday and Wednesday, 10:30 a.m.–4 p.m.; Monday and Tuesday and Thursday–Saturday,
11 a.m.–4 p.m. **Dinner** Daily, 4 p.m.–park closing.
Everyone gets a kick out of this unusual dining room—a facsimile of a drive-in from the 1950s, with
faux classic cars instead of tables. You hop in, order, and watch cartoons and clips of vintage horror and
sci-fi movies, such as *Attack of the 50 Ft. Woman, Robot Monster,* and *Son of the Blob.* Servers, some on
roller skates, take your order from the driver's seat. Lunch fare consists of sandwiches, burgers, salads,
and shakes. Dinner offerings include pasta, ribs, and steak. We recommend making late-afternoon or
late-evening Advance Reservations and ordering only dessert—the Sci-Fi is an attraction, not a good
dining opportunity. If you don't have Advance Reservations, try walking in at 11 a.m. or around 3 p.m.

Shula's Steak House ★★★★

STEAK EXPENSIVE QUALITY ★★★★ VALUE ★★
READER-SURVEY RESPONSES 60% ⚬ 40% ⚬ DISNEY DINING PLAN No

Walt Disney World Dolphin; 407-934-1362
Reservations Recommended. **When to go** Anytime. **Cost range** $24–$85. **Service ★★★★**.
Dinner Daily, 5–11 p.m.
In a word, meat—really expensive but very high-quality meat. Only certified Angus beef is served:
filet mignon, porterhouse (including a 48-ounce cut), and prime rib. This is part of a chain owned
by former Miami Dolphins football coach Don Shula. The menu is printed on the side of a football
and placed on a kickoff tee in the center of the table. Clubby and masculine is the atmosphere.

Shutters at Old Port Royale ★★

STEAK/SEAFOOD MODERATE QUALITY ★★½ VALUE ★★
READER-SURVEY RESPONSES 59% ⚬ 41% ⚬ DISNEY DINING PLAN Yes

Caribbean Beach Resort; 407-939-3463
Reservations Recommended. **Dining Plan credits** 1 per person, per meal. **When to go** Anytime.
Cost range $16–$28 (child $5–$9). **Service ★★★**. **Dinner** Daily, 5–10 p.m.
The small dining areas are claustrophobia-inducing. New York strip steak, plantain-crusted red
snapper, chicken wings with habanero sauce, and tamarind-glazed roasted chicken are house
specialties. Practically no one except resort guests dines here.

Teppan Edo ★★★½

JAPANESE EXPENSIVE QUALITY ★★★★ VALUE ★★★
READER-SURVEY RESPONSES 95% ⚬ 5% ⚬ DISNEY DINING PLAN Yes

Japan, World Showcase, Epcot; 407-939-3463
Reservations Recommended. **Dining Plan credits** 1 per person, per meal. **When to go** Anytime.
Cost range $19–$30 (child $9.50–$12.50). **Service ★★★★★**. **Lunch** Daily, noon–3:45 p.m.
Dinner Daily, 4 p.m.–park closing.
Upscale Japanese, compliments of a beautiful renovation, serving chicken, shrimp, beef, scal-
lops, and Asian vegetables stir-fried on a teppan grill by a knife-juggling chef. The menu
includes sushi and appetizers such as edamame and seaweed salad. Be aware that diners at the
teppan tables (large tables with a grill in the middle) are seated with other parties.

Tokyo Dining ★★★

JAPANESE MODERATE QUALITY ★★★★ VALUE ★★★
READER-SURVEY RESPONSES 83% ⚬ 17% ⚬ DISNEY DINING PLAN Yes

Japan, World Showcase, Epcot; 407-939-3463
Reservations Recommended. **Dining Plan credits** 1 per person, per meal. **When to go** Lunch.
Cost range $18–$25 (child $9.50). **Service ★★★★**. **Lunch** Daily, noon–3:45 p.m. **Dinner** Daily,
4 p.m.–park close.
Modern Asian decor with a beautifully lighted sushi bar. Grilled meats and seafood; tempura-
battered deep-fried foods, featuring chicken, shrimp, scallops, and vegetables; sushi and sashimi;

and six kinds of sake appear on the menu. It's a relatively quiet space in the Japan Pavilion. You can't beat a window seat here at fireworks time.

Tony's Town Square Restaurant ★★½

ITALIAN MODERATE QUALITY ★★★ VALUE ★★
READER-SURVEY RESPONSES 70% 👍 30% 👎 DISNEY DINING PLAN Yes

Main Street, U.S.A., Magic Kingdom; 407-939-3463
Reservations Recommended. **Dining Plan credits** 1 per person, per meal. **When to go** Late lunch or early dinner. **Cost range** Lunch $11.50–$17 (child $7.50), dinner $17–$28 (child $7.50). **Service ★★★★. Lunch** Daily, 11:30 a.m.–2:45 p.m. **Dinner** Daily, 5 p.m.–park closing.
Tony's is a bit worn on the edges, with memorabilia from the Disney classic *Lady and the Tramp* on the walls. The nicest seats are on the glass-windowed porch. For lunch, flatbreads, paninis, and spaghetti; for dinner, shrimp scampi and New York strip. Tony's does a decent job with pasta. And the chef keeps gluten-free pasta on hand. Go at lunch, when the prices aren't so steep.

Trail's End Restaurant ★★★

AMERICAN/BUFFET MODERATE QUALITY ★★★ VALUE ★★★
READER-SURVEY RESPONSES 90% 👍 10% 👎 DISNEY DINING PLAN Yes

Fort Wilderness Resort; 407-939-3463
Reservations Recommended. **Dining Plan credits** 1 per person, per meal. **When to go** Breakfast or dinner. **Cost range** Breakfast $14, (child $9), lunch $15 (child $10), dinner $21 (child $12). **Service ★★★. Breakfast** 7:30–11:30 a.m. **Lunch** 11:30 a.m.–2 p.m. **Dinner** 4:30–9:30 p.m. Sunday–Thursday, 4:30–10 p.m. Friday and Saturday.
Trail's End is what a pioneer buffet would have looked like had America's settlers built one out of a log cabin. Breakfast features eggs, sausage, bacon, waffles, pancakes, biscuits, fruit, and pastries. Lunch includes soup, fried chicken, chili, pulled pork, mac and cheese, and a salad bar. At dinner try fried chicken, ribs, pasta, fish, peel-and-eat shrimp, carved meats, pizza, and cobbler. Trail's End makes a great midday break from the Magic Kingdom; take the boat from the park.

T-REX ★★★

AMERICAN MODERATE QUALITY ★★ VALUE ★★
READER-SURVEY RESPONSES 82% 👍 18% 👎 DISNEY DINING PLAN No

Downtown Disney Marketplace; 407-828-8739
Reservations Accepted. **When to go** Anytime. **Cost range** $12–$30 (child $7–$8). **Service ★★★. Lunch and dinner** Daily, 11 a.m.–11 p.m.; open until midnight Friday and Saturday.
A cavernous dining room with life-size robotic dinosaurs, giant fish tanks, bubbling geysers, waterfalls, fossils in the bathrooms, and crystals in the walls. Volume: loud and louder, with meteor showers, growling dinos, and overstimulated kids. Colosso Nachos, Ice Age Salmon Salad, and Bronto Burger are some of the offerings. Expect a wait unless there's an empty seat at the bar. The coolest spot for dining is the Ice Cave at the back of the restaurant, with glowing blue walls.

Turf Club Bar & Grill ★★

AMERICAN MODERATE QUALITY ★★ VALUE ★★
READER-SURVEY RESPONSES 82% 👍 18% 👎 DISNEY DINING PLAN Yes

Saratoga Springs Resort; 407-824-1100
Reservations Recommended. **Dining Plan credits** 1 per person, per meal. **When to go** Lunch or dinner. **Cost range** Lunch $10.50–$19 (child $7.50), dinner $12–$28 (child $7.50). **Service ★★★. Lunch** Daily, noon–4 p.m. **Dinner** Daily, 5–9 p.m.
When the weather's nice, ask for an outdoor table; you can spot golfers on the adjacent Lake Buena Vista Golf Course while eating steamed mussels; penne with shrimp, artichokes, and sun-dried tomatoes; or grilled chicken Caesar salad. Turf Club is worth the trip on a sunny day for a drink and appetizers on the shady terrace. The best Caesar salad in Disney World.

Tusker House Restaurant ★½

AMERICAN/AFRICAN/BUFFET MODERATE QUALITY ★ VALUE ★★
READER-SURVEY RESPONSES 90% 👍 10% 👎 DISNEY DINING PLAN Yes

Africa, Animal Kingdom; 407-939-3463
Reservations Required for character breakfast. **Dining Plan credits** 1 per person, per meal. **When to go** Anytime. **Cost range** Breakfast $20 (child $11), lunch $21 (child $11), dinner $28 (child $13). **Service ★★★. Breakfast** Daily, 8–10:30 a.m. **Lunch** Daily, 11:30 a.m.–3:30 p.m. **Dinner** Daily, 4 p.m.–park closing.

144   In Harambe Village. Donald's Safari Breakfast features Donald, Daisy, Mickey, and Goofy. The setting is a bit austere and the food (roasted meats, rotisserie chicken, salmon) unexciting, but it's fine for filling up families and a visit with the Disney characters. The menu mixes comfort food with more-exotic selections for lunch and dinner. The usual bacon, eggs, fruit, and pastries are served for breakfast.

Tutto Italia   ★★½

ITALIAN   EXPENSIVE   QUALITY ★★½   VALUE ★★½
READER-SURVEY RESPONSES 78% 👍 22% 👎   DISNEY DINING PLAN Yes

Italy, World Showcase, Epcot; 407-939-3463
Reservations Accepted. **Dining Plan credits** 1 per person, per meal. **When to go** Midafternoon. **Cost range** Lunch $15–$28 (child $9), dinner $24–$36 (child $9). **Service** ★★★★. **Lunch** Daily, 11:30 a.m.–3:30 p.m. **Dinner** Daily, 4:30–park closing.

The Roman decor features huge murals of an Italian piazza along the wall behind the upholstered banquettes. If the weather is pleasant, request a table on the piazza, away from the noisy dining room. Spaghetti with veal meatballs and pomodoro sauce and *paccheri* (pasta tubes) with calamari, peas, and a light tomato sauce are delicious. A little pricey, but the cuisine is authentic, and the servings are ample.

Victoria & Albert's   ★★★★★

GOURMET   EXPENSIVE   QUALITY ★★★★★   VALUE ★★★★
READER-SURVEY RESPONSES 86% 👍 14% 👎   DISNEY DINING PLAN Yes

Grand Floridian Resort & Spa; 407-939-3463
Reservations Mandatory; must confirm by noon the day of your seating; credit card required to reserve; call at least 180 days in advance to reserve. **Dining Plan credits** 2 per person, per meal. **When to go** Anytime. **Cost range** Fixed price, $125 per person or $185 with wine pairings; Chef's Table, $175 or $245 with wine pairings. **Service** ★★★★★. **Dinner** 2 seatings nightly at 5:45–6:30 p.m. and 9–9:45 p.m., plus 1 seating at 6 p.m. for the Chef's Table. Children below age 10 admitted only at Chef's Table.

Frette linens, Riedel crystal, Christofle silver—with only 18 tables in the main dining room and the private Fireplace Room with 5 tables, this is the top dining experience at Disney World. A winner of AAA's Five Diamond Award (the only restaurant in central Florida so honored), Victoria & Albert's is civilized, lavish, and expensive. The menu changes daily, but favorites include Jamison Farm lamb, Florida seafood, and Australian Kobe beef. The Stilton "cheesecake" with Bosc pears is divine. A harpist or violinist entertains from the foyer. But the best show is in the kitchen when you book the Chef's Table, where chef Hunnel starts the evening with a Champagne toast and crafts a personal menu.

The Wave   ★★★

NEW AMERICAN   MODERATE   QUALITY ★★   VALUE ★★
READER-SURVEY RESPONSES 80% 👍 20% 👎   DISNEY DINING PLAN Yes

Contemporary Resort; 407-939-3463
Reservations Accepted. **Dining Plan credits** 1 per person, per meal. **When to go** Anytime. **Cost range** Breakfast $8.50–$18, lunch $12–$21, dinner $18–$29. **Service** ★★★. **Breakfast** Daily, 7:30–11 a.m. **Lunch** Daily, noon–2 p.m. **Dinner** Daily, 5:30–10 p.m.

The Wave has one of the coolest lounges at Disney World, adjoining a dining room with the feel of an upscale coffee shop. Unusual drinks such as the Antioxidant Cocktail and the strawberry-lychee margarita; for breakfast, Supercharged Tropical Smoothie, multigrain pancakes, make-your-own muesli; for lunch, avocado-and-citrus salad, Italian chef salad, Reuben; for dinner, sustainable fish, braised lamb shank. Organic beers, organic coffees, hip cocktails, and New World wines poured in stingy portions. The creations coming out of the kitchen aren't executed nearly as well as the drinks.

Whispering Canyon Cafe ★★★

AMERICAN MODERATE QUALITY ★★★½ VALUE ★★★★
READER-SURVEY RESPONSES 81% 👍 19% 👎 DISNEY DINING PLAN Yes

Wilderness Lodge and Villas; 407-939-3463
Reservations Accepted. **Dining Plan credits** 1 per person, per meal. **When to go** Anytime. **Cost range** Breakfast skillets $15 (child $6.50), all-you-can-eat lunch skillets $18 (child $9.50), all-you-can-eat dinner skillets $27 (child $9.50). **Service ★★★★**. **Breakfast** Daily, 7:30–11:30 a.m. **Lunch** Daily, 11:30 a.m.–2:30 p.m. **Dinner** Daily, 5–10 p.m.
All-you-can-eat skillets with cornbread, ribs, pulled pork, smoked brisket, roast chicken, mashed potatoes, baked beans, coleslaw, salad, and seasonal vegetables. There is also an à la carte option for those who don't care to share. Wait staff engage children in impromptu parades and other rowdy demonstrations.

Wolfgang Puck Cafe ★★

CREATIVE CALIFORNIAN EXPENSIVE QUALITY ★½ VALUE ★½
READER-SURVEY RESPONSES 84% 👍 16% 👎 DISNEY DINING PLAN No

Downtown Disney West Side; 407-938-9653
Reservations Accepted. **When to go** Early evening. **Cost range** Cafe $12–$29 (child $5–$9), upstairs $25–$43 for 4 courses (child $10–$17). **Service ★★★**. **Hours** *Cafe:* Daily, 11:30 a.m.–11 p.m. *Upstairs:* Sunday–Wednesday, 6–9 p.m.; Thursday–Saturday, 6–10 p.m.
This is actually two restaurants in one—four if you count the attached Wolfgang Puck Express and the sushi bar that flows into the restaurant's lounge area. Downstairs is the actual cafe. The upstairs is a more formal dining room, but in name only. Both spaces are inordinately loud, making conversation difficult. Puck's has wood-fired pizzas, including barbecue chicken and his signature smoked-salmon pie. Sushi is also a good bet. Upstairs, the menu features fresh fish, chicken, and beef.

Yachtsman Steakhouse ★★★

STEAK EXPENSIVE QUALITY ★★★½ VALUE ★★
READER-SURVEY RESPONSES 80% 👍 20% 👎 DISNEY DINING PLAN Yes

Yacht Club Resort; 407-939-3463
Reservations Required. **Dining Plan credits** 2 per person, per meal. **When to go** Anytime. **Cost range** $24–$47 (child $6–$12). **Service ★★★★**. **Dinner** Daily, 5:30–10:30 p.m.
Take in the view of the sandy lagoon at the resort. The menu features seafood, lamb, fowl, and vegetarian creations. The adjacent Crew's Cup Lounge, with 40 types of beer and fine wine by the glass, is a fun place to start the evening. Start with seared scallops or Caesar salad. All steaks are cut and trimmed on the premises. Everything is significantly overpriced. For the money, Shula's Steakhouse at the Dolphin is far superior.

Yak & Yeti ★★★

PAN-ASIAN EXPENSIVE QUALITY ★★★½ VALUE ★★★
READER-SURVEY RESPONSES 85% 👍 15% 👎 DISNEY DINING PLAN Yes

Asia, Animal Kingdom; 407-939-3463
Reservations Recommended. **Dining Plan credits** 1 per person, per meal. **When to go** Dinner. **Cost range** $17–$25 (child $8). **Service ★★★★**. **Lunch** Daily, 11 a.m.–3:30 p.m. **Dinner** Daily, 4 p.m.–park closing.
A rustic two-story Nepalese inn . . . with seating for hundreds. Windows on the second floor overlook the Asia section of the park.
Seared miso salmon, crispy mahimahi, glazed duck, and fried wontons with pineapple for dessert are good choices. The steak-and-shrimp combo is also quite good, but the chicken dishes are just average.

PART 5

THE
MAGIC KINGDOM

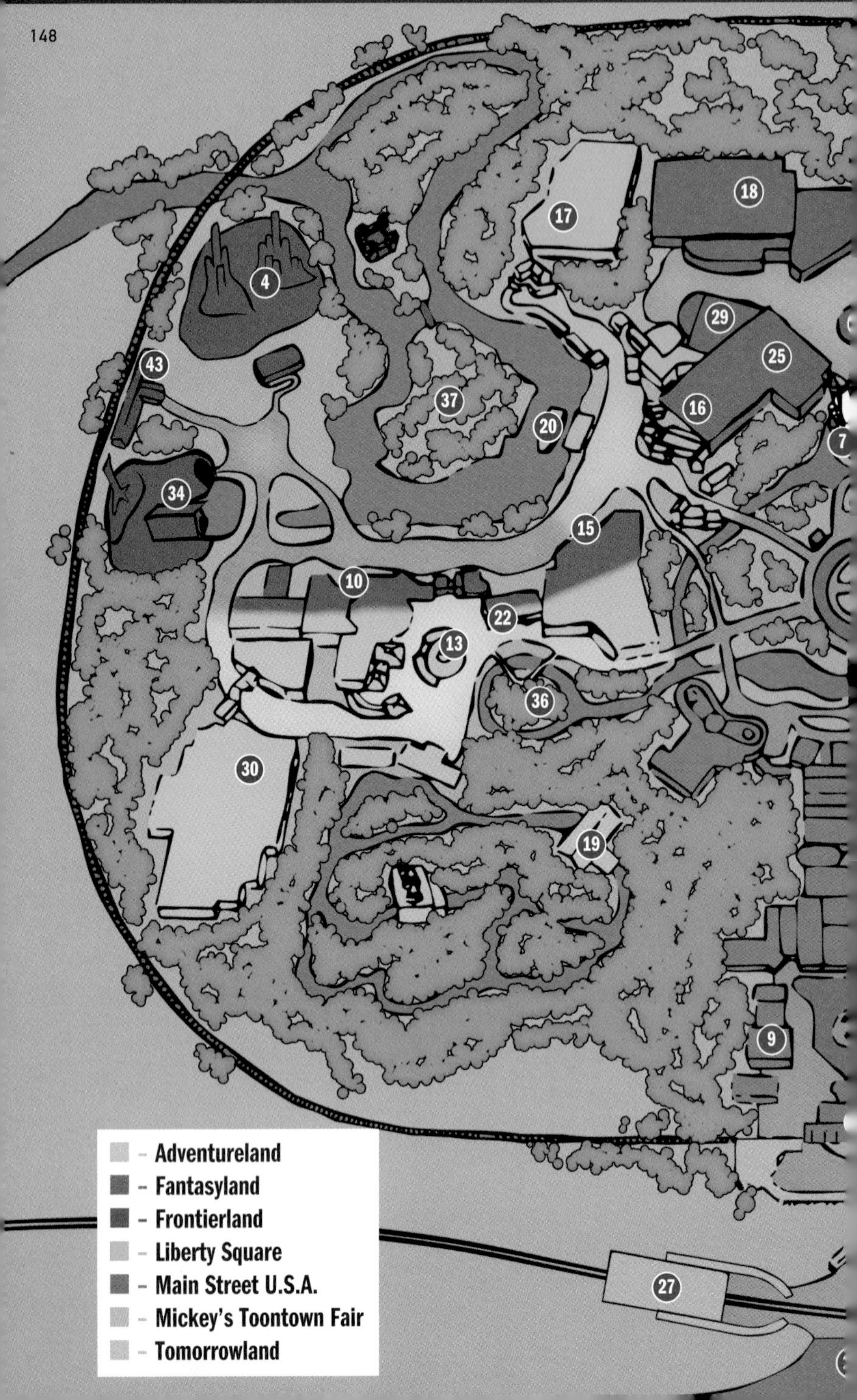
4
43
34
37
20
17
18
29
25
16
7
15
10
22
13
36
30
19
9
27
– Adventureland
– Fantasyland
– Frontierland
– Liberty Square
– Main Street U.S.A.
– Mickey's Toontown Fair
– Tomorrowland

Not to Be Missed at the Magic Kingdom

ADVENTURELAND	**Pirates of the Caribbean**
FANTASYLAND	**The Many Adventures of Winnie the Pooh** *Mickey's PhilharMagic* **Peter Pan's Flight**
FRONTIERLAND	**Big Thunder Mountain Railroad** **Splash Mountain**
LIBERTY SQUARE	**The Haunted Mansion**
SPECIAL EVENTS	**Evening Parade**
TOMORROWLAND	**Space Mountain**

Opened in 1971, the Magic Kingdom was the first of the current four Walt Disney World theme parks built. Many of the attractions found here are originals from that park opening, and a few—including Cinderella Castle, Pirates of the Caribbean, and Splash Mountain—have helped define the basic elements of theme park attractions the world over. Indeed, the Magic Kingdom is undoubtedly what most people think of when Walt Disney World is mentioned.

Much of the Magic Kingdom was built by the same Disney staff that had built Disneyland a little more than a decade earlier. The remarkable achievement that Disney wrought in Orlando isn't that they could build a second, equally compelling theme park; it's that they could do so on a much larger scale while keeping many of the fine details that make visiting a Disney park such a completely immersive experience.

►**UNOFFICIAL TIP** If you don't already have a handout guide map of the park, get one at City Hall or entrance turnstiles.

The Magic Kingdom is divided into seven themed lands arranged around a circular hub. At the bottom of the hub is Main Street, replicating small-town American life, where all visitors enter and exit the park. Main Street leads to a central hub around which the other lands are distributed. Going clockwise from Main Street at the bottom, next is Adventureland, with its exotic jungle theme, and then Frontierland, Disney's take on the American West. Liberty Square follows, seamlessly integrating Frontierland's architecture with that of the early United States. At the top of the circular hub is Fantasyland, home of Cinderella Castle and the visual center of the park. Rounding out the lands are Mickey's Toontown Fair and Tomorrowland, one of the most popular areas of the park.

►**UNOFFICIAL TIP** Because Cinderella Castle is large, designate a very specific meeting spot, such as the entrance to Cinderella's Royal Table restaurant at the rear of the castle.

MAIN STREET, U.S.A.

Begin and end your visit on Main Street, which may open a half hour before and close a half hour to an hour after the rest of the park. The Walt Disney World Railroad stops at Main Street. Get on to tour the park or ride to Frontierland or Mickey's Toontown Fair.

Main Street is a Disney-fied turn-of-the-19th-century small-town American street. Its buildings are real, not elaborate props. Along the street are shops, eating places, City Hall, and a fire station. What many visitors don't know, however, is that virtually all of the shops and restaurants are connected, and it's possible to walk almost from one end of Main Street to the other indoors. This is especially useful during parades and inclement weather. On most mornings, horse-drawn trolleys, fire engines, and horseless carriages transport visitors along Main Street to the central hub.

Main Street Services

Most park services are centered on Main Street, including:

Baby Center/Baby Care Needs: Next to The Crystal Palace, left around the central hub (toward Adventureland)
First Aid: Next to The Crystal Palace
Live Entertainment and Parade Information: City Hall at railroad-station end of Main Street
Lost and Found: City Hall
Lost Persons: City Hall
Storage Lockers: Underneath Main Street railroad station; all lockers cleaned out each night
Wheelchair and Stroller Rental: Ground floor of the railroad station at the end of Main Street

WALT DISNEY WORLD RAILROAD ★★½

! APPEAL	Preschool ★★★★	Grade School ★★½	Teens ★★★
BY AGE	Young Adults ★★★	Over 30 ★★	Seniors ★★★

What it is Scenic railroad ride around perimeter of Magic Kingdom, and transportation to Frontierland and Mickey's Toontown Fair. **Scope and scale** Minor attraction. **When to go** Anytime. **Comments** Main Street is usually the least congested station. **Authors' rating** Plenty to see; ★★½. **Duration of presentation** About 20 minutes for a complete circuit. **Average wait in line per 100 people ahead of you** 8 minutes; assumes 2 or more trains operating. **Loading speed** Moderate.

The Walt Disney World Railroad is a scenic trip around the perimeter of the Magic Kingdom, aboard an actual steam-powered train. The primary boarding area is the two-story train station on Main Street, but alternate stops are in Frontierland and Mickey's Toontown. The ride provides a glimpse of all lands except Adventureland, with most of the interesting stuff (Native American village, animatronic animals, frontier structures) on the leg between Frontierland and Toontown.

As a transportation method, the railroad is more effective in saving your feet than saving time. That is, it's probably faster to walk anywhere within the park, but the train is useful if you're just plain worn out. Parents, for example, who find themselves at the far end of Toontown when it's time to go home, should hop on the train at the Toontown station and ride to Main Street, where they can exit the park immediately after exiting the station. Note that Disney strollers aren't allowed on the train (although folding strollers are fine). Take your name card and receipt with you, and a new one will be issued at your destination.

TRANSPORTATION RIDES

In addition to the railroad, trolleys, horseless carriages, and horse-drawn wagons bring guests from one end of Main Street to the other from park opening until midmorning on most days. As with the railroad, these are more fun than efficient transportation.

This horse has been down Main Street so many times that it doesn't need its human guide.

DISNEY DESIGN with Sam Gennawey

The experience of entering Main Street parallels that of entering a movie theater, almost certainly due to the filmmaking experience of Walt Disney and the first Imagineers who built Disneyland.

The movie-going analogy begins at the front gate, where you present your ticket and enter the lobby. In this case, the lobby is the forecourt in front of the train station. Notice the red bricks beneath your feet, which represent a movie theater's red carpet. Also notice that the train station now blocks your view of everything behind it, in the way a movie curtain restricts your view of the screen.

You enter the Magic Kingdom through a tunnel under the railroad. Walking through the tunnel simulates the raising of the movie curtain and provides a transition from the lobby to the "theater." It's no accident that these tunnel passages are built wide, deep, and dark; they delay your view of an open and colorful Main Street, U.S.A. until the last moment.

With this initial glimpse of Main Street, it's clear that you're now truly in "Disney's World." Orientation in this new world is Main Street's Town Square, providing guide maps and advice to newcomers. By design, Guest Services are on the left-hand side of most Disney theme parks.

The use of forced perspective is what makes the Main Street buildings seem taller than they really are and the castle seem farther away. If you turn around, the full-scale train station does the reverse, making the walk to the exit seem much closer for weary guests at the end of the day. The results are optical illusions that trick your mind and feet.

ADVENTURELAND

The design of Adventureland blends together many different architectural styles. In the span of about one city block, you'll travel from the Victorian-era trappings of Swiss Family Treehouse and 1920s Jungle Cruise, past Middle Eastern bazaars and Polynesian tiki huts, to the Colonial forts of the Spanish Main.

It's also the home of the Dole Whip, a pineapple and soft-serve ice cream treat that is, by itself, proof that American civilization was still advancing in the last years of the 20th century.

DISNEY DESIGN *with Sam Gennawey*

The Imagineers make the transition from Main Street's small-town America to Adventureland's jungles of your imagination by using the vocabulary of Victorian architecture, the dominant style in America of the time period represented by Main Street as well as 19th-century British Colonial rule. The Crystal Palace, located at the end of Main Street, is the visual bridge to Adventureland and is modeled after historic Victorian buildings, including New York's Crystal Palace, San Francisco's Conservatory of Flowers, and England's Royal Botanic Gardens.

Adventureland's main pathway winds past the Victorian-era Swiss Family Treehouse, eventually opening onto an Arabian bazaar containing the Magic Carpets of Aladdin. This attraction has added a strong center to the area and helps to orient you. The Jungle Cruise is below you to the left and Spanish Main beckons just ahead.

The plaza in front of Pirates of the Caribbean is a traditional element of towns created during the great age of Spanish exploration. The buildings on your left reflect the Spanish architectural style found throughout the Caribbean. On your right, the Imagineers reinterpret the same architectural vocabulary as Spanish-influenced buildings typical of the America Southwest circa 1850. This creates the equivalent of a filmmaker's cross-dissolve transition from the jungles of Adventureland to the deserts of the American frontier West without creating any visual contradictions to spoil your journey.

©Mona Collentine (center)

Adventureland's architecture seamlessly transitions from the Victorian style of Main Street into an exotic blend of jungle landscapes, South Pacific tikis, and Spanish forts.

ENCHANTED TIKI ROOM ★★★½

! **APPEAL**   Preschool ★★★   Grade School ★★★   Teens ★★★
• **BY AGE**   Young Adults ★★½   Over 30 ★★★   Seniors ★★★

What it is Audio-animatronic Pacific-island musical-theater show. **Scope and scale** Minor attraction. **When to go** Before 11 a.m. or after 3:30 p.m. **Comments** Frightens some preschoolers. **Authors' rating** Very, very unusual; ★★★1/2. **Duration** 15½ minutes. **Preshow** Talking birds. **Probable waiting time** 15 minutes.

If we didn't love *Tiki Room* so much, we'd be tempted to call it strange. Let's just say that it's quaint. One of the original Magic Kingdom attractions, *Enchanted Tiki Room* is a musical show that stars four mechanical male birds, accompanied by a flock of feathered females. Guests are seated in a thatched-roof tiki hut and surrounded by tropical foliage. Tiki statues and carvings cover most of the remaining space, and the entire room's furnishings come alive for the finale.

Tiki Room's appeal, however, isn't from the music or the now-decades-old effects. Rather, it seems to come from the fact that around 40 years ago, someone decided that the best way to show off the then-new audio-animatronic technology was by building an elaborate Polynesian-themed attraction and populating it with a hundred miniature mechanical birds. At that time, the only folks thinking in that direction were Disney.

Parts of the *Tiki Room*'s soundtrack—the good parts—date back to the original Disneyland version of 1963. In 1998, Imagineers cut the original show's soundtrack and added dialog featuring Iago from Disney's animated film Aladdin. To quote another *Guide* author, this has made a lot of people angry and has been widely regarded as a bad move.

MAGIC CARPETS OF ALADDIN ★★★

! **APPEAL**   Preschool ★★★★½   Grade School ★★★   Teens ★★★
• **BY AGE**   Young Adults ★★   Over 30 ★★★   Seniors ★★

What it is Elaborate midway ride. **Scope and scale** Minor attraction. **When to go** Before 10 a.m. or in the hour before park closing. **Authors' rating** A visually appealing children's ride; ★★★. **Duration** 1½ minutes. **Average wait in line per 100 people ahead of you** 16 minutes. **Loading speed** Slow.

Magic Carpets is a virtual clone of Fantasyland's Dumbo, except you ride a carpet instead of an elephant. Its one different feature is that Magic Carpets features a water-spitting camel, which soaks unsuspecting riders and passers-by. As with Dumbo, you have some control over the ride: Those who sit up front control the carpet's height, while those in the back control tilt. Kids sitting up front naturally try to get everyone wet. It's their job.

JUNGLE CRUISE (FASTPASS) ★ ★ ★

| ❗ APPEAL | Preschool ★★★★ | Grade School ★★★★ | Teens ★★★½ |
| ● BY AGE | Young Adults ★★★½ | Over 30 ★★★★ | Seniors ★★★★ |

What it is Outdoor safari-themed boat-ride adventure. Scope and scale Major attraction. When to go Before 10 a.m. or 2 hours before closing. Special comments A lot of fun to ride at night! Authors' rating A long-enduring Disney classic; ★★★. Duration of presentation 8–9 minutes. Average wait in line per 100 people ahead of you 3 minutes; assumes 10 boats operating. Loading speed Moderate.

Forget that the animals aren't real and the boat is tethered to a track. The genius of the Jungle Cruise is that every square inch of the ride is filled with humor. Corny jokes and puns abound, from the radio banter playing in the queue's background to the stand-up comedians that double as your boat skippers. Regarding the skippers, no two have the same script, and the best way to experience the attraction is to go along with your captain's gags, even if the jokes are older than they are.

Of course we've acted like this. It was called college.

Another boatload of guests returning from their two-week jungle cruise.

158

PIRATES OF THE CARIBBEAN ★★★★★

APPEAL	Preschool ★★★½	Grade School ★★★★	Teens ★★★★
BY AGE	Young Adults ★★★★½	Over 30 ★★★★½	Seniors ★★★★

What it is Indoor pirate-themed boat ride. **Scope and scale** Headliner. **When to go** Before noon or after 5 p.m. **Comments** Frightens some children. **Authors' rating** Disney audio-animatronics at their best; not to be missed; ★★★★★. **Duration** About 7½ minutes. **Average wait in line per 100 people ahead of you** 1½ minutes; assumes both waiting lines operating. **Loading speed** Fast.

If there's one attraction that you'd live in for the rest of your life, it's got to be Pirates of the Caribbean. As Disney theme-park blogger Greg Maletic observed, Pirates is one of the most influential theme park attractions of all time, and its elaborate queuing, grand scope, and storytelling set the standard by which subsequent theme-park rides are judged. Plus, it's one of the first attractions to have a catchy song: "Yo Ho (A Pirate's Life for Me)."

The Pirates ride itself is a virtual crash course in Disney attraction design. The line guides you through an old Caribbean fort, complete with cannon defenses and jail cells holding the skeletons of captured pirates. The line ends at a small wood pier, where you board a boat and set sail. We won't spoil the story for you, but first-time riders should notice how the first set of scenes, which take place in a series of caves, transition the mood from sleepy backwater dock to cursed pirate treasure hunt.

One other thing we love about Pirates: It's one of the Magic Kingdom's most efficient attractions and can handle roughly 2,000 guests per hour. Unless the park is packed like a sardine can, wait times should be low.

The redhead in this scene is referenced in the *Pirates* movies.

SWISS FAMILY TREEHOUSE ★★★

! APPEAL	Preschool ★★★	Grade School ★★★	Teens ★★½
• BY AGE	Young Adults ★★½	Over 30 ★★★	Seniors ★★½

What it is **Outdoor walk-through treehouse.** Scope and scale **Minor attraction.** When to go **Anytime.** Comments **Requires climbing a lot of stairs.** Authors' rating **Incredible detail and execution; ★★★** Duration **10–15 minutes.** Average wait in line per 100 people ahead of you **7 minutes.**

The hallmark of Adventureland's attractions is their attention to setting and detail. It would have been impressive enough if Disney had merely created this 60-foot-tall treehouse and built upon it the bedrooms, kitchen, and other parts of the Robinson abode you see. (The water wheel is particularly clever.) For us, the best part of the attraction is how the tree's limbs and leaves work with the rest of Adventureland's buildings and landscape to ensure that what you see is consistent with the treehouse's tropical setting. Because you're far off the ground, it's possible to get a glimpse of Tomorrowland or beyond, but for the most part the tree works to guide your eye either inward to the family's rooms, or outside to the plant life or water features that surround the attraction. That's impressive work considering that the attraction was designed before the advent of computers, so Disney's architects had to imagine what the views would be from the upper reaches of the tree before the first branch was built.

FRONTIERLAND

It may be argued that Frontierland is the Magic Kingdom's best land. Themed to mimic the architecture of the American West, Frontierland includes two of the Magic Kingdom's headliner rides (Splash Mountain and Big Thunder Mountain), one of the Magic Kingdom's best spots to relax and unwind (Tom Sawyer Island), arguably the park's best counter-service restaurant (Pecos Bill Tall Tale Inn and Cafe), and some of the best spots for viewing the afternoon and evening parades.

DISNEY DESIGN with Sam Gennawey

Frontierland is designed to be a journey through time and distance, celebrating America's great westward expansion following the Louisiana Purchase. Frontierland's story begins where Liberty Square ends and takes you on a journey from St. Louis in the early 1840s to a ghost town after the gold rush boom in the 1880s. Each building moves you farther west through the use of different architectural styles and materials. In addition, the building addresses themselves are clues to the year many of the building facades were erected.

The first building in Frontierland is, appropriately, Liberty Square's Diamond Horseshoe Saloon, a grand show palace common in St. Louis in 1830, when St. Louis was known as the gateway to the American West.

Moving westward, time passes into the 1850s. Here we find a north woods union hall featuring the *Country Bear Jamboree*. Farther down, the Town Hall came in 1867, and Pecos Bill's saloon is dated 1878. The Frontier Trading Post is owned by "Texas" John Slaughter, a real-life person and Disney TV character from the 1870s. Turning the corner, we come to Splash Mountain, set in the antebellum South.

The last stop on our westward journey is the little mining town of Big Thunder. The mountain is influenced by the peaks of Monument Valley, and the designers have used forced perspective to make them seem larger.

Since our journey was from east to west, it is appropriate that the last thing you see in Frontierland is the Walt Disney World Railroad train station. The Rivers of America and the *Liberty Belle* Riverboat are a symbolic link between Liberty Square and Frontierland, highlighting the importance of rivers and canals to the start of the American expansion. The railroad station, in contrast, represents the completion of the transcontinental railroad and the end to the great expansion.

There is one more design element unique to Frontierland: the use of multiple pathways to provide variety to your experience. You can walk along the raised wooden plank sidewalk along the building frontier facades, in the street with the great masses migrating "West," or along the boardwalk at the edge of the Rivers of America to get a taste of the rural life. Not only does this provide a set of options for the guests, but it also creates huge capacity to move people without looking like a giant sidewalk.

BIG THUNDER MOUNTAIN (FASTPASS) ★ ★ ★ ★

! APPEAL BY AGE

Preschool ★ ★ ★ ★	Grade School ★ ★ ★ ★½	Teens ★ ★ ★ ★½
Young Adults ★ ★ ★ ★	Over 30 ★ ★ ★ ★½	Seniors ★ ★ ★½

What it is Western mining–themed roller coaster. Scope and scale Headliner. When to go Before 10 a.m., the hour before closing, or use FASTPASS. Comments Must be 40" tall to ride; children younger than age 7 must ride with an adult; switching-off option (see page 107). Authors' rating Great effects; relatively tame ride; not to be missed; ★ ★ ★ ★. Duration About 3½ minutes. Average wait in line per 100 people ahead of you 2½ minutes; assumes 5 trains operating. Loading speed Moderate–fast.

Big Thunder Mountain is a roller coaster ride through a decaying western mining town. The queue winds through the upper part of the mine and offers a good look at the mountains and canyons you'll be screaming through. The effects are even better at night, when colored lights cast shadows on the jagged rocks and landscape, and create a completely different ride dynamic. It's also

Of course there's a landslide involved. Why wouldn't there be?"

possible to see the Magic Kingdom's nighttime fireworks from Big Thunder, if you 163 can time it correctly.

Many Disney rides feature a transition scene, which sets the story and mood for the ride as you depart from the ride's loading area. Big Thunder is one of these, with a transition scene that takes you inside a mountain cave complete with stalactites and mineral-colored pools. At the top of the cave is the basis for a clever ride effect: A fissure in the cave ceiling mists water on you from above, just before you're launched down the mountain. Then as you're riding and the wind whips by, the mist on your skin evaporates. Besides cooling you off, the evaporation makes you feel like you're going faster than you really are.

As roller coasters go, Big Thunder is tamer than Space Mountain, and certainly less intimidating than many headliner coasters found at regional amusement parks around the country. The ride does have a lot of side-to-side movement, however, which some readers find uncomfortable. But because most of the ride takes place outdoors, where riders can see the track, many families find that Big Thunder is a good introduction for grade-school children to Disney's brand of thrill rides.

WARNING: THIS RIDE WILL MUSS YOUR DO

Another day, another runaway industrial vehicle.

COUNTRY BEAR JAMBOREE ★★★

! APPEAL   Preschool ★★★½   Grade School ★★★   Teens ★★½
• BY AGE   Young Adults ★★½   Over 30 ★★★   Seniors ★★★½

What it is Audio-animatronic country-hoedown theater show. Scope and scale Major attraction. When to go Before 11:30 a.m., before a parade, or during the 2 hours before closing. Comments Shows change at Christmas. Authors' rating Old and worn but pure Disney; ★★★. Duration 15 minutes. Probable waiting time Moderately popular but comparatively small capacity. Waiting time between noon and 5:30 p.m. on a busy day will average 15–45 minutes.

Country Bear Jamboree is a country-music themed variety show featuring animatronic singing bears. It's roughly the equivalent of Adventureland's *Enchanted Tiki Room*, with bears and country music instead of birds and Hawaiian songs. *Country Bear*

Jamboree, like *Enchanted Tiki Room*, was conceived by Disney in the 1960s, and *Country Bear* has remained little changed since then. Unlike *Tiki Room*, however, many readers think the *Bear* show has passed from charming and quaint to stale. It's still a good attraction when you're trying to get out of the midday sun or when your feet need a break, and the waits are usually short.

FRONTIERLAND SHOOTIN' ARCADE ★½

! APPEAL   Preschool ★★½   Grade School ★★★★   Teens ★★★
• BY AGE   Young Adults ★★½   Over 30 ★★   Seniors ★★

What it is Electronic shooting gallery. Scope and scale Diversion. When to go Whenever convenient. Comments Costs $1 per play. Authors' rating Very nifty shooting gallery; ★1/2.

Perhaps it's because the arcade is one of the few interactive experiences in the park, but there's something satisfying about hitting a target and sending it spinning. In the Frontierland Shootin' Arcade, your rifles shoot beams of light at targets about 10 to 30 feet away. The rifles are a bit heavy for smaller children, and even adults will need to rest their arms after a few rounds. Still, it's a hoot.

TOM SAWYER ISLAND AND FORT LANGHORN ★★★

APPEAL BY AGE

| Preschool ★★★★ | Grade School ★★★★ | Teens ★★★ |
| Young Adults ★★½ | Over 30 ★★★ | Seniors ★★★ |

What it is Outdoor walk-through exhibit/rustic playground. **Scope and scale** Minor attraction. **When to go** Midmorning–late afternoon. **Comments** Closes at dusk. **Authors' rating** The place for rambunctious kids: ★★★.

Tom Sawyer Island isn't one of the Magic Kingdom's more celebrated attractions, but it's one of the park's better conceived ones. Attention to detail is excellent, and the island is bigger than you might think. While the windmill is visible from almost all of Frontierland, the island hides a cave, climbing hills, barrel bridges, and children's play areas, as well as a replica pioneer fort (Fort Langhorn). It's a delight for adults and a godsend for children who have been in tow and closely supervised all day.

A relatively unknown secret about Tom Sawyer Island is that Disney cast members hide a few paintbrushes—in reference to the whitewashed fence from the novel—all around the island every morning before the park opens. Find one and return it to the nearest cast member, and you'll receive a prize ranging from free FASTPASSes to free soft drinks. Most of the paintbrushes have brightly colored handles and can be hidden on shelves, rooftops, and (of course) near fences.

© Meghan Gerc

One of Tom Sawyer Island's many bridges—this one is made of barrels floating in the water.

SPLASH MOUNTAIN (FASTPASS) ★★★★★

| ❗ APPEAL | Preschool ★★★★ † | Grade School ★★★★½ | Teens ★★★★★ |
| BY AGE | Young Adults ★★★★★ | Over 30 ★★★★½ | Seniors ★★★★ |

† Many preschoolers are too short to ride, and others are intimidated when they see the attraction from the waiting line. Among preschoolers who actually ride, most give it high marks.

What it is Indoor/outdoor water-flume adventure ride. Scope and scale Superheadliner. When to go As soon as the park opens, during afternoon or evening parades, just before closing, or use FASTPASS. Comments Must be 40″ tall to ride; children younger than age 7 must ride with an adult. Switching-off option provided (see page 107). Authors' rating A soggy delight, and not to be missed; ★★★★★. Duration About 10 minutes. Average wait in line per 100 people ahead of you 3½ minutes; assumes ride is operating at full capacity. Loading speed Moderate.

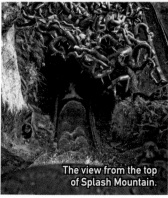

The view from the top of Splash Mountain.

One of the *Guide*'s authors (Len) thinks Splash Mountain is the best attraction in Walt Disney World. Writes Len: "The best Disney attractions combine five key traits: a grand scope or scale, attention to detail, a dynamic element that rewards repeated visits, the right amount of thrills for the family, and a ride long enough to justify the wait in line." Splash Mountain succeeds on every count. In terms of scope and scale, Splash is among Disney's largest and longest rides, covering more than half a mile and including swamps, caves, and briar patches. There's plenty of detail, too—from the story of how Bre'r Rabbit leaves home to the grand showboat scene in his triumphant return. An especially nice touch is in an underground cave

Dad's "See no water, feel no water" theory fails its big test.

scene, where water jumps from geyser to geyser just in front of your ride vehicle. And there are plenty of hidden Mickeys to be found along the way.

Also, since your journey takes place in a water-borne log, each ride is slightly different, depending on the weight of passengers with you, speed of current, and a dozen other variables. The result is that you'll end up somewhere between slightly damp and completely soaked, with riders at the front of the log generally getting wetter.

Splash Mountain contains a couple of long drops, but don't let the view from outside the ride intimidate you or your kids—even the big drop is mild by any thrill ride standard, and many families report that Splash is their kindergartener's favorite attraction. Finally, Splash lasts anywhere from 10 to 12 minutes—an impressive amount of time for any thrill ride and an ample reward for most waits in line. It's hard to find a better theme-park ride anywhere.

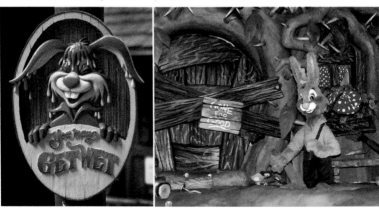

LIBERTY SQUARE

Liberty Square re-creates America at the time of the Revolutionary War. The architecture is Federal or Colonial and provides a seamless transition from the edge of Fantasyland to Frontierland. A real 130-year-old live oak, the Liberty Tree, lends dignity and grace to the setting.

DISNEY DESIGN with Sam Gennawey

Despite being one of the smallest lands in any Disney park, Liberty Square requires an unusual level of detail because it reflects the qualities of places that really exist and would be accessible to many of Disney World's visitors. The challenge for the design team was to create, in the Imagineers' words, an "enhanced reality" that is "better than real."

Just like Frontierland, the use of architectural details provides the clues for our trip through time and geography. For Liberty Square, our trip begins in New York along the banks of the Hudson River in the early 1700s, where the Haunted Mansion is based on the Gothic architecture used in the New York region when it was known as Dutch New Amsterdam.

The nearby Columbia Harbour House would feel right at home in the port city of Boston in the mid-1700s. Traveling south, the buildings begin to take on the Georgian style popular in Williamsburg during the late 1700s. The Hall of Presidents is modeled after buildings in Philadelphia at the time of the Constitution's adoption in 1787. Liberty Square ends at the edge of the American frontier with the Diamond Horseshoe Saloon, which could have been in St. Louis during the 1830s. The westward expansion continues in Frontierland.

HALL OF PRESIDENTS ★★★

! APPEAL BY AGE	Preschool ★½	Grade School ★★½	Teens ★★★
	Young Adults ★★★	Over 30 ★★★½	Seniors ★★★★

What it is **Audio-animatronic historical theater presentation.** Scope and scale **Major attraction.** When to go **Anytime.** Authors' rating **Impressive and moving; ★★★.** Duration **Almost 23 minutes.** Probable waiting time **The lines for this attraction look intimidating, but they're usually swallowed up as the theater exchanges audiences. Even during the busiest times, wait times rarely exceed 40 minutes.**

© Disney

President Barack Obama was added in 2009, and the show was revamped with a new narration by Morgan Freeman and speech by George Washington. It remains, however, strongly inspirational (for Americans) and patriotic, highlighting milestones in American history.

The roll call of presidents, in which the name of every man ever to hold the office is read in the order in which he served, has long been an opportunity to boo or cheer the recent occupants of the White House. We're here to encourage you to take this one step further by catcalling more of the earlier presidents when their names are announced. It's time to give Grover Cleveland what-for about the free coinage of silver, for example, and jeer William Howard Taft's support of the Sixteenth Amendment, which instituted the income tax.

LIBERTY BELLE RIVERBOAT ★★½

! APPEAL BY AGE	Preschool ★★★	Grade School ★★★	Teens ★★
	Young Adults ★★★	Over 30 ★★★	Seniors ★★★½

What it is **Outdoor scenic boat ride.** Scope and scale **Major attraction.** When to go **Anytime.** Authors' rating **Slow, relaxing, and scenic; ★★1/2.** Duration **About 16 minutes.** Average wait to board **10–14 minutes.**

The *Liberty Belle* is a massive paddle-wheel riverboat that takes passengers on a spin around Tom Sawyer Island and Fort Langhorn, passing settler cabins, old mining paraphernalia, a Plains Indian village, and some animatronic wildlife. It's not the fastest way around, and during summer it can be hot and humid. It's better at dusk, however, and the upper deck offers some especially good views of Liberty Square and Frontierland.

THE HAUNTED MANSION ★★★★

| APPEAL | Preschool ★★★ | Grade School ★★★★ | Teens ★★★★ |
| BY AGE | Young Adults ★★★★½ | Over 30 ★★★★½ | Seniors ★★★★½ |

What it is Haunted-house dark ride. Scope and scale Major attraction. When to go Before 11:30 a.m. or after 8 p.m. Comments Frightens some very young children. Authors' rating Some of Walt Disney World's best special effects; not to be missed; ★★★★. Duration 7-minute ride plus a 1½-minute preshow. Average wait in line per 100 people ahead of you 2½ minutes; assumes both "stretch rooms" operating. Loading speed Fast.

Although its roots are in the haunted houses of small amusement parks everywhere, Disney's is done on a scale big enough to justify use of the word mansion. The Haunted Mansion is a masterpiece of detail, starting with the gravestones lining the lawn next to the exterior waiting area and extending into the wallpaper and paintings in pre-show areas. Even the cast members get into the act as they gravely announce, "Your time has come," to enter the ride, and exhort you to move to the "dead center" of the foyer to begin the show.

The mansion is filled with room after room of visual effects, most of which are no more threatening than a whoopee cushion. Only the graveyard scene, which features a handful

One of the grave markers seen in the queue.

Men lose their heads over the Haunted Mansion's bride.

The Haunted Mansion sits alone atop a hill in Liberty Square.

of skulls popping up from behind tombstones, might be considered mildly scary. Other rooms include a clever tribute to M.C. Escher and a ballroom dancing scene that ranks among Disney's best (and oldest) effects. As with Disney's other classic attractions, the Haunted Mansion also features a catchy soundtrack ("Grim Grinning Ghosts") that will keep you humming on your way to the next attraction.

You'd think the Haunted Mansion would be better at night, but the attraction is already so dark that it makes no difference once you get inside. Once you're done riding, however, check out the pet cemetery on your left just after you exit the building.

FANTASYLAND

Fantasyland is the center of the action in most Disney theme parks, both literally (in terms of crowds) and figuratively (in terms of theming and storytelling). Walt Disney World's version is modeled after an Alpine village tucked behind the steepled towers of Cinderella Castle.

DISNEY DESIGN with Sam Gennawey

Fantasyland is at the heart of the Magic Kingdom, and it represents a chance to visit with some of our favorite Disney characters. To get there you must pass through the gates of Cinderella Castle, which is influenced by French Gothic castles and an ornamental style based on French chateaus. The castle is the only fully realized four-sided building that is not a spinning ride in Fantasyland. Behind the castle walls, you enter a medieval courtyard surrounded by a Gothic village that has been decorated for a celebration.

In creating Fantasyland, the Imagineers faced a design dilemma. They wanted to re-create elements from architecture found in Disney cartoons, but they feared chaos as the variety of styles might collide. The solution was to wrap the facades of English Tudor, French Gothic, and other styles with decorative elements from a medieval tournament. These elements include tents, flags, and banners and supports that look like lances.

From a guest's point of view, the Fantasyland courtyard appears to be a collection of small stores and larger attraction queues. In reality, as you can see from an aerial photo, the land is made up of three very large buildings that are wrapped in thematic materials. This concept of wrapping buildings was relatively new at the time the Magic Kingdom was built and has become very common today. The design details along the roofline of the buildings surrounding the courtyard support the design elements of Cinderella Castle and confirm that you are within the walls of the castle.

A lot has changed over the years, but the facades have remained relatively the same. Winnie the Pooh took over the lease from Mr. Toad, and the audio-animatronic *Mickey Mouse Revue* kept with the same great idea and morphed into the 3-D film *Mickey's PhilharMagic*. The loss of the lagoon for the 20,000 Leagues Under the Sea submarines has greatly weakened the boundaries of the courtyard. The proposed Fantasyland expansion may go a long way in repairing that damage.

ARIEL'S GROTTO ★★★

❗ APPEAL BY AGE   Preschool ★★★★½   Grade School ★★★½   Teens ★★
             Young Adults ★   Over 30 ★★   Seniors ★½

What it is Interactive fountain and character-greeting area. **Scope and scale** Minor attraction. **When to go** Before 11 a.m. or after 9 p.m. **Authors' rating** One of the most elaborate of the character-greeting venues; ★★★. **Average wait in line per 100 people ahead of you** 50 minutes.

On the lagoon side of Dumbo, Ariel's Grotto consists of a small children's play area with an interactive fountain and a rock grotto where Ariel, the Little Mermaid, poses for photos and signs autographs. The best times to go are as soon as the grotto opens (typically 10 a.m.) or during parades.

If interactive fountain is new to you, it means an opportunity for your children to get as wet as a trout. That's fine during summer, but can induce hypothermia even during Florida's mild winters.

CINDERELLA'S GOLDEN CARROUSEL ★★★

❗ APPEAL BY AGE   Preschool ★★★★   Grade School ★★★½   Teens ★★½
             Young Adults ★★★   Over 30 ★★★   Seniors ★★★

What it is Merry-go-round. **Scope and scale** Minor attraction. **When to go** Before 11 a.m. or after 8 p.m. **Comments** Adults enjoy the beauty and nostalgia of this ride. **Authors' rating** A beautiful ride for children; ★★★. **Duration** About 2 minutes. **Average wait in line per 100 people ahead of you** 5 minutes. **Loading speed** Slow.

One of the most elaborate and beautiful merry-go-rounds you'll ever have the pleasure of seeing, especially when its lights are on. Don't be intimidated by a crowd of people standing near the entrance—unless the line stretches back to Peter Pan, the wait is probably under ten minutes.

Unofficial Royalty Field Guide

Prince

Princess

Queen

The King

DUMBO ★★★

! APPEAL   Preschool ★★★★★   Grade School ★★★★   Teens ★★½
. BY AGE   Young Adults ★★   Over 30 ★★★   Seniors ★★

What it is **Disneyfied midway ride**. Scope and scale **Minor attraction**. When to go **Before 10 a.m. or after 9 p.m.** Authors' rating **Disney's signature ride for children; ★★★**. Duration of ride **1½ minutes**. Average wait in line per 100 people ahead of you **20 minutes**. Loading speed **Slow**.

A tame, happy children's ride based on the lovable flying elephant, Dumbo. Despite being little different from rides at state fairs and amusement parks, Dumbo is the favorite Magic Kingdom attraction of many younger children. If Dumbo is essential to your child's happiness, make it your first stop, preferably within 15 minutes of park opening.

IT'S A SMALL WORLD ★★★

| APPEAL | Preschool ★★★★½ | Grade School ★★★★ | Teens ★★★ |
| • BY AGE | Young Adults ★★★ | Over 30 ★★★½ | Seniors ★★★★ |

What it is World-brotherhood-themed indoor boat ride. **Scope and scale** Major attraction. **When to go** Anytime. **Authors' rating** Exponentially cute; ★★★. **Duration** Approximately 11 minutes. **Average wait in line per 100 people ahead of you** 11 minutes; assumes busy conditions with 30 or more boats operating. **Loading speed** Fast.

It's a Small World is one of the rides most frequently maligned by critics of Disney theme parks, American culture, or indeed, anyone who's ever heard the theme song. Truth be told (and we're not exactly strangers to any of those aforementioned groups), the ride gets a bum rap mainly because it's an easy target. Yes, the Walt Disney World version plays second fiddle to the original Disneyland attraction, which is larger and features Mary Blair's iconic design. Yes, the imagery and message are trite, with your boat gliding past Hawaiian dancers predictably doing the hula and French kids in front of the Eiffel Tower, accompanied by the song's "wouldn't it be great if we all just got along" lyrics (of course, sung by small children).

All of that being said, however, we're not sure that we could have come up with a better attraction given the scope, cost, and schedule constraints that Disney's Imagineers were surely under when the ride was being built. While it's nice to think that we would have gone with some sort of highbrow concept, our initial reaction to the first budget cut or schedule delay would have been to yell at Bret the intern, "You know what Peru's all about? Llamas. Get me some llamas!"

MAD TEA PARTY ★★

! **APPEAL** Preschool ★★★★ Grade School ★★★★ Teens ★★★★
• **BY AGE** Young Adults ★★★ Over 30 ★★★ Seniors ★★

What it is Midway-type spinning ride. **Scope and scale** Minor attraction. **When to go** Before 11 a.m. or after 5 p.m. **Comments** Turn the wheel in the center of the cup to make the teacups spin faster. **Authors' rating** Fun, but not worth the wait; ★★. **Duration** 1½ minutes. **Average wait in line per 100 people ahead of you** 7½ minutes. **Loading speed** Slow.

It looks so cute—oversized teacups! Inside every extra-large teacup, however, is a metal wheel of death. OK, not death in the literal sense, but the Guide's marketing reps note that metal wheel of gastrointestinal discomfort isn't as catchy. And our lawyers say the aesthetics justify the hyperbole.

The faster you spin the metal wheel, the faster your teacup spins about its central axis. And while your cup is spinning around its central axis, it's also spinning in a larger circle with two other cups. And all of the cups are spinning on one giant orbit around the middle of the ride. It's circles within circles within circles. Needless to say, the row of green hedges you see around the outside of the ride while you're waiting in line are there for you to vomit in afterward, without having to get janitors to clean it up. We write from experience. Sad, sad experience. Whatever you do, don't go on this ride with anyone to whom you've helped give birth.

Although they're years apart, and you can't tell it on film, both of these girls are laughing their evil "Mwah ha ha ha—I've got you now!" laughs.

MOTION SICKNESS WARNING

THE MANY ADVENTURES OF WINNIE THE POOH (FASTPASS) ★★★½

! APPEAL   Preschool ★★★★½   Grade School ★★★★   Teens ★★★
• BY AGE   Young Adults ★★★   Over 30 ★★★½   Seniors ★★★½

What it is Indoor track ride. Scope and scale Minor attraction. When to go Before 10 a.m., in the 2 hours before closing, or use FASTPASS. Authors' rating As cute as the Pooh Bear himself; ★★★½. Duration About 4 minutes. Average wait in line per 100 people ahead of you 4 minutes. Loading speed Moderate.

Tigger tails are made for bouncing!

© MrChrisCornwell/Matt Shirky

Pooh is mostly sunny, upbeat, and fun— that is, more like Peter Pan's Flight than Snow White's Scary Adventures. You ride a honey pot through the pages of a huge picture book into the Hundred Acre Wood, where you encounter Pooh, Piglet, Eeyore, Owl, Rabbit, Tigger, Kanga, and Roo as they contend with a blustery day. Small children may be frightened by one short part of the ride, which contains dramatic lighting, Pooh talking in a worried tone, and an appearance by Heffalumps and Woozles. It all ends well, however, with the gang joining together for a big party.

POOH'S PLAYFUL SPOT ★★½

! APPEAL   Preschool ★★★★   Grade School ★★★   Teens ½
• BY AGE   Young Adults ★½   Over 30 ★★   Seniors ★

What it is Playground for children. Scope and scale Minor attraction. When to go Anytime. Comments Good resting place for adults. Authors' rating A favorite of the 7-and-under crowd; ★★1/2.

Located directly across from The Many Adventures of Winnie the Pooh, Pooh's Playful Spot is a playground imaginatively landscaped as a mini version of the Hundred Acre Wood. An oasis from the bustle of Fantasyland, the playground is small enough and sufficiently enclosed for tired parents to easily keep an eye on their kids. And speaking of tired parents, you can plop yourself down on one of the thoughtfully placed rustic benches. Fun features for the kids include spurting water fountains, honey pots, crawl-through logs, a treehouse for climbing, and a slide.

MICKEY'S PHILHARMAGIC
(FASTPASS SEASONALLY) ★ ★ ★ ★

❗ APPEAL
• BY AGE

Preschool ★ ★ ★ ★   Grade School ★ ★ ★ ★ ½   Teens ★ ★ ★ ★ ½
Young Adults ★ ★ ★ ★ ½   Over 30 ★ ★ ★ ★ ½   Seniors ★ ★ ★ ★ ★

What it is 3-D movie. **Scope and scale** Major attraction. **When to go** Before 11 a.m., during parades. **Comments** Not to be missed. **Authors' rating** A zany masterpiece; ★ ★ ★ ★. **Duration** About 20 minutes. **Probable waiting time** 12–30 minutes.

The newest (and best) of Disney World's 3-D movies, *Mickey's PhilharMagic* tells the tale of Donald Duck frantically trying to find Mickey Mouse's orchestra conductor's hat after losing it in a self-inflicted (what else?) tornado of time and space. Disney film buffs will recognize that the premise owes a lot to the 1935 Mickey Mouse short *The Band Concert*.

In *PhilharMagic*, Donald whips through scenes from many of Disney's pre-Pixar animated films, including *The Little Mermaid*, *Beauty and the Beast*, and *The Lion King*, in a wide-angle 3-D presentation that is remarkably well done, both in terms of visual appeal and soundtrack. If you've got small children and own these movies, you'll catch yourself singing along with the score, possibly at near operatic levels. Don't worry—everyone else is either singing along or watching the movie. In addition to sight and sound, there's something for your senses of smell and touch too.

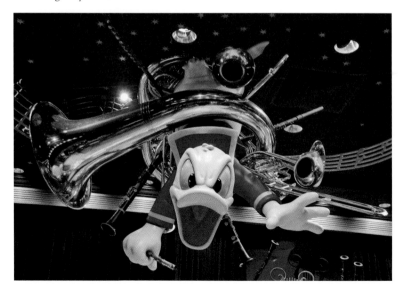

PETER PAN'S FLIGHT (FASTPASS) ★ ★ ★ ★

! APPEAL
• BY AGE

Preschool ★★★½	Grade School ★★★★	Teens ★★★½
Young Adults ★★★★	Over 30 ★★★★	Seniors ★★★★

What it is **Indoor track ride.** Scope and scale **Minor attraction.** When to go **Before 10 a.m., or use FASTPASS after 6 p.m.** Authors' rating **Nostalgic, mellow, and well done; ★★★★.** Duration **A little over 3 minutes.** Average wait in line per 100 people ahead of you **5½ minutes.** Loading speed **Moderate–slow.**

Peter Pan's Flight is the best of Fantasyland's midway-style attractions. Instead of a ride that pushes you around a track on the floor, Peter Pan's Flight launches you into the London night sky on board a miniature pirate ship suspended from a rail

in the ceiling. Perhaps because you're up high, many of the effects had to be three-dimensional, rather than the painted flat panels you'll find in other Fantasyland attractions. Other neat tricks include simulated moving cars on the London streets (courtesy of a bicycle chain dotted with luminescent paint) and a neat fly-by of some imaginative mountain ranges.

Hard to say. They won't sit still while we count them.

SNOW WHITE'S SCARY ADVENTURES ★★½

APPEAL BY AGE	Preschool ★★★	Grade School ★★★	Teens ★★★
	Young Adults ★★★	Over 30 ★★★	Seniors ★★★

What it is Indoor track ride. **Scope and scale** Minor attraction. **When to go** Before 11 a.m. or after 6 p.m. **Comments** Terrifying to many young children. **Authors' rating** Worth seeing if the wait isn't long; ★★½. **Duration** Almost 2½ minutes. **Average wait in line per 100 people ahead of you** 6¼ minutes. **Loading speed** Moderate–slow.

© MrChrisCornwell/Matt Shirky

One of Fantasyland's prototypical "dark rides," with a ride vehicle attached to a track on the ground, spinning you through comic book–style story panels and various animatronics. In this case, the ride vehicles are mine cars, and the story shows Snow White as she narrowly escapes harm at the hands of the wicked witch. Action and effects are not as good as Peter Pan's Flight or Winnie the Pooh.

We jokingly mentioned highbrow attraction ideas in It's a Small World, but as Disney historian Jim Hill noted, Snow White's Scary Adventures actually tried one: the idea that as you went through the attraction, you were supposed to be Snow White. Thus, your ride vehicle went through the story, past dwarves and evil queens, without ever showing Snow White. Not many people got the concept, however, and Disney reluctantly added Snow White to the story a few years back.

FANTASYLAND EXPANSION: VIVE LA REVOLUTION!

Compared to California's Disneyland and Disneyland Paris, the Magic Kingdom's version of Fantasyland was far smaller in both size and scope. We'd not thought much of it, but apparently it had been a source of discontent for Disney princesses for quite some time. In 2009, the princesses, led by Cinderella and Ariel, staged a revolution against the established character aristocracy that resulted in the biggest land grab in Magic Kingdom history. With a small but fabulously dressed army of princesses and fairies, Cinderella and Ariel claimed a huge chunk of undeveloped acreage outside of Fantasyland, while their sympathetic forest friends stormed Toontown. It was all over in a matter of hours, when Mickey and Minnie fled their country houses for exile on Main Street. If there is any doubt about who wields power in the Magic Kingdom, one only need look at who now has the castle and the most land.

Soon after claiming control, Cinderella began divvying up the spoils of war. Ariel, who served as Cindy's consigliere during the coup and coined the phrase sleep with the fishes, will be rewarded with a new ride-through attraction using the story

and characters from Disney's The Little Mermaid film. Belle, who led the storming of France (not technically part of the Magic Kingdom, but still on any reasonably complete list of places to invade), will get her own character-greeting area. In addition, Belle's old country pal Gaston muscled in on the restaurant business in Fantasyland. We hear he's opening up a new place that'll serve fast food to the masses at lunch and convert to pricey sit-down meals for dinner. It's sure to be a hit—no one eats or drinks like Gaston.

Princess Aurora, who kept the trains running on schedule (and the rest of the characters at bay) during the revolution, gets a dedicated greeting area themed after her forest home and has announced plans to re-do the Toontown train station in Fantasyland decor. The Tinker Bell–led fighting fairies also get their own meet-and-greet location, dubbed Pixie Hollow, as well as a play area that looks suspiciously like an after-hours obstacle course training ground for the new Cinderella Youth Brigade.

Dumbo the Flying Elephant, once part of Mickey's inner circle, proved to be an agent working for Cinderella. The reward for his treachery is a second Dumbo attraction—a clone of the first—on what was ironically Mickey's old property. We hear Dumbo will also get a new interactive queue and waiting area.

Donald Duck, who used to store his boat in Toontown across from Mickey's house, hasn't been heard from since the revolt. We're pretty sure his ship's bell has rung for the last time, if you know what we mean. The only Toontown attraction that appears to have been spared is The Barnstormer at Goofy's Wiseacres Farm. Said Goofy, "Hey, I'm just excited to be part of Cinderella's plans. She's a visionary, you know? That stuff with Mickey—it was just business."

MICKEY'S TOONTOWN FAIR

Much of Toontown is slated for demolition as part of the Fantasyland expansion. For now, however, Toontown holds most of the formal character-greeting areas in the Magic Kingdom, as well as a play area and a kid-friendly miniature roller coaster.

GOOFY'S BARNSTORMER ★★

! APPEAL   Preschool ★★★★   Grade School ★★★★   Teens ★★★
• BY AGE   Young Adults ★★   Over 30 ★★★   Seniors ★★

What it is Small roller coaster. Scope and scale Minor attraction. When to go Before 10:30 a.m., during parades, or just before the park closes. Comments Must be 35″ or taller to ride. Authors' rating Great for little ones, but not worth the wait for adults; ★★. Duration About 53 seconds. Average wait in line per 100 people ahead of you 7 minutes. Loading speed Slow.

The Barnstormer is a miniature roller coaster designed for small children as an introduction into thrill rides. The coaster moves at a relatively slow speed, but the experience lasts less than a minute. Most kids love the attraction—it's small enough in size not to intimidate them, and the entire track is visible from Toontown's street. It's another example of Disney designers knowing their audience.

DONALD'S BOAT ★★½

! APPEAL   Preschool ★★★½   Grade School ★★★   Teens ★½
• BY AGE   Young Adults ★   Over 30 ★   Seniors ★

What it is Playground and (when the water is running) interactive fountain. Scope and scale Diversion. When to go Anytime. Authors' rating A favorite of the 5-and-under set; ★★½ .

Donald's Boat is a small interactive playground themed as a fat, cartoon-style tugboat. It's a great opportunity for small children to run around and blow off some steam. Donald's Boat used to feature a few interactive fountains in the play area, but they very rarely run now.

MINNIE'S COUNTRY HOUSE ★★

! APPEAL   Preschool ★★★★   Grade School ★★★★   Teens ★★½
• BY AGE   Young Adults ★★½   Over 30 ★★★   Seniors ★★★

What it is Walk-through exhibit. Scope and scale Minor attraction. When to go Before 11:30 a.m. or after 4:30 p.m. Authors' rating Getting personal with Minnie; ★★. Duration About 10 minutes. Average wait in line per 100 people ahead of you 12 minutes. Touring speed Slow.

Minnie's Country House is a self-guided tour through the rooms and backyard of Mickey's main squeeze. It's similar to Mickey's Country House, but more feminine. However, unlike Mickey's Country House, which ends with meeting Mickey, there's no chance to meet Minnie at her house.

MICKEY'S COUNTRY HOUSE AND JUDGE'S TENT ★★★

APPEAL Preschool ★★★★★ Grade School ★★★★½ Teens ★★★
BY AGE Young Adults ★★★ Over 30 ★★★★ Seniors ★★★★

What it is **Walk-through tour of Mickey's house and meeting with Mickey.** Scope and scale **Minor attraction.** When to go **Before 11:30 a.m. or after 4:30 p.m.** Authors' rating **A glimpse at Mickey's private life; ★★★.** Duration **15–30 minutes (depending on the crowd).** Average wait in line per 100 people ahead of you **20 minutes.** Touring speed **Slow.**

Mickey's Country House serves as an elaborate queuing area for meeting Mickey Mouse himself. The queue winds through Mickey's front door, past his living room and kitchen, and out into the garden. There you see the plants Mickey is preparing for the big Toontown agricultural contest. Your path ends in the Judge's Tent to meet Mickey. Mickey's Country House is well conceived and contains a lot of Disney memorabilia, and it shows Mickey on a more personal level rather than some corporate symbol.

FSBO: 1BR, 0BA. Roof needs work. Large garden.

TOONTOWN HALL OF FAME ★★

APPEAL Preschool ★★★★½ Grade School ★★★★ Teens ★★★
BY AGE Young Adults ★★ Over 30 ★★★ Seniors ★★

What it is **Character-greeting venue.** Scope and scale **Minor attraction.** When to go **Before 10:30 a.m. or after 5:30 p.m.** Authors' rating **You want characters? We got 'em! ★★.** Duration **About 7–10 minutes.** Average wait in line per 100 people ahead of you **35 minutes.** Touring speed **Slow.**

The Toontown Hall of Fame is at the end of a small plaza between Mickey's and Minnie's houses. It offers one of the largest and most dependably available collection of characters in Walt Disney World. Just inside to the right are entrances to several queuing areas; signs over each indicate which set of characters you will meet. Two lines are almost always dedicated to Disney's princesses (Sleeping Beauty, Snow White, Cin-

derella, and others) and fairies (Tinker Bell and her posse). If a third greeting area is running, character assortments may change when the others need a break.

Each category of characters occupies a greeting room where 15 to 20 guests are admitted at a time. They're allowed to stay 7 to 10 minutes, long enough for a photo, autograph, and hug with each character.

TOMORROWLAND

Tomorrowland's original vision was to showcase how man had developed technology and what that technology might hold for the future. Problem was, technology developed faster than Disney could keep up, so Tomorrowland eventually became a walk-through of what the future might look like from Watergate-era designers—the same people who brought you polyester pants and puffy disco shirts.

In the mid-1990s, however, Disney took that "what the future might look like" idea and pushed it back a few more decades, changing Tomorrowland's theme to what artists of the late 1800s and early 1900s had envisioned for their future. The new Tomorrowland features lots of Buck Rogers–like mechanical rockets, with plenty of brass fittings and other metallic bits. Several attractions feature characters from recent Disney films, too, and they've more or less been worked into the new theming.

DISNEY DESIGN with Sam Gennawey

One of the signature hallmarks of Tomorrowland is all of the vehicles moving about. Moving vehicles dominate the land at all levels. On the ground plain, constantly queuing up are the cars of the Speedway. Up one level are the Tomorrowland Transit Authority trains. The TTA trains continue throughout the land and become a thread that ties many of the Tomorrowland structures together. Flying high overhead are the Astro Orbiter rockets. And when the *Carousel of Progress* is spinning, even the buildings add to the movement. There is no other spot in the Magic Kingdom with such diversity of vehicles on display.

This movement is due to the original Tomorrowland, which lived until 1994. In the relatively brief history of the Magic Kingdom, only Tomorrowland has received a significant makeover. What you see today is the Imagineers' solution to a longtime vexing problem. How do you create the world of tomorrow when tomorrow happens so fast? What happens when the design and construction process takes so long that by the time the project is done, it isn't relevant anymore?

The first Tomorrowland, in Disneyland in 1955, was set in 1986, the return year for Haley's Comet. It was updated in 1967 to no specific date, but the place was the "world on the move." The Magic Kingdom's Tomorrowland 1.0 was the next generation of that concept. But 20 years later the "world on the move" was looking dated.

So the solution in 1994 was to rethink the entire question. Instead of projecting a place set into the future, why not just create a fantasy place influenced by visions of the future? The Imagineers decided to borrow elements from Disneyland Paris's Discoveryland and create "a future that never was." This created a place that is less about anticipating the future than creating a more timeless setting. To this end, the Imagineers borrowed heavily from predictions of Jules Verne, H.G. Wells, and Buck Rogers to create a Spaceport, a place where visitors from throughout the universe come and go. In some respects Tomorrowland is the first postmodern land.

ASTRO ORBITER ★★

| ! APPEAL | Preschool ★★★★ | Grade School ★★★½ | Teens ★★½ |
| ● BY AGE | Young Adults ★★ | Over 30 ★★½ | Seniors ★ |

What it is Buck Rogers–style rockets revolving around a central axis. Scope and scale Minor attraction. When to go Before 11 a.m. or after 5 p.m. Comments This attraction is not as innocuous as it appears. Authors' rating Not worth the wait; ★★. Duration 1½ minutes. Average wait in line per 100 people ahead of you 13½ minutes. Loading speed Slow.

The Astro Orbiter is conceptually the same kind of spinning ride as Fantasyland's Dumbo or Adventureland's Magic Carpets, but with fanciful rocket ships instead of elephants or carpets. The other major difference is that while those attractions take off from ground level, Astro Orbiter's ride vehicles start on the third floor of the ride building and go up from there. The result is that you get some great views of Tomorrowland and the Contemporary Resort, but the experience frightens a fair number of children and adults. Besides the fright factor, Astro Orbiter is one of the slowest loading rides in any Disney park, so expect long lines throughout the day.

MONSTERS, INC. LAUGH FLOOR ★★★½

| ! APPEAL | Preschool ★★★½ | Grade School ★★★★½ | Teens ★★★★ |
| ● BY AGE | Young Adults ★★★★ | Over 30 ★★★★ | Seniors ★★★★ |

What it is Interactive animated comedy routines. Scope and scale Major attraction. When to go Before 11 a.m. or after 4 p.m. Comments Audience members may be asked to participate in skits. Authors' rating Good concept. Jokes are hit-and-miss; ★★★½. Duration About 15 minutes.

We learned in Disney/Pixar's *Monsters Inc.*, that children's screams could be converted into electricity, which was used to power a town inhabited by monsters. During the film, the monsters discovered that children's laughter was an even better source of energy. The concept behind this attraction is that the monsters have set up a comedy club to capture as many laughs as possible. Mike Wazowski, the one-eyed character from the film, serves as the emcee to the club's three comedy acts. Each consists of an animated monster (most not seen in the film) trying out

Most of the Laugh Floor's comedians are computer generated, but look at the kid in the last row.

various bad puns, knock-knock jokes, and Abbott and Costello–like routines. Using the same technology as Epcot's popular *Turtle Talk with Crush*, behind-the-scenes Disney employees voice the characters and often interact with audience members during the skits. As with any comedy club, some performers are funny and some are not. A good thing about this attraction is that Disney has shown a willingness to try new routines and jokes, so the show has remained relatively fresh to repeat visitors.

BUZZ LIGHTYEAR'S
SPACE RANGER SPIN (FASTPASS) ★★★★

❗ APPEAL Preschool ★★★★½   Grade School ★★★★½   Teens ★★★★½
BY AGE Young Adults ★★★★   Over 30 ★★★★½   Seniors ★★★★

What it is **Whimsical space travel–themed indoor ride.** Scope and scale **Minor attraction.** When to go **Before 10:30 a.m., after 6 p.m., or use FASTPASS.** Authors' rating **Surreal shooting gallery; ★★★★.** Duration **About 4½ minutes.** Average wait in line per 100 people ahead of you **3 minutes.** Loading speed **Fast.**

Buzz Lightyear is a moving shooting gallery in which you board rocket ships equipped with two cartoon-style laser "cannons" and shoot at round orange targets in various configurations. Through a small joystick mounted in between the cannon, you can spin the entire ride vehicle around to get better aim at the targets. Of course, the ones hardest to hit are typically worth the most points.

The ride features characters from Disney/Pixar's *Toy Story* film, including Emperor Zurg, the little green aliens, and of course, Buzz Lightyear. Buzz Lightyear's Space Ranger Spin is the first generation of Disney's ride-through target practice attractions, and the 3-D *Toy Story* Mania at Disney's Hollywood Studios is the latest. Despite being older, the game play within Buzz Lightyear is great (even for small children), and it remains one of Tomorrowland's most popular attractions.

Focus your laser cannon on the z-lettered targets.

¹⁹⁰

SPACE MOUNTAIN (FASTPASS) ★ ★ ★ ★

! APPEAL   Preschool ★★½ †   Grade School ★★★★½   Teens ★★★★★
• BY AGE   Young Adults ★★★★½   Over 30 ★★★★½   Seniors ★★★

† Some preschoolers love Space Mountain; others are frightened by it.

What it is Roller coaster in the dark. Scope and scale Superheadliner. When to go When
the park opens, 6–7 p.m., during the hour before closing, or use FASTPASS. Comments
Great fun and action; much wilder than Big Thunder Mountain Railroad. Must be 44″ tall
to ride; children younger than age 7 must be accompanied by an adult. Switching-off
option provided (see page 107). Authors' rating An unusual roller coaster with excellent
special effects; not to be missed; ★★★★. Duration Almost 3 minutes. Average wait in
line per 100 people ahead of you 3 minutes; assumes 2 tracks, one dedicated to FAST-
PASS riders, dispatching at 21-second intervals. Loading speed Moderate–fast.

WARNING:
THIS RIDE WILL
MUSS YOUR DO

Totally enclosed in a mammoth futuristic structure, Space Mountain has always been
the Magic Kingdom's most popular attraction. It remains a rite of passage for Disney
theme-park fans, most of whom can still recite details from their first few rides. The
theme is a space flight through dark recesses of the galaxy. Effects are superb, and
the ride is the fastest and wildest in the Magic Kingdom. It's much zippier than Big
Thunder Mountain, but much less than Rock 'n' Roller Coaster at Disney's Hollywood Studios or Expedition Everest at Animal Kingdom.

Conceptually, Space Mountain is an overgrown version of the small coasters found
at local and regional amusement parks throughout the country for the past 50 years.
Disney's is much bigger, of course, as well as indoors in the dark, and with much more
elaborate special effects. Still, Space Mountain's thrills come from tight turns and unexpected drops, not from endless loops, corkscrews, or skin-flapping high speeds that
other coaster designs turn to when they can't come up with a good storyline.

In 2009 Space Mountain received an extensive refurbishment, adding new lighting and effects, an improved sound system, and a completely redesigned queuing area
with interactive games to help pass the time in line.

STITCH'S GREAT ESCAPE (FASTPASS SEASONALLY) ★★

! APPEAL Preschool ★½   Grade School ★★½   Teens ★★½
• BY AGE Young Adults ★★   Over 30 ★★   Seniors ★½

What it is Theater-in-the-round sci-fi adventure show. Scope and scale Major attraction. When to go Before 11 a.m. or after 6 p.m., during parades. Comments Frightens children of all ages. 40" minimum height requirement. Authors' rating A cheap coat of paint on a broken car; ★★. Duration About 12 minutes plus a 6-minute preshow. Probable waiting time 12–35 minutes.

> Dear Stitch,
> We have to talk. We tried to make this work. We really did. But you're just not the kind of theme-park character we need in our lives right now. We were happy for you when your parents gave you your own attraction after one mediocre film and TV series. And the ride's story about you escaping as prisoner of the galactic authorities when they tried to transfer you to another prison — we totally get the whole "bad boy" thing. But no one likes what you've become. What's with all the spitting and burping you do on the audience during the show? You never used to do that when we were just hanging out. And why is it that the audience has to sit there, strapped to their seats in the dark, so that parents can't help when their kids start screaming? Is that what you want? Because it's like...it's like we don't even know you anymore.
> You say you've tried to improve — keeping the lights on low so kids can see what's going on, for example, and making some of the story scenes less scary. But it's too late. It's not you; it's us. We've changed, and we don't want that kind of ride anymore. We just hope that we can be friends.
> Best, Bob and Len

TOMORROWLAND SPEEDWAY ★

! APPEAL Preschool ★★★★   Grade School ★★★★   Teens ★★★
• BY AGE Young Adults ★★½   Over 30 ★★★   Seniors ★★½

What it is Drive-'em-yourself miniature cars. Scope and scale Major attraction. When to go Before 11 a.m. or after 5 p.m. Comments Kids must be 54" tall to drive unassisted. Authors' rating Boring for adults ★★; great for preschoolers. Duration About 4¼ minutes. Average wait in line per 100 people ahead of you 4½ minutes; assumes 285-car turnover every 20 minutes. Loading speed Slow.

The Speedway is an elaborate miniature raceway with gasoline-powered cars that travel up to seven miles per hour. With its sleek cars and racing noises, it is quite alluring. Unfortunately, the cars poke along on a guide rail, leaving the driver little to do. Even with the guide rail, however, the steering wheel seems to be completely unconnected to the actual bits that steer the car. We're not the best drivers in the world, but we're always thrashed side to side on the Speedway like some sort of children's toy caught in the washing machine. And you spend so much energy pushing down the gas pedal in a futile attempt to go faster that your right leg is useless quivering jelly for an hour after you ride. (When asked why you're limping, mutter something about an old character-meal injury and say that you don't want to talk about it. Then throw in, "I'll get you, Mary Poppins," in a barely audible whisper.) The 54" height requirement to drive excludes small children who would most enjoy the ride.

We're so doing this when we get home!

TOMORROWLAND TRANSIT AUTHORITY ★★★

! APPEAL Preschool ★★★★ Grade School ★★★½ Teens ★★★½
• BY AGE Young Adults ★★★★ Over 30 ★★★★ Seniors ★★★★

What it is Scenic tour of Tomorrowland. Scope and scale Minor attraction. When to go Anytime, but especially during hot, crowded times of day (11:30 a.m.–4:30 p.m.). Comments A good way to check out the FASTPASS line at Space Mountain. Authors' rating Scenic and relaxing; ★★★. Duration 10 minutes. Average wait in line per 100 people ahead of you 1½ minutes; assumes 39 trains operating. Loading speed Fast.

A once-unique prototype of a linear-induction mass-transit system, the authority's trams take you on a spin past most of Tomorrowland, through Space Mountain, and past Buzz Lightyear's Space Ranger Spin on a covered, elevated track on Tomorrowland's second story.

Besides the view, the best things about the TTA are that there's rarely a wait for it, you get to sit on comfortable padded seats for around ten minutes, and there's enough combined breeze and air-conditioning to cool off in that time. If you make especially pathetic faces to the cast members at the unloading area, they may let you ride again without getting off.

WALT DISNEY'S CAROUSEL OF PROGRESS ★★★

! APPEAL Preschool ★★★ Grade School ★★★ Teens ★★★
• BY AGE Young Adults ★★★½ Over 30 ★★★½ Seniors ★★★★

What it is Audio-animatronic theater production. Scope and scale Major attraction. When to go Anytime. Authors' rating Nostalgic, warm, and happy; ★★★. Duration 18 minutes. Preshow Documentary on the attraction's long history. Probable waiting time Less than 10 minutes.

Walt Disney's *Carousel of Progress* showcases how modern family life has evolved over the past century, using kitchen appliances as a backdrop for discussing social and familial changes in a four-act script. Originally conceived for the 1964–5 World's Fair, *Carousel of Progress* has gone through regular updates over the past 40 years; however, the underlying story is relatively unchanged, tracing how family life has improved for a father, mother, daughter, and son. Though the story spans roughly a hundred years, the characters age only slightly. *Carousel* is a great ride in the middle of the day. Because of its unique theater setup, waits are usually minimal at any time.

Hats are all the rave at Walt Disney World, and as you can see, there's more than one Mad Hatter.

LIVE ENTERTAINMENT

Besides the attractions and shows, Disney character appearances, parades, fireworks, singing, and dancing further enliven the Magic Kingdom. Because so many things are going on in any day, check the live-entertainment schedule in your guide map (free as you enter the park or at City Hall) or in the *Times Guide* available along with the guide map. Following is a sample of the best live entertainment offerings in the park.

Parades The Magic Kingdom offers at least an afternoon parade every day, and most nights include an evening parade as well. Both are major productions. The afternoon parade, which typically starts at Main Street and works its way toward Frontierland, features bands, floats, and Disney characters who sing and dance to contemporary and classic Disney music. The theme usually changes every year or two, along with the music. If you're not going to be in the park at night, try to catch at least a few minutes of the afternoon parade.

The Magic Kingdom's evening parade is, in our opinion, far superior to the afternoon version and the single best parade in all of Walt Disney World. Titled SpectroMagic, the evening parade is a high-tech affair that employs electro-luminescent and fiber-optic technologies, light-spreading thermoplastics (don't try this at home!), and clouds of underlit liquid-nitrogen smoke. The parade also offers a memorable-in-a-good-way soundtrack, all the major characters (including Mickey Mouse), and thousands of sparkling lights.

▶**UNOFFICIAL TIP** Frontierland offers some of the best parade-viewing spots. We like to sit along the shops rather than along the waterside, as the shops are usually in the shade, and during summer months you can catch some of the cool air-conditioning wafting out of the stores. Finally, note that both parades occasionally incorporate seasonal themes, especially during the winter holidays.

Wishes **Fireworks** *Wishes* features memorable vignettes and music from beloved Disney films, along with a stellar fireworks display, while Jiminy Cricket narrates a lump-in-your-throat story about making wishes come true. Cinderella Castle is used as a backdrop for various mood lighting. If *Wishes* is being performed during your stay, be sure you catch the show.

Disney Character Shows and Appearances Usually, a number of characters are on hand to greet guests when the park opens. Most days, a character is on duty for photos and autographs from 9 a.m. to 10 p.m. next to City Hall. Mickey and an assortment of other characters are available most of the day at Mickey's Toontown Fair. Shows at the Castle Forecourt Stage feature Disney characters several times daily (check the *Times Guide*). In Fantasyland, Ariel can be found in her grotto daily, while others can be seen at the Character Festival next to Dumbo. Assorted characters also roam the park.

▶**UNOFFICIAL TIP** For information on character whereabouts on the day you visit, check the Character Greeting Guide printed on the inside of the handout park map or the *Times Guide.*

Bay Lake and Seven Seas Lagoon Floating Electrical Pageant Performed at nightfall (about 9 p.m. most of the year) on Seven Seas Lagoon and Bay Lake, this is one of our favorites among the Disney extras, but it's necessary to leave the Magic Kingdom to view it. The pageant is a stunning electric-light show aboard small barges and set to nifty electronic music. Leave the Magic Kingdom and take the monorail to the Polynesian Resort. Get yourself a drink and walk to the end of the pier to watch the show.

The Magic Kingdom has its own marching band, performing here on Main Street.

To watch *Wishes* with family and friends is to experience everything good that a Walt Disney World park has to offer.

Magic Kingdom Special Treats Menu

You can sure work up a mighty appetite pounding the pavement of the Magic Kingdom. If you've had a cravin' flung on but you don't know what for, consider these popular Magic Kingdom taste treats.

Cinderella Castle Cone

Comes with a signed photo of Ben and Jerry in their bathing suits at the Peoria YMCA. Six generous dips of ice cream hang over the side of the cone and, frankly, could use a little extra buttressing (and so will you if you eat one of these humdingers).

.............$10.95 ($9.95 *without flags*)

Captain Hook Shish-Ka-Bob

If you're a real carnivore this one's for you. Tucker in for a whole pound of real cow meat grilled on a stainless steel prosthetic device over an open grill. Try it once and you'll be hooked! Gluten free.

...............................$11.37

Goofy Burger

Observing the sausage factory code of silence, we can't tell you what's in it. But it's served on a bun, golden brown, and makes your lips jump up and down! Comes with fries and a medium-size drink.

....$8.95 ($10.95 with super-size ears)

Peter Pancakes

This dapper artery-clogger is served at all Magic Kingdom character breakfasts and consists of six hearty flapjacks smothered in extra-gooey maple syrup. The hat is yours to keep and is guaranteed to stick on your head, even on roller coasters.

.................................$12.95

Tinkerburger

Peter Pancakes won't hop off your plate and fly around the room, but the Tinker-burger sure will. Served with Monterey Jack cheese, chipotle sauce, and a heap-ing measure of Pixie Dust, this is a burger you can't put (or keep) down.

.....$8.95 ($12.95 with butterfly net).

COUNTER-SERVICE RESTAURANTS

For all that can be said about the Magic Kingdom, with its lovingly crafted attractions, beautiful buildings, and timeless stories, dining is not one of the park's strengths. More than likely, your dining choices for lunch are going to be made simply by finding the closest restaurant to where you are when you're hungry. It's not that counter-service food in the park is necessarily bad, but you probably won't find many places worth walking across the park for.

Our favorite restaurant is Frontierland's Pecos Bill Tall Tale Inn and Cafe. A couple of notable exceptions (which operate seasonally) are the Mexican-themed El Pirata y El Perico in Adventureland and the Asian-inspired Tomorrowland Terrace Noodle Station. The food at these two places is sufficiently different from the usual theme-park fare, so we try to visit them whenever they're open.

Casey's Corner

QUALITY Good VALUE B PORTION Medium LOCATION Main Street, U.S.A.
READER RESPONSES 88% ⌕ 12% ⌕ DINING PLAN Yes

Quarter-pound hot dogs, fries, and brownies. A little pricey on the dogs and very crowded—keep walking.

Columbia Harbour House

QUALITY Fair VALUE C+ PORTION Medium LOCATION Liberty Square
READER RESPONSES 90% ⌕ 10% ⌕ DINING PLAN Yes

Fried fish and chicken strips; hummus and tuna-salad sandwiches; child's plate with macaroni and cheese or garden chicken salad with grapes and child's beverage; New England clam chowder and vegetarian chili; coleslaw; chips; fries; garden salad; chocolate cake. No trans fats in the fried items; a nice change from the usual pizza and burger fare. The quickest service within spitting distance of Fantasyland.

Cosmic Ray's Starlight Cafe

QUALITY Good VALUE B PORTION Large LOCATION Tomorrowland
READER RESPONSES 84% ⌕ 16% ⌕ DINING PLAN Yes

Rotisserie chicken and ribs; turkey-bacon and vegetarian wraps; hot dogs; hamburgers, including veggie burgers; Caesar salad with chicken; chicken-noodle soup; chili; carrot cake and no-sugar-added brownies for dessert. Kosher choices include a burger, chicken strips, and corned beef on rye. Out-of-this-world entertainment on stage.

El Pirata y el Perico *(open seasonally)*

QUALITY Fair VALUE B PORTION Medium–large LOCATION Adventureland
READER RESPONSES 73% ⌕ 27% ⌕ DINING PLAN Yes

Beef taco salad, vegetarian and beef tacos, quesadillas for kids. Large, shaded eating area.

Golden Oak Outpost

QUALITY Good VALUE B+ PORTION Medium–large LOCATION Frontierland
READER RESPONSES *TOO NEW TO RATE* DINING PLAN Yes

Chicken nuggets, fried-chicken-breast sandwich, vegetarian flatbread wrap, served with apple slices or French fries.

The Lunching Pad

QUALITY Good **VALUE** B– **PORTION** Medium **LOCATION** Tomorrowland
READER RESPONSES 76% 👍 24% 👎 **DINING PLAN** Yes

Smoked turkey legs, pretzels, frozen sodas.

Mrs. Potts' Cupboard

QUALITY Good **VALUE** B **PORTION** Medium **LOCATION** Fantasyland
READER RESPONSES 93% 👍 7% 👎 **DINING PLAN** No

Sundaes, including fudge brownie and strawberry shortcake; floats and shakes; cookies; drinks.

Pecos Bill Tall Tale Inn and Cafe

QUALITY Good **VALUE** B **PORTION** Medium–large **LOCATION** Frontierland
READER RESPONSES 90% 👍 10% 👎 **DINING PLAN** Yes

Cheeseburgers, veggie burgers, chicken wraps, chicken salad, chili, child's plate with hamburger or salad with grilled chicken and child's beverage, fries and chili-cheese fries, peanut-butter-brownie mousse. Use the great fixin's station to garnish your burger. Combos come with fries or carrots.

The Pinocchio Village Haus

QUALITY Fair **VALUE** C **PORTION** Medium **LOCATION** Fantasyland
READER RESPONSES 77% 👍 23% 👎 **DINING PLAN** Yes

Personal pizzas, chicken nuggets, Caesar salad with chicken, Mediterranean salad, kids' meals of mac and cheese or PB&J, fries plain or with toppings. The Village Haus is always filled with families taking a Fantasyland break. Consider Columbia Harbour House or Pecos Bill Tall Tale Inn and Cafe, both only a few minutes' walk away.

Scuttle's Landing

QUALITY Good **VALUE** B **PORTION** Medium **LOCATION** Fantasyland
READER RESPONSES 78% 👍 22% 👎 **DINING PLAN** No

Frozen Cokes, soft pretzels, chips. Essentially a snack bar, but not a bad place to grab a drink.

Tomorrowland Terrace Noodle Station

QUALITY Good **VALUE** B **PORTION** Medium–large **LOCATION** Tomorrowland
READER RESPONSES 64% 👍 36% 👎 **DINING PLAN** Yes

Chicken or vegetable noodle bowl, fried-chicken nuggets, orange chicken with rice, beef and broccoli, Caesar salad, child's plate of chicken nuggets or beef and mac. Chocolate cake for dessert; beverage selections include iced green teas and hot teas. Good if you're looking for something beyond dogs and burgers.

EPCOT

It's probably safe to say that Epcot was what Walt Disney most wanted to build after the success of Disneyland. Designed to demonstrate new technology and innovation, Walt envisioned it as a sort of permanent world's fair for companies, universities, and governments to show off their latest creations.

On paper, that doesn't sound like the recipe for a fun vacation. Indeed, Epcot's educational theme and corporate imagery lacks some of the obvious warmth and charm of the Magic Kingdom. And unlike the Magic Kingdom's attractions, many of which assume you're going to sit passively and watch whatever is in front of you, Epcot is a theme park about ideas, such as ecologies, energy sources, and the role communication systems play in human societies. Epcot's attractions work best when you consider the impact these ideas have—and will have—on the lives of everyday people.

Besides futuristic attractions, half of Epcot is devoted to World Showcase, a collection of elaborate pavilions representing the landmarks and cultures of various countries from around the world. Each country is staffed by young adults from that nation, so it's possible your children will hear French spoken in the France pavilion or Mandarin in the China pavilion. Every country has at least one restaurant, too, making Epcot home to the most diverse set of dining options on property. For adults, Epcot may have the best nighttime fireworks display and music in *IllumiNations*. Given these, Epcot may be the best theme park ever built.

Not to Be Missed at Epcot

WORLD SHOWCASE	**The American Adventure**	*IllumiNations*
FUTURE WORLD	*Honey, I Shrunk the Audience*	**Living with the Land**
Soarin'	**Mission: Space**	**The Seas**
	Spaceship Earth	**Test Track**

▶**UNOFFICIAL TIP** Plan to arrive at the turnstiles 30 to 40 minutes before official opening time. Give yourself an extra 10 minutes or so to park and make your way to the entrance.

DISNEY DESIGN with Sam Gennawey

The popular story of Epcot's design is that Imagineers John Hench and Marty Sklar pushed two models of two separate projects together—Future World plus a permanent world's fair called the World Showcase—into one massive 260-acre park, more than twice as large as the Magic Kingdom and three times as large as Disneyland.

The gateway for this new park would be a time machine, just like the entrance at the Magic Kingdom. To illustrate my point, you might recall that at the Magic Kingdom, you pass below the railroad, through a small tunnel, and enter an idealistic American town circa 1900. The tunnel is like a time machine. At Epcot, no matter how you arrive—whether it's by auto, bus, or monorail—you always enter into the future. And you do it through Spaceship Earth.

Everyone passes under this unifying theme element, Spaceship Earth, and everyone shares that experience as a community in a park that celebrates the interdependence between our minds, bodies, and Earth. The front half of the figure eight–shaped park teaches us about the past and anticipates the future. The back half celebrates the cultures of the world.

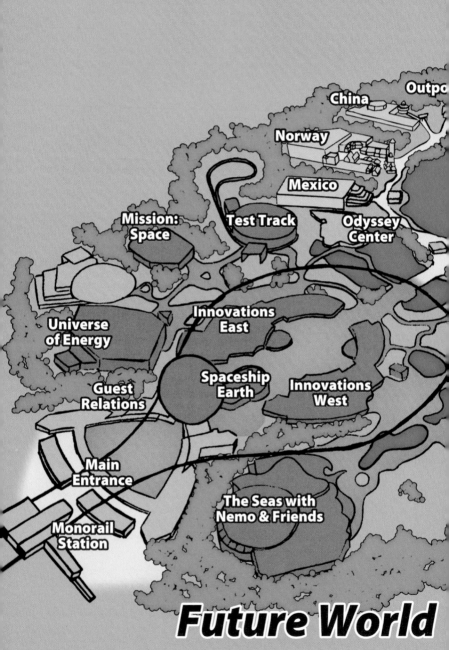

China

Outpo

Norway

Mexico

Mission:
Space

Test Track

Odyssey
Center

Innovations
East

Universe
of Energy

Guest
Relations

Spaceship
Earth

Innovations
West

Main
Entrance

The Seas with
Nemo & Friends

Monorail
Station

Future World

World Showcase

How much does Epcot weigh?

Huh?

FUTURE WORLD

Gleaming futuristic structures of immense proportions define the first themed area beyond the main entrance. Broad thoroughfares are punctuated with billowing fountains—all reflected in shiny space-age facades. Everything, including landscaping, is sparkling clean and seems bigger than life. Front and center is Spaceship Earth, flanked by Innoventions East and West, while pavilions dedicated to mankind's past, present, and future technological accomplishments ring the perimeter of Future World.

Future World Services

Epcot's service facilities in Future World include:

Baby Center/Baby Care Needs: On the World Showcase side of the Odyssey Center

Banking Services: ATMs outside the main entrance near the kennels, on the Future World bridge, and in World Showcase at the Germany Pavilion

Dining Reservations: At Guest Relations, to the left of Spaceship Earth

First Aid: Next to the Baby Center on the World Showcase side of the Odyssey Center

Live Entertainment Information: At Guest Relations

Lost and Found: At the main entrance at the gift shop

Lost Persons: At Guest Relations and the Baby Center on the World Showcase side of the Odyssey Center

Storage Lockers: Turn right at Spaceship Earth (lockers emptied nightly)

Wheelchair and Stroller Rental: Inside the main entrance and to the left, toward the rear of the Entrance Plaza

Most Epcot services are concentrated in Future World's Entrance Plaza, near the main gate.

CLUB COOL

Attached to the fountain side of Innoventions West is a retail space–soda fountain called Club Cool. It doesn't look like much, but inside, this Coca-Cola–sponsored exhibit provides free unlimited samples of soft drinks from around the world. Some of the selections will taste like medicine to an American (Italy's offering, Beverly, could peel paint off walls), but others will please. Because it's centrally located in Future World, it makes a good meeting or break place, and you can slake your thirst while you wait for the rest of your party.

INNOVENTIONS ★★★½

| ! APPEAL | Preschool ★★★½ | Grade School ★★★★ | Teens ★★★½ |
| • BY AGE | Young Adults ★★★ | Over 30 ★★★ | Seniors ★★★ |

What it is Static and hands-on exhibits relating to products and technologies of the near future. **Scope and scale** Major diversion. **When to go** On your second day at Epcot or after you've seen all the major attractions. **Comments** Most exhibits demand time and participation to be rewarding—there's not much gained here by a quick walk-through. **Authors' rating** Something for everyone; ★★★½.

Innoventions—a huge, busy collection of walk-through, hands-on exhibits sponsored by corporations—consists of two huge, crescent-shaped, glass-walled structures separated by a central plaza. Dynamic, interactive, and forward-looking, the area resembles a high-tech trade show. Products preview consumer and industrial goods of the near future. Electronics, communications, and entertainment technology play a prominent role. Exhibits, many of which are changed each year, demonstrate such products as virtual-reality games, high-definition television, voice-activated appliances, future cars, medical diagnostic equipment, and Internet applications. Each of the major exhibit areas is sponsored by a different manufacturer or research lab, emphasizing the effect of the products or technology on daily living.

Exhibits change periodically, and there is a definite trend toward larger, more elaborate exhibits, almost mini-attractions. The newer exhibits are certainly more compelling, but they require waiting in line to be admitted. The most popular new attraction is The Sum of All Thrills, a ride in which guests use math skills to create a virtual roller coaster track before boarding a giant robot arm to "ride" their creation.

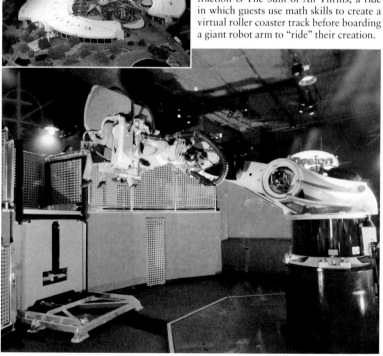

SPACESHIP EARTH ★★★★

! APPEAL
• BY AGE

Preschool ★★★★	Grade School ★★★★	Teens ★★★★
Young Adults ★★★★	Over 30 ★★★★	Seniors ★★★★½

What it is **Educational dark ride through past, present, and future.** Scope and scale **Headliner.** When to go **Before 10 a.m. or after 4 p.m.** Comments **If lines are long when you arrive, try again after 4 p.m.** Authors' rating **One of Epcot's best; not to be missed; ★★★★.** Duration **About 16 minutes.** Average wait in line per 100 people ahead of you **3 minutes.** Loading speed **Fast.**

This ride spirals through the 18-story interior of Epcot's premier landmark, taking visitors past audio-animatronic scenes depicting mankind's developments in communications. Key scenes in those developments are re-created in incredible detail, including everything from Phoenician merchants' invention of the alphabet, Greek theater, the moveable type printing press and its path to the Renaissance, and modern television, space communications, and computer networks. The ride is well done and an amazing use of the geosphere's interior.

Besides the story, Spaceship Earth has a few more features that make it one of Disney World's best rides. One is that there's rarely a long wait to board, since its ride vehicles are loaded continuously. In addition, the ride's narration is available in a variety of languages. And the ride ends with an interactive, animated cartoon that lets you choose how your lifestyle might look in a Jetsons-like future.

IMAGINATION! PAVILION

This glass pyramid-shaped pavilion is on the west side of Innoventions West and down the walk from The Land. Outside is an upside-down waterfall and one of our favorite Future World landmarks, the "jumping water," a fountain that hops over the heads of unsuspecting passersby. Imagination! is home to two attractions and a post-show area with interactive computer art and music stations.

HONEY, I SHRUNK THE AUDIENCE ★★★★½

! APPEAL   Preschool ★★★★½   Grade School ★★★★   Teens ★★½
● BY AGE   Young Adults ★★   Over 30 ★★½   Seniors ★★

What it is 3-D film with special effects. Scope and scale Headliner. When to go Before noon or after 4 p.m. Comments Adults should not be put off by the sci-fi theme. The loud, intense show with tactile effects frightens some young children. Authors' rating An absolute hoot! Not to be missed; ★★★★½. Duration About 17 minutes plus 8-minute preshow. Probable waiting time 15 minutes (at suggested times).

Honey, I Shrunk the Audience is a 3-D offshoot of Disney's feature film *Honey, I Shrunk the Kids. Honey, I Shrunk the Audience* features an array of special effects, including simulated explosions, smoke, fiber optics, lights, water spray, and moving seats. While some of the scenes may be intense for small children, most of the attraction is played strictly for laughs.

This is a Disney press photo. The actual dog that licks you is much smaller.

© Disney

JOURNEY INTO IMAGINATION
WITH FIGMENT ★★½

! APPEAL   Preschool ★★★★   Grade School ★★★½   Teens ★★★
• BY AGE   Young Adults ★★★   Over 30 ★★★   Seniors ★★★

What it is **Dark fantasy-adventure ride.** Scope and scale **Major-attraction wannabe.** When to go **Anytime.** Authors' rating **★★½.** Duration **About 6 minutes.** Average wait in line per 100 people ahead of you **2 minutes.** Loading speed **Fast.**

In 2002, the attraction was retooled to add Figment, everyone's favorite dragon. This attraction draws on the Imagination Institute theme from *Honey, I Shrunk the Audience* (in the same pavilion) and takes you on a tour of the zany institute. Sometimes you're a passive observer, and sometimes you're a test subject, as the ride provides a glimpse of the fictitious lab's inner workings. Stimulating all your senses and then some, you are hit with optical illusions, an experiment in which noise generates colors, a room that defies gravity, and other brainteasers. The ride features Figment, a purple winged dinosaur that is among the parks' most popular residents.

After the ride, you're led through an interactive exhibit area offering some hands-on imagery technology. One of the coolest interactive exhibits is a photo-morphing computer. First the machine takes your picture, and then you select an image (such as an animal) from several categories into which your photo is integrated. You can then e-mail the photo to friends and family, at no charge. We sent a number of photos in which our faces were morphed into pandas, lions, lizards, and even a great owl!

At home in the Imagination labs,
sitting down on the ceiling.

THE LAND PAVILION

The Land is a huge themed area containing three attractions, a guided tour of a greenhouse, and several food court–style restaurants. When the pavilion was originally built, its emphasis was on farming, but it now focuses on the environment.

THE CIRCLE OF LIFE ★★★½

! APPEAL BY AGE	Preschool ★★★	Grade School ★★★	Teens ★★★
	Young Adults ★★★	Over 30 ★★★	Seniors ★★★½

What it is Film exploring man's relationship with his environment. Scope and scale Minor attraction. When to go Before 11 a.m. or after 2 p.m. Authors' rating Highly interesting and enlightening; ★★★½. Duration About 12½ minutes. Preshow Ecological slide show and trivia. Probable waiting time 10–15 minutes.

This playful yet educational film, starring Simba, Timon, and Pumbaa from Disney's animated feature *The Lion King*, spotlights the environmental interdependency of all creatures, demonstrating how easily the ecological balance can be upset. The message is sobering, but one that enlightens.

LIVING WITH THE LAND (FASTPASS) ★★★★

! APPEAL
• BY AGE

Preschool ★★★½	Grade School ★★★½	Teens ★★★★
Young Adults ★★★★	Over 30 ★★★★	Seniors ★★★★

What it is Indoor boat-ride adventure chronicling the past, present, and future of farming and agriculture in the United States. **Scope and scale** Major attraction. **When to go** Before 10:30 a.m. or after 5 p.m., or use FASTPASS. **Comments** Go early in the morning and save other Land attractions (except for Soarin') for later in the day. The ride is located on the pavilion's lower level. **Authors' rating** Interesting, fun, and not to be missed; ★★★★. **Duration** About 12 minutes. Average wait in line per 100 people ahead of you 3 minutes; assumes 15 boats operating. **Loading speed** Moderate.

Living with the Land is a relaxing boat ride through the history of (mostly American) agriculture. As you float past swamps and inhospitable farm environments, you're shown how technology such as mechanization, fertilizers, and pest management help produce the food we eat.

The second half of the attraction showcases a futuristic greenhouse, where everything from fish and alligators to exotic and everyday plant crops are grown. Each room in the greenhouse displays innovative ways to grow these crops: In areas with little land space, for example, vertical walls grow lettuce. In areas with little natural rain, techniques are shown that limit the amount of water used by spraying the liquid directly on the plant's roots. And vegetables and gourds that typically sit on the soil are made rot-resistant by growing them in strong nets several feet off the ground.

It's inspiring and educational, with excellent effects and good narrative. Stars of the greenhouse include giant pumpkins and a tomato tree that has produced a world-record harvest of more than 20,000 tomatoes with a total weight in excess of 850 pounds. A walking tour of the greenhouse is also available for a small cost. If you're into this sort of thing, it's like a visit to the Willie Wonka chocolate factory (and you can sneak the occasional sample, too).

Many Epcot guests who read about Living with the Land in guidebooks decide that it sounds too dry and educational for their tastes. We find smaller children to be much more engaged if they're asked to guess what kind of food comes from the plants being grown.

© Jeff Bergman

SOARIN' (FASTPASS) ★ ★ ★ ★ ½

! APPEAL	Preschool ★ ★ ★ ★	Grade School ★ ★ ★ ★ ★	Teens ★ ★ ★ ★ ★
• BY AGE	Young Adults ★ ★ ★ ★ ★	Over 30 ★ ★ ★ ★ ★	Seniors ★ ★ ★ ★ ★

What it is Flight-simulation ride. **Scope and scale** Superheadliner. **When to go** First 30 minutes the park is open or use FASTPASS. **Comments** Entrance on the lower level of the Land Pavilion. May induce motion sickness; 40" minimum height requirement; switching off available (see page 107). **Authors' rating** Exciting and mellow at the same time; ★ ★ ★ ★ ½. Not to be missed. **Duration** 5½ minutes. **Average wait in line per 100 people ahead of you** 4 minutes; assumes 2 concourses operating. **Loading speed** Moderate.

Soarin' is a thrill ride for all ages, exhilarating as a hawk on the wing and as mellow as swinging in a hammock. If you are fortunate enough to have experienced flying dreams in your sleep, you'll have a sense of how Soarin' feels.

Once you enter the main theater, you are secured in a seat not unlike those on inverted roller coasters (where the coaster is suspended from above). When everyone is in place, the rows of seats swing into position, making you feel as if the floor has dropped away, and you are suspended with your legs dangling. Thus hung out to dry, you embark on a simulated hang-glider tour with IMAX-quality images projected all around you, and with the flight simulator moving in sync with the movie.

The IMAX images are well chosen and drop-dead beautiful. Special effects include wind, sound, and even olfactory stimulation. The ride itself is thrilling but perfectly smooth. We're not sure what an attraction about hang-gliding over California is doing in a place called Future World, but nonetheless, it's the most popular attraction in all of Walt Disney World. We think Soarin' is a must-experience for guests of any age who meet the height requirement. And yes, we interviewed senior citizens who tried the ride and were crazy about it.

We're not sure what it's doing in Future World, but Soarin' is fun for everyone.

© Disney

Reader Questions We Can Answer

How far has the Disney monorail traveled since Walt Disney World opened in 1971?

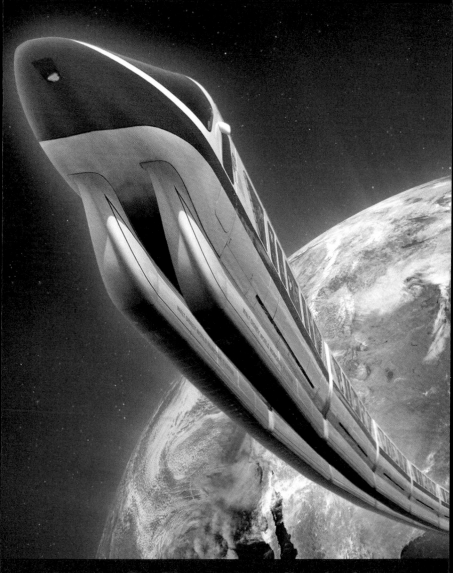

Answer: The Disney monorail trains have logged mileage equal to more than 30 round-trips to the moon.

214

THE SEAS WITH NEMO AND FRIENDS PAVILION

This area comprises one of America's top marine aquariums, a ride that tunnels through the aquarium, an interactive animated film, and a number of first-class educational walk-through exhibits.

Altogether it's a stunning package, one we rate as not to be missed. A comprehensive makeover featuring characters from the animated feature Finding Nemo brought some whimsy and much-needed levity to what theretofore was educationally brilliant but somewhat staid.

TURTLE TALK WITH CRUSH ★★★★

! APPEAL
• BY AGE

Preschool ★★★★½   Grade School ★★★★½   Teens ★★★★
Young Adults ★★★★   Over 30 ★★★★   Seniors ★★★★

What it is An interactive animated film. Scope and scale Minor attraction. When to go Before 11 a.m. or after 5 p.m. Authors' rating A real spirit lifter; ★★★★. Duration 17 minutes. Probable waiting time 10–20 minutes before 11 a.m. and after 5 p.m.; as much as 40–60 minutes during the more crowded part of the day.

Turtle Talk with Crush is an interactive theater show starring the 153-year-old surfer-dude turtle from the Disney/Pixar film *Finding Nemo*. Although it starts like a typical Disney theme-park movie, *Turtle Talk* quickly turns into a surprise interactive encounter as

All Crush needs is some tasty waves, kids.

the on-screen Crush begins to have actual conversations with guests in the audience. Real-time computer graphics are used to accurately move Crush's mouth when forming words, and he's voiced by a guy who went to the *Fast Times at Ridgemont High* school of diction.

THE SEAS MAIN TANK AND EXHIBITS ★★★½

! APPEAL | Preschool ★★★★ | Grade School ★★★★ | Teens ★★★★
• BY AGE | Young Adults ★★★★ | Over 30 ★★★★ | Seniors ★★★★

What it is A huge saltwater aquarium, plus exhibits on oceanography, ocean ecology, and sea life. **Scope and scale** Major attraction. **When to go** Before 11:30 a.m. or after 5 p.m. **Authors' rating** An excellent marine exhibit; ★★★½. **Average wait in line per 100 people ahead of you** 3½ minutes. **Loading speed** Fast.

The Seas is among Future World's most ambitious offerings. Scientists and divers conduct actual marine experiments in a 200-foot-diameter, 27-foot-deep main tank containing fish, mammals, and crustaceans in a simulation of an ocean ecosystem. Visitors can watch the activity through eight-inch-thick windows below the surface (including some in the Coral Reef restaurant). On entering The Seas, you're directed to the loading area for The Seas with Nemo & Friends, an attraction that conveys you via a Plexiglas tunnel through the Seas' main tank.

The Seas' fish population is substantial, but the strength of this attraction lies in the dozen or so exhibits offered after the ride. Visitors can view fish-breeding experiments, watch short films about sea life, and more. A delightful exhibit showcases clownfish (Nemo), regal blue tang (Dory), and other species featured in Disney/Pixar's *Finding Nemo*. Other highlights include a haunting, hypnotic jellyfish tank; a sea horse aquarium; a stingray exhibit; and a manatee tank.

About two-thirds of the main aquarium is home to reef species, including sharks, rays, and a number of fish that you've seen in quiet repose on your dinner plate. The other third, separated by an inconspicuous divider, houses bottle-nosed dolphins and sea turtles.

© Disney

216 THE SEAS WITH NEMO & FRIENDS ★★★

APPEAL   Preschool ★★★★½   Grade School ★★★★   Teens ★★★
BY AGE   Young Adults ★★★½   Over 30 ★★★½   Seniors ★★★★

What it is Ride through a tunnel in The Seas' main tank. Scope and scale Major attraction. When to go Before 11 a.m. or after 5 p.m. Authors' rating ★★★. Duration 4 minutes. Average wait in line per 100 people ahead of you 3½ minutes. Loading speed Fast.

The Seas with Nemo & Friends is a high-tech ride featuring characters from the animated hit *Finding Nemo*. The ride likewise deposits you at the heart of The Seas, where the exhibits, *Turtle Talk with Crush*, and viewing platforms for the main aquarium are located.

Upon entering The Seas, you're given the option of experiencing the ride or proceeding directly to the exhibit area. If you choose the ride, you'll be ushered to its loading area, where you'll be made comfortable in a "clam mobile" for your journey through the aquarium. The attraction features technology that makes it seem as if the animated characters are swimming with live fish. Very cool.

Almost immediately you meet Mr. Ray and his class and learn that Nemo is missing. The remainder of the odyssey consists of finding Nemo with the help of Dory, Bruce, Marlin, Squirt, and Crush, all characters from the animated feature. Unlike the film, however, the ride ends with a musical finale.

Nemo's gone missing again? How unusual.

© Disney

UNIVERSE OF ENERGY:
ELLEN'S ENERGY ADVENTURE ★★★★

! APPEAL Preschool ★★★   Grade School ★★★   Teens ★★★
• BY AGE Young Adults ★★★   Over 30 ★★★½   Seniors ★★★½

What it is Combination ride–theater presentation about energy. Scope and scale Major attraction. When to go
Before 11:15 a.m. or after 4:30 p.m. Comments Don't be dismayed by long lines; 580 people enter the pavilion
each time the theater changes audiences. Authors' rating The most unique theater in Walt Disney World;
★★★★. Duration About 26½ minutes plus 8-minute preshow. Probable waiting time 20–40 minutes.

This pavilion focuses on energy sources, primarily the origin of fossil fuels. What
would be an otherwise ponderous discussion is greatly enhanced by the addition of
Ellen DeGeneres and Bill Nye, in both the preshow film and in narration throughout the presentation.

For the presentation, you're seated in what appears to be an ordinary theater. A
short movie sets up the premise of the ride: Ellen falls asleep watching *Jeopardy*—her
favorite game—and she dreams of competing on the show when all of the question
categories involve energy. Bill Nye plays Ellen's neighbor in the film and appears in
her dream to provide educational tips about the origins, types, and relative merits of
energy in all its forms.

During all of this, you'll notice the theater
seats divide into six 97-passenger traveling cars that
glide among the swamps and reptiles of a prehistoric forest. Special effects include the feel of warm,
moist air from the swamp, and the smell of sulfur
from an erupting volcano.

If you enjoy Ellen's humor (and we do), parts
of the ride are downright funny. For kids, Universe of Energy remains a toss-up. The
dinosaurs frighten some preschoolers, and kids of all ages lose the thread during the
educational segments. And no matter what, we recommend avoiding the ride right
after lunch—the combination of arcane subject matter; smooth, dark ride; and air-
conditioning is too great an opportunity to nap for many, many people.

TEST TRACK PAVILION

Test Track, presented by General Motors, contains the Test Track ride and Inside Track, a collection of transportation-themed stationary exhibits and multimedia presentations. The pavilion is the last on the left before crossing into the World Showcase. Many readers tell us that Test Track "is one big commercial" for General Motors. We agree that promotional hype is more heavy-handed here than in most other business-sponsored attractions. But Test Track is one of the most creatively conceived and executed attractions in Walt Disney World.

The Test Track Pavilion is filled with various machines that build and test automobile subassemblies.

TEST TRACK (FASTPASS) ★★★½

! **APPEAL**   Preschool ★★★★   Grade School ★★★★½   Teens ★★★★★
• **BY AGE**   Young Adults ★★★★½   Over 30 ★★★★½   Seniors ★★★★

What it is **Automobile test-track simulator ride.** Scope and scale **Superheadliner.** When to go **The first 30 minutes the park is open, just before closing, or use FASTPASS.** Comments **40" height minimum.** Authors' rating **Not to be missed; ★★★½.** Duration **About 4 minutes.** Average wait in line per 100 people ahead of you 4½ minutes. Loading speed **Moderate–fast.**

Visitors board a future-model car as it runs through a series of tests designed to stress various components, such as shocks (by driving over rough terrain), anti-lock brakes (skidding through high-speed turns), and paint (by passing through superhot and freezing-cold rooms). The tests culminate in a high-speed lap around the exterior of the pavilion, and you can hear the cars whoosh by as you're walking inside. If you're visiting Epcot with your lead-footed, text-talk-and-steer brother-in-law, don't worry: The Test Track car is affixed to a track, and no actual driving is necessary.

It's never too soon to brace for impact.

WARNING: THIS RIDE WILL MUSS YOUR DO

The ride vehicle is designed to simulate speeds of up to 100 miles per hour.

MISSION: SPACE (FASTPASS) ★★★★

! APPEAL   Preschool ★★½   Grade School ★★★★   Teens ★★★★½
• BY AGE   Young Adults ★★★★   Over 30 ★★★★   Seniors ★★★

What it is Space-flight-simulation ride. Scope and scale Superheadliner. When to go First hour the park is open or use FASTPASS. Comments Not recommended for pregnant women or people prone to motion sickness or claustrophobia; 44" minimum height requirement. Authors' rating ★★★★. Duration About 5 minutes plus preshow. Average wait in line per 100 people ahead of you 4 minutes.

MOTION SICKNESS WARNING

Mission: Space, among other things, is Disney's reply to all the cutting-edge attractions introduced over the past few years by crosstown rival Universal. The first truly groundbreaking Disney attraction since *The Twilight Zone* Tower of Terror, Mission: Space was one of the hottest tickets at Walt Disney World until two guests died after riding it in 2005 and 2006. While neither death was linked directly to the attraction, the negative publicity caused many guests to skip it entirely. In response, Disney added a tamer nonspinning version of Mission: Space in 2006.

Disney's lawyers probably clocked as much time as the ride engineers in designing the lite version. Even before you walk into the building, you're asked whether you want your ride with or without spin. Choose the spinning version, and you're on the orange team; the green team trains on the no-spin side. Either way, you're immediately handed the appropriate launch ticket containing the first of myriad warnings about the attraction. (In case you're wondering, the nonspinning version typically has much shorter wait times.)

Guests for both versions of the attraction enter the NASA Mission: Space Training Center, where they are introduced to the deep-space exploration program and then divided into groups for flight training.

After orientation, you are strapped into space capsules for a simulated flight, where, of course, the unexpected happens. Each capsule accommodates a crew consisting of a group commander, pilot, navigator, and engineer, with a guest functioning in each role. The crew's skill and finesse (or, more often, lack thereof) in handling their respective responsibilities have no effect on the outcome of the flight. The capsules are small, and both ride versions are amazingly realistic. The nonspinning version does not subject your body to g-forces, but it does bounce and toss you around in a manner roughly comparable to other Disney motion simulators.

Along with the flight controls, motion sickness bags are within reach on the control panels, too.

Space Station replica

The queuing area and preshow are pretty dazzling. En route to the main event, guests pass space hardware, astronaut tributes and memorials, a cutaway of a huge space wheel showing crew working and living compartments, and a manned mission control where cast members actually operate the attraction. The postshow area features an electronic game called Mission: Space Race that almost three dozen guests, divided into two teams, can play at once. The winning team beats the other team's spaceship back from Mars to the home base. Individuals on each team are responsible for certain tasks essential to the mission and make their ship fly faster by hitting the correct keyboard buttons.

WORLD SHOWCASE

World Showcase, Epcot's second themed area, is an ongoing world's fair encircling a picturesque 40-acre lagoon. The cuisine, culture, history, and architecture of almost a dozen countries are permanently displayed in individual national pavilions spaced along a 1.2-mile promenade. Pavilions replicate familiar landmarks and present representative street scenes from the host countries. Critics might say that one cannot gain a full appreciation of any diverse nation by visiting a two-acre theme park pavilion. We agree, but think they're missing the point. As with Future World, inspiration is a main goal of World Showcase—the inspiration to actually visit these countries. You'll be the judge as to whether it works. One way to tell is if you utter, "Oslo looks like a lot of fun!" after leaving the Norway exhibit.

Besides the pavilions, World Showcase features some of the loveliest gardens in the United States. Located in Germany, France, England, Canada, and to a lesser extent, China, they are sometimes tucked away and out of sight of pedestrian traffic on the World Showcase promenade. These are best appreciated during daylight hours. The World Showcase offers some of the most diverse and interesting shopping at Walt Disney World.

DISNEY DESIGN with Sam Gennawey

So how do you bring peace and harmony to the world? The formula at the World Showcase is to host countries in a suburban-like cul-de-sac around a lagoon and give each country the same amount of waterfront footage.

Instead of being a collection of exact replicas of famous buildings, the Imagineers use a cinematic trick called "shrink and edit." This technique takes well-known iconic buildings, changes the scale and some of the details, and then arranges the structures to make the most compelling composition.

Architectural aficionados will have a field day strolling the 1.3-mile promenade around the lagoon. Going clockwise, you start with an Aztec-style pyramid with a Mexican village tucked inside. Next door, a Norwegian castle and village are out front with a Stave Church and sod roofs. A scale model of 1420 Hall of Prayer for Good Harvest dominates China, while Germany heavily leans on Bavarian influences. In Italy, the reproduction of Venice's Piazza of San Marco is reversed.

The American Adventure's Georgian manor uses forced perspective to hide its huge show building and to make the structure look smaller than it really is. The traditional torii gate along the waterfront and the 83-foot pagoda outside the entrance of a palace defines the Japan pavilion. The King of Morocco brought over his own artists to create the amazing hand-made terracotta tile mosaics that line the rooms and corridors that connect the ville novelle section to the Medina section in Morocco.

France celebrates the La Belle Époque period and includes a one-tenth scale model of the Eiffel tower. A replica of the long-gone Pont des Arts Bridge connects France to the United Kingdom. The UK pavilion is a history lesson in British architecture and includes examples of Elizabethan, Tudor, Regency, Yorkshire, and Victorian buildings plus a Shakespearian cottage. Finally, Canada presents nothing less than the Rockies and one of that country's most famous gardens.

Kidcot Fun Stops

Designed to make Epcot more interesting for the 5- to 12-year-old crowd, Kidcot allows children to make small craft projects related to the host pavilion. While the setup usually consists of nothing more than a couple of tables, some chairs, and craft items, Kidcot Stops are an inexpensive way for your child to collect souvenirs from the park and to spend a few minutes in air-conditioning. Our favorite recent Kidcot Stops include a Velcro exhibit in Innoventions (is there nothing this wonder material cannot do?) and Mexico in World Showcase.

It's called Kidcot, not Adultcot, but it's hard for anyone to resist free tchotchkes in Disney World.

226 Now, moving clockwise through the World Showcase promenade, here are the nations represented and their attractions.

MEXICO

Pre-Colombian pyramids dominate the architecture of this exhibit. One forms the pavilion's facade, and the other overlooks the restaurant and plaza alongside the boat ride, Gran Fiesta Tour, inside the pavilion. Romantic and exciting testimony to Mexico's charms, the pyramids contain a large number of authentic and valuable artifacts. Many people zip past these treasures without stopping to look.

The interior of the pavilion is designed as a nighttime village scene. It is beautiful and exquisitely detailed. The right half of the inner pavilion holds shops, while the left half has an open, cheerful two-floor space housing Mexico's Kidcot stop, plus hands-on exhibits of Mexico's food, culture, and geography. Be sure to send a video postcard of yourself cliff-diving in Acapulco to your friends back home. At the rear of the pavilion is a restaurant, with some very romantic seats overlooking the water and boat ride.

© Linda O'Keefe

GRAN FIESTA TOUR STARRING
THE THREE CABALLEROS ★★½

! APPEAL   Preschool ★★★★   Grade School ★★★½   Teens ★★★
• BY AGE   Young Adults ★★★   Over 30 ★★★   Seniors ★★★

What it is **Indoor scenic boat ride.** Scope and scale **Minor attraction.** When to go **Before noon or after 5 p.m.**
Authors' rating **Visually appealing, light, and relaxing; ★★½.** Duration **About 7 minutes (plus 1½-minute
wait to disembark).** Average wait in line per 100 people ahead of you **4½ minutes; assumes 16 boats in
operation.** Loading speed **Moderate.**

The Gran Fiesta Tour is a slow boat ride through an elaborate tour of Mexican
landmarks. Gran Fiesta features animated versions of Donald Duck, José Carioca,
and Panchito—an avian singing group called The Three Caballeros, from Disney's
1944 film of the same name—to enliven what some consider a Mexican-style It's a
Small World.

The ride's premise is that the Caballeros are scheduled to perform at a fiesta later
that day, but Donald has gone missing. Large video screens show Donald off enjoying
Mexico's pyramids, monuments, and water sports while José and Panchito search
other Mexican points of interest. Everyone is reunited in time for a rousing concert
near the end of the ride. All of the scenes are done in eye-catching colors. At the risk
of sounding like the Disney geeks we are, we must point out that Panchito is technically the only Mexican Caballero; José Carioca is from Brazil, and Donald is from
Burbank. Either way, more of the ride's visuals seem to be situated on the left side of
the boat. Have small children sit nearer to that side to keep their attention, and listen
for Donald's humorous dialogue as you wait to disembark at the end of the ride.

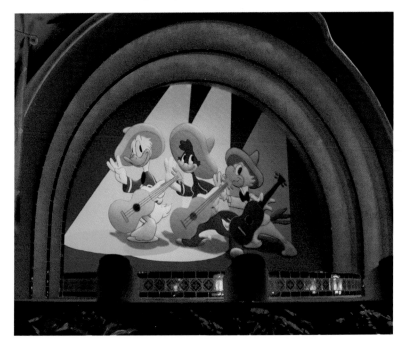

228

NORWAY

The Norway pavilion is complex, beautiful, and architecturally diverse. Surrounding a courtyard is an assortment of traditional Scandinavian buildings, including a replica of the 14th-century Akershus Castle, a wooden stave church (which you can enter—try the door!), red-tiled cottages, and replicas of historic buildings representing the traditional designs of Bergen, Alesund, and Oslo. Attractions include an adventure boat ride in the mold of Pirates of the Caribbean, a movie about Norway, and a gallery of art and artifacts. The pavilion houses Akershus Royal Banquet Hall, a sit-down eatery that hosts princess character meals for breakfast, lunch, and dinner; breakfast here is one of the most popular character meals in the World. An open-air cafe and a bakery cater to those on the run. Shoppers find abundant native handicrafts.

MAELSTROM (FASTPASS) ★ ★ ★

| **!** APPEAL | Preschool ★ ★ ★ | Grade School ★ ★ ★½ | Teens ★ ★ ★½ |
| **.** BY AGE | Young Adults ★ ★ ★½ | Over 30 ★ ★ ★½ | Seniors ★ ★ ★½ |

What it is Indoor-adventure boat ride. Scope and scale Major attraction. When to go Before noon, after 4:30 p.m., or use FASTPASS. Authors' rating Too short but has its moments; ★ ★ ★. Duration 4½ minutes, followed by a 5-minute film with a short wait in between; about 14 minutes for the whole show. Average wait in line per 100 people ahead of you 4 minutes; assumes 12 or 13 boats operating. Loading speed Fast.

In one of Disney World's shorter water rides, guests board dragon-headed ships for a voyage through the fabled rivers and seas of Viking history and legend. They brave trolls, rocky gorges, waterfalls, and a storm at sea. A second-generation Disney water ride, the Viking voyage assembles an impressive array of special effects, combining visual, tactile, and auditory stimuli in a fast-paced and often humorous odyssey. You disembark the boat and step into a small theater where you'll see a five-minute film on Norway. It's worth seeing once.

CHINA

A half-sized replica of the Temple of Heaven in Beijing identifies this pavilion. Gardens and reflecting ponds simulate those found in Suzhou, and an art gallery features a lotus-blossom gate and formal saddle roofline. Inside the temple is a short film about the history and people of China, shown on screens that form a complete 360-degree circle around the viewing area. Surprisingly well done (and with some really powerful air-conditioning), the only things the theater lacks are seats. Which is all for the best, since we'd probably end up asleep here after lunch. Exiting the film, you're deposited in one of the largest and prettiest gift shops on Disney property.

The pavilion also hosts regularly updated exhibits on Chinese history, culture, or trend-setting developments. Past exhibits have covered everything from China's indigenous peoples to the layout of Hong Kong Disneyland. The current exhibit features a look at Chinese funeral sculptures, including miniature clay warriors who protect the tombs' occupants.

REFLECTIONS OF CHINA ★★★½

APPEAL Preschool ★★½	Grade School ★★★	Teens ★★★
BY AGE Young Adults ★★★	Over 30 ★★★½	Seniors ★★★½

What it is Film about the Chinese people and culture. Scope and scale Major attraction. When to go Anytime Comments Audience stands throughout performance. This beautifully produced film was introduced in 2003. Authors' rating ★★★½ . Duration About 14 minutes. Probable waiting time 10 minutes.

Pass through the Hall of Prayer for Good Harvest to view the Circle-Vision 360 film *Reflections of China*. Warm and appealing, it's a brilliant (albeit politically sanitized) introduction to the people and natural beauty of China.

GERMANY

A clock tower, adorned with boy and girl figures, rises above the *platz* (plaza) marking the Germany pavilion. Dominated by a fountain depicting St. George's victory over the dragon, the platz is encircled by buildings in the style of traditional German architecture.

Germany has no film or attraction, and the main draw seems to be the popular (and tasty) Biergarten restaurant, where yodeling, folk dancing, and oompah-band music are part of the mealtime festivities. You know, just like the spread mom used to put out. Lederhosen are optional.

Be sure to check out the large and elaborate model railroad located just beyond the restrooms as you walk from Germany toward Italy.

ITALY

The entrance to Italy is marked by a 105-foot-tall campanile (bell tower) said to mirror the tower in St. Mark's Square in Venice. Left of the campanile is a replica of the 14th-century Doge's Palace, also in the famous square. The architectural detail in these buildings is incredible. The pavilion extends to a waterfront on the lagoon, where gondolas are tied to striped moorings, and this area offers some spectacular views of both Italy and other parts of World Showcase.

Like Germany, the Italy pavilion has no film or attraction, and most of the space is dedicated to retail shops and a sit-down restaurant. The shops closest to the United States pavilion often sell relatively inexpensive, individually wrapped candies and cookies, in case you're looking for a sugar boost to get you through to dinner. You'll have to make it to Morocco, however, to get coffee with them.

UNITED STATES

THE AMERICAN ADVENTURE ★★★★

❗ APPEAL • BY AGE	Preschool ★★½ Young Adults ★★★★	Grade School ★★★ Over 30 ★★★★	Teens ★★★ Seniors ★★★½

What it is Patriotic mixed-media and audio-animatronic theater presentation on U.S. history. **Scope and scale** Headliner. **When to go** Anytime. **Authors' rating** Disney's best historic/patriotic attraction; not to be missed; ★★★★. **Duration** About 29 minutes. **Preshow** Voices of Liberty choral singing. **Probable waiting time** 25 minutes.

The United States pavilion, generally referred to as The American Adventure, consists (not surprisingly) of a fast-food restaurant and a patriotic show.

The pavilion is an imposing brick structure reminiscent of colonial Philadelphia. The right wing of the building holds a small garden area often used for special events, and the left holds the restaurant. Inside the pavilion is a marble-floored gallery displaying artwork and crafts from American hands. Inside, under the rotunda, a singing group named The Voices of Liberty perform American classics (think "She'll Be Comin' Round the Mountain," not "Purple Rain") a capella prior to each show.

The American Adventure production is a composite of everything Disney does best. The 29-minute show is a stirring, but sanitized, rendition of American history narrated by an audio-animatronic Mark Twain (who carries a smoking cigar) and Ben Franklin (who climbs a set of stairs to visit Thomas Jefferson). Behind a stage (almost half the size of a football field) is a 28-by-55-foot rear-projection screen (the largest ever used) on which motion-picture images are interwoven with action on stage.

The sets are among the most ambitious ever constructed for a Disney attraction, considering they're all moved on and off stage. A detailed room in colonial Philadelphia, the World's Fair of 1876, and a Depression-era gas station are among the best.

Americans affected by the collapse of the housing market . . .
no, wait . . . the tech bubble of the '90s? The '80s recessions?
The '70s oil crisis? Whatever it is, the U.S. generally finds a way
to get through.

234

JAPAN

The five-story, blue-roofed pagoda, inspired by a 17th-century shrine in Nara, sets this pavilion apart. A hill garden behind it features waterfalls, rocks, flowers, lanterns, paths, and rustic bridges. The building on the right (as one faces the entrance) was inspired by the ceremonial and coronation hall at the Imperial Palace at Kyoto. It contains restaurants and a large retail store. Through the center entrance and to the left is the Bijutsu-kan Gallery, exhibiting some exquisite Japanese artifacts. Tasteful and elaborate, the pavilion creatively blends simplicity, architectural grandeur, and natural beauty.

At Japan, you'll find an artist who creates sculpture out of candy. They're almost too pretty to eat. Almost.

MOROCCO

The bustling market, winding streets, lofty minarets, and stuccoed archways re-create the romance and intrigue of Marrakesh and Casablanca. Attention to detail makes Morocco one of the most exciting World Showcase pavilions. It also has a museum of Moorish art and the Restaurant Marrakesh, which serves some unusual and difficult-to-find North African specialties, as well as belly dancers at dinnertime.

Another interesting item in Morocco is the water wheel in World Showcase Lagoon that provides irrigation to the flowerbeds opposite the pavilion. Unlike the scoop-and-dump mechanisms with which most people are familiar, the water here is actually carried inside the wheel. Through a complex combination of baffles, chambers, and gravity, the water emerges at the highest point of the circle through a spout perpendicular to the wheel's motion. One can only imagine the number of late espresso-filled nights it took to come up with this design.

Restaurant Marrakesh has some of the best food in Epcot, but for some reason it took us a couple of visits to realize they had, you know, menus. Not sure why.

236

FRANCE

Naturally, a replica of the Eiffel Tower (a big one) is this pavilion's centerpiece. In the foreground, streets recall Belle Époque, France's "beautiful age" between 1870 and 1910. Detail and the evocation of a bygone era enrich the atmosphere of this pavilion. Streets are small—just like Paris—and the pavilion holds a popular coffee shop and bakery. This probably explains why readers rank the France pavilion as the best in World Showcase. Less-explored areas of the pavilion include the perfume store and gardens, both featured prominently during Epcot's annual spring Flower and Garden Festival.

"That's the third Eiffel Tower I've seen this year."—actual quote from *Unofficial Guide* statistician Fred Hazelton, who saw versions in Epcot and Las Vegas prior to beginning research for the Disneyland Paris guidebook. Many thanks for the worldwide laughs, Fred.

IMPRESSIONS DE FRANCE ★★★½

APPEAL	Preschool ★★★	Grade School ★★½	Teens ★★★
BY AGE	Young Adults ★★★½	Over 30 ★★★½	Seniors ★★★★

What it is Film essay on the French people and country. **Scope and scale** Major attraction. **When to go** Anytime. **Authors' rating** Exceedingly beautiful film; not to be missed; ★★★½. **Duration** About 18 minutes. Probable waiting time **15 minutes (at suggested times).**

Impressions de France is an 18-minute movie projected over 200 degrees onto five screens. Unlike the films at China and Canada, the audience sits to view this well-made film introducing France's people, cities, and natural wonders.

UNITED KINGDOM

A variety of period architecture attempts to capture Britain's city, town, and rural atmospheres. One street alone has a thatched-roof cottage, a four-story timber-and-plaster building, a pre-Georgian plaster building, a formal Palladian exterior of dressed stone, and a city square with a Hyde Park bandstand (whew!).

The pavilion is composed mostly of shops. The Rose & Crown Pub and Dining Room is the only World Showcase full-service restaurant with dining on the waterside of the promenade. The pub doesn't require reservations. For fast food try Harry Ramsden Fish & Chips and sit by the water.

CANADA

Canada's cultural, natural, and architectural diversity is reflected in this large and impressive pavilion. Thirty-foot-tall totem poles embellish a Native American village at the foot of a magnificent château-style hotel. Nearby is a rugged stone building said to be modeled after a famous landmark near Niagara Falls and reflecting Britain's influence on Canada. Behind the facades are rugged mountain rock formations, complete with a waterfall. These are hidden photo-op gems for your family.

Le Cellier, a steak house on the pavilion's lower level, is one of Disney World's most popular restaurants. It almost always requires reservations; you'd have to be incredibly lucky to get a walk-in spot, but it doesn't hurt to ask.

O CANADA! ★★★½

! **APPEAL** Preschool ★★ | Grade School ★★★ | Teens ★★★
● **BY AGE** Young Adults ★★★ | Over 30 ★★★½ | Seniors ★★★★

What it is Film essay on the Canadian people and their country. **Scope and scale** Major attraction. **When to go** Anytime. **Comments** Audience stands during performance. **Authors' rating** Makes you want to catch the first plane to Canada! ★★★½. **Duration** About 18 minutes. **Probable waiting time** 10 minutes.

O Canada! showcases Canada's natural beauty and population diversity and demonstrates the immense pride Canadians have in their country. Visitors leave the theater through Victoria Gardens, which was inspired by the famed Butchart Gardens of British Columbia.

Speaking of Canada's immense pride, cast members often run a preshow quiz on Canadian trivia outside the theater before the show. Helpful tips for Americans: Canada's capital is Ottawa; its $1 coin is nicknamed the Loonie, after the bird engraved on it; and the $2 coin is the Toonie—not, unfortunately, the Doubloonie.

KIM POSSIBLE WORLD SHOWCASE ADVENTURE ★★★★

! APPEAL Preschool ★★½   Grade School ★★★★   Teens ★★★½
• BY AGE   Young Adults ★★★½ Over 30 ★★★[1]   Seniors ★★½

What it is Interactive scavenger hunt in select World Showcase pavilions. Scope and scale Minor attraction. When to go Anytime Authors' rating One of our favorite additions to the parks; ★★★. Duration Allow 30 minutes per adventure.

Disney Channel's *Kim Possible* show follows a teen heroine as she battles the forces of evil in exotic locations while trying to navigate typical teen challenges such as proms, parents, and homework. In the Kim Possible World Showcase Adventure, you play the part of Kim and are given a cell phone–like Kimmunicator before being dispatched on a mission to your choice of seven World Showcase pavilions. Once you arrive at the pavilion, the Kimmunicator's video screen and audio provide various clues about the adventure. As you discover each clue, you'll find special effects such as talking statues and flaming lanterns, plus the occasional live secret agents stationed in the pavilions just for this game.

   Kim Possible is Disney's attempt at making static World Showcase pavilions more interactive and kid-friendly. It succeeds wildly, even as Disney is still ironing out all the technological kinks. The adventures have relatively simple clues, fast pacing, and neat rewards for solving the puzzles. Disney clearly put a lot of thought into game play and substantial investment into the effects.

LIVE ENTERTAINMENT

Live entertainment in Epcot is more diverse than in the Magic Kingdom. In World Showcase, it reflects the nations represented. Future World provides a perfect setting for new and experimental offerings. Information about live entertainment on the day you visit is contained in the Epcot guide map, often supplemented by a *Times Guide*.

Here are some performers and performances you'll encounter:

America Gardens Theatre This large amphitheater, near The American Adventure, faces World Showcase Lagoon. International talent plays limited engagements there. Many shows spotlight the programs feature Disney characters.

Around the World Showcase Impromptu performances take place in and around the World Showcase pavilions. They include a strolling mariachi group in Mexico; street actors in Italy; a fife-and-drum corps or singing group (The Voices of Liberty) at The American Adventure; traditional songs, drums, and dances in Japan; street comedy and a Beatles-impersonation band in the United Kingdom; white-faced mimes in France; and bagpipes in Canada, among other offerings. Street entertainment occurs about every half hour.

Kilter plays Celtic-inspired music with a rock-and-roll edge. One of Epcot's most popular bands, it's found near the Canada pavilion.

Disney Characters Once believed to be inconsistent with Epcot's educational focus, Disney characters have now been imported in significant numbers. Characters appear throughout Epcot and in live shows at the America Gardens Theatre and the Showcase Plaza between Mexico and Canada. Times are listed in the Times Guide available upon entry and at Guest Relations. Finally, The Garden Grill Restaurant in the Land Pavilion and Akershus Royal Banquet Hall in Norway offer character meals.

In Future World A musical crew of drumming janitors work near the front entrance and at Innoventions Plaza (between the two Innoventions buildings and by the fountain) according to the daily entertainment schedule. They're occasionally complemented by an electric-keyboard band playing what today's wouldn't-know-good-music-if-it-bit-them-on-the-keister kids would call oldies.

Innoventions Fountain Show Numerous times each day, the fountain situated between the two Innoventions buildings comes alive with pulsating, arching plumes of water synchronized to a musical score.

ILLUMINATIONS

IllumiNations is Epcot's great outdoor spectacle, integrating fireworks, laser lights, neon, and music in a stirring tribute to the nations of the world. It's the climax of every Epcot day. The show has a plot as well as a theme and is loaded with symbolism. We'll provide the CliffsNotes version here, because it all sort of runs together in the show itself.

The show kicks off with colliding stars that suggest the big bang, following which "chaos reigns in the universe." This display is soon replaced by twittering songbirds and various other manifestations signaling the nativity of the Earth. Next comes a brief history of time, from the dinosaurs to ancient Rome, all projected in images on a huge, floating globe. Man's art and inspiration then flash across the globe "in a collage of creativity." All this stimulates the globe to unfold "like a massive flower," bringing on the fireworks crescendo heralding the dawn of a new age. Although only the artistically sensitive will be able to differentiate all this from, say, the last five minutes of any Bruce Willis movie, we thought you'd like to know what Disney says is happening. The soundtrack is excellent and can often be heard throughout the Guide's offices while we're working on the book.

IllumiNations provides the perfect ending to a great day at a great park.

COUNTER-SERVICE RESTAURANTS

For the most part, Epcot's restaurants have always served decent food, although World Showcase restaurants have occasionally been timid about delivering an honest representation of the host nation's cuisine. While these eateries have struggled with authenticity and have sometimes shied away from challenging the meat-and-potatoes palate of the average tourist, they are bolder now, encouraged by America's expanding appreciation of ethnic dining. True, the less adventuresome can still find sanitized and homogenized meals, but the same kitchens will serve up the real thing for anyone with a spark of curiosity and daring.

Africa Coolpost

QUALITY Good VALUE B– PORTION Small LOCATION Between Germany and China
READER RESPONSES 89% 🖒 11% 🖓 DINING PLAN Yes

Hot dogs, ice cream (waffle cone), fresh fruit, frozen slushes (frozen soda), coffee or tea, draft Safari Amber beer ($6.25). Mainly prepackaged food for a quick drink or snack.

Boulangerie Pâtisserie

QUALITY Good VALUE B PORTION Small–medium LOCATION France
READER RESPONSES 92% 🖒 8% 🖓 DINING PLAN Yes

Coffee, croissants, pastries, chocolate mousse, sandwiches, baguettes, cheese plate, ham-and-cheese croissant, quiche. The French pastries are tempting at this tucked-away spot. A few shaded outside tables provide a place to relax and savor sweets.

Cantina de San Angel

QUALITY Fair–good VALUE C+ PORTION Medium LOCATION Mexico
READER RESPONSES 78% 🖒 22% 🖓 DINING PLAN Yes

Tacos, burritos, quesadillas, ensalada mexicana, nachos, churros, draft beer, and frozen margaritas. Most meals served with refried beans and salsa. Tables are outdoors. The margaritas pack a punch—sip slowly.

Crêpes des Chefs de France

QUALITY Good VALUE B+ PORTION Medium LOCATION France
READER RESPONSES 78% 🖒 22% 🖓 DINING PLAN No

Crêpes with chocolate, strawberry, or sugar; vanilla and chocolate ice cream; specialty beer (Kronenbourg 1664); espresso. Kiosk treats made while you watch.

Electric Umbrella Restaurant

QUALITY Fair–good VALUE B– PORTION Medium LOCATION Innoventions East
READER RESPONSES 79% 🖒 21% 🖓 DINING PLAN Yes

Burgers and chicken nuggets with fries; vegetable wrap; island chicken salad; grilled-chicken sandwich; child's plate with cheeseburger or turkey-and-cheese pinwheels; fruit cups; cookies; cheesecake. One of the busiest restaurants in Future World. There's more-interesting fast food in the World Showcase.

Fife and Drum Tavern

QUALITY Fair VALUE C PORTION Large LOCATION United States
READER RESPONSES 87% 👍 13% 👎 DINING PLAN Yes

Turkey legs, pretzels, ice cream, and smoothies. Better for a quick snack to tide you over than for an actual meal. Seating is available in and around the Liberty Inn, behind the Fife and Drum.

Kringla Bakeri og Kafé

QUALITY Good–excellent VALUE B PORTION Small–medium LOCATION Norway
READER RESPONSES 88% 👍 12% 👎 DINING PLAN Yes

Pastries; no-sugar-added chocolate mousse; lefse (traditional potato bread); cakes and cookies; rice cream; open-faced sandwiches (smoked ham, turkey, or salmon); green salad; fruit cup; sweet pretzels with raisins and almonds; imported beers (Carlsberg beer for $7.50). Pricey but good (try the rice cream). Shaded outdoor seating.

Liberty Inn

QUALITY Fair VALUE C PORTION Medium LOCATION United States
READER RESPONSES 75% 👍 25% 👎 DINING PLAN Yes

Bacon double cheeseburger; barbecued pork; hot dogs; veggie burgers; chicken nuggets; Caesar chicken salad; child's plate of grilled chicken over romaine lettuce, chicken nuggets with fries, or PB&J with applesauce. The menu offers more than dogs and burgers; kosher items also available. Still, World Showcase has more-inspired selections.

Lotus Blossom Cafe

QUALITY Fair VALUE C PORTION Medium LOCATION China
READER RESPONSES 59% 👍 41% 👎 DINING PLAN Yes

Egg rolls, pot stickers, veggie stir-fry, sesame chicken salad, shrimp fried rice, orange chicken with steamed rice, and beef-noodle soup bowl.

Promenade Refreshments

QUALITY Fair VALUE C PORTION Large LOCATION Between World Showcase
and Future World READER RESPONSES 89% 👍 11% 👎 DINING PLAN Yes

Hot dogs, pretzels, chips, ice cream, and smoothies. Best for a quick snack, especially if you have a reservation at one of the World Showcase's full-service restaurants. Seating is limited to nonexistent, depending on whether cast members have put out tables and chairs—be prepared to walk and chew.

Refreshment Port

QUALITY Good VALUE B PORTION Medium LOCATION Between World Showcase and Future World READER RESPONSES 98% 👍 2% 👎 DINING PLAN Yes

Chicken nuggets, fries, ice cream. Convenient place for a snack.

Rose & Crown Pub

QUALITY Good VALUE C PORTION Medium LOCATION United Kingdom READER RESPONSES 94% 👍 6% 👎 DINING PLAN Yes

Fish-and-chips; turkey sandwich; Guinness, Harp, and Bass beers, as well as other spirits. The attractions here are the pub atmosphere and the draft beer. Note that the restaurant usually requires Advance Reservations while the pub does not. See the full-service restaurant profile for the Rose & Crown Dining Room on page 141.

Sommerfest

QUALITY Good VALUE B– PORTION Medium LOCATION Germany READER RESPONSES 88% 👍 12% 👎 DINING PLAN Yes

Bratwurst and frankfurter sandwiches with kraut, soft pretzels, apple strudel, German wine and beer (Löwenbrau, Franziskaner Weissbier, and Spaten Optimator). Tucked in the entrance to the Biergarten restaurant, Sommerfest is hard to find from the street. Very limited seating. Not for picky eaters, but a good place to grab a cold brew and bratwurst.

Sunshine Seasons Food Fair

QUALITY Excellent VALUE A PORTION Medium LOCATION The Land READER RESPONSES 93% 👍 7% 👎 DINING PLAN Yes

Comprises the following four areas: (1) wood-fired grills and rotisseries; (2) made-to-order sandwiches; (3) Asian shop, with noodle bowls and various stir-fry combos; (4) and soup-and-salad shop, with unusual creations such as seared tuna on mixed greens with sesame–rice wine vinaigrette. No fried food, no pizza, no burgers—everything is prepared fresh as you watch. Diverse choices are perfect for picky eaters.

Tangierine Cafe

QUALITY Good VALUE B PORTION Medium LOCATION Morocco READER RESPONSES 88% 👍 12% 👎 DINING PLAN Yes

Chicken and lamb shawarma; hummus; tabbouleh; lentil salad; chicken and tabbouleh wraps; olives; child's meal of pizza, hamburger, or chicken tenders with carrot sticks and apple slices and small beverage; Moroccan wine and beer; baklava. Good food with an authentic flavor. The best seating is at the outdoor tables.

Yakitori House

QUALITY Excellent VALUE B PORTION Small–medium LOCATION Japan READER RESPONSES 80% 👍 20% 👎 DINING PLAN Yes

Shogun combo meal with beef and chicken teriyaki, vegetables, and rice (adult and child versions); beef curry; vegetable tempura with shrimp and udon noodles; side salad; sushi; miso soup; green tea; sponge cake with ginger-flavored frosting; Kirin beer, sake, and plum wine. A great place for a light meal. Limited seating.

Yorkshire County Fish Shop

QUALITY Good VALUE B+ PORTION Medium LOCATION United Kingdom READER RESPONSES 91% 👍 9% 👎 DINING PLAN Yes

Fish-and-chips, shortbread, Bass Ale draft. A convenient fast-food window attached to the Rose & Crown Pub (see profile above). Outdoor seating overlooks the lagoon.

PART 7

ANIMAL KINGDOM

With its lush flora, winding streams, meandering paths, and exotic setting, Animal Kingdom is a stunningly beautiful theme park. The landscaping conjures images of rain forests, velds, and formal gardens. Add to this loveliness a population of more than 1,000 animals, replicas of Africa's and Asia's most intriguing architecture, and a diverse array of original attractions, and you have the most distinctive of all Disney theme parks.

Although it is the fourth Disney theme park built in Orlando, the wildlife exhibits at Animal Kingdom do break some new ground. For starters, there's lots of space, thus allowing for the sweeping vistas that Discovery Channel viewers would expect in, say, an African veld setting. The enclosures, natural in appearance, have few or no apparent barriers between you and the animals. The operative word, of course, is *apparent*. That flimsy stand of bamboo separating you from a gorilla is actually a neatly disguised set of steel rods embedded in concrete. The Imagineers even take a crack at certain animals' stubborn unwillingness to be on display. A lion that would rather sleep out of sight under a bush, for example, is lured to center stage with nice, cool, climate-controlled artificial rocks. Your journey into these exhibits begins just past the park entrance at The Oasis.

▶**UNOFFICIAL TIP** Three attractions—Dinosaur, Expedition Everest, and Kilimanjaro Safaris—are among the best in the Disney repertoire.

Not to Be Missed at Animal Kingdom

AFRICA	**Kilimanjaro Safaris**
ASIA	**Expedition Everest**
CAMP MINNIE-MICKEY	*Festival of the Lion King*
DINOLAND U.S.A.	**Dinosaur**
	Finding Nemo—The Musical
DISCOVERY ISLAND	*It's Tough to Be a Bug!*

- Africa
- Asia
- Camp Minnie-Mickey
- DinoLand U.S.A.
- Discovery Island
- Main Entrance

1. The Boneyard
2. Character Greeting Area
3. Conservation Station
4. Dinosaur
5. Expedition Everest
6. *Festival of the Lion King*
7. *Flights of Wonder*
8. Gibbon Pool
9. Guest Relations
10. Harambe Village
11. Kali River Rapids
12. Kilimanjaro Safaris
13. Maharaja Jungle Trek
14. Main Entrance
15. Pangani Forest
    Exploration Trail
16. Primeval Whirl
17. Rafiki's Planet Watch
18. Theater in the Wild/
    *Finding Nemo—
    The Musical*
19. Ticket Booths
20. The Tree of Life/*It's
    Tough to Be a Bug!*
21. TriceraTop Spin
22. Wildlife Express Train

Animal Kingdom's breathtaking natural scenery begins at The Oasis. Unlike other Disney theme-park entrances, there's not a gift shop in sight.

THE OASIS

Your first look at The Oasis should tell you that the Animal Kingdom is a different kind of Disney theme park. Once past the turnstiles, there's no clear road to follow. Instead, you see two garden paths heading in seemingly opposite directions. Each path leads you to Discovery Island, but the path you choose and what you see on the way is up to you. This transition experience is unique among Disney's parks, and the lesson is that the Animal Kingdom is a park to linger and appreciate. If it's critical for your family's happiness that they have FASTPASSes for Expedition Everest, then by George, send the husband or teenagers off to the races while you maintain your serenity.

DISNEY DESIGN with Sam Gennawey

From the time you arrive, Disney Imagineers use contrast to signal that Animal Kingdom is going to be different than any other theme park. The parking lot is a barren, treeless, lifeless field. Not a very inviting first impression. Off in the distance, beyond the edge of the parking lot, is a lush forest—The Oasis.

Functionally, The Oasis serves the same purpose as Main Street, U.S.A., Hollywood Boulevard, or walking under Spaceship Earth: to create a shared experience that sets up the adventures that lie ahead. The pathways meander and cross under a land bridge acting like a curtain to set up the big reveal—your first view of the Tree of Life.

Here's something to watch for throughout the park: In the field of ecology, naturalists use the concept of transects—a series of zones that transition from one type of land to another—to describe the characteristics of an ecosystem and how it changes. When the transition is sudden or is severely disrupted, significant environmental impacts can be felt. Virtually every attraction in the Animal Kingdom and every land deals with a disruption in the natural transect to move the story along.

Animal Kingdom Services

Most of the park's service facilities are located inside the main entrance and on Discovery Island as follows:

Baby Center/Baby Care Needs: On Discovery Island, next to the Creature Comforts Shop
Banking Services: ATMs located at the main entrance and on Discovery Island
Film and Cameras: Just inside the main entrance at Garden Gate Gifts and in Africa at Duka La Filimu
First Aid: On Discovery Island, next to the Creature Comforts Shop
Guest Relations and Information: Inside the main entrance to the left
Live Entertainment and Parade Information: Included in the park guide map, available free at Guest Relations
Lost and Found: Inside the main entrance to the left
Lost Persons: Can be reported at Guest Relations and at the Baby Center on Discovery Island
Storage Lockers: Inside the main entrance to the left
Wheelchair and Stroller Rental: Inside the main entrance to the right

These children are going into the FBI's witness protection program.

DISCOVERY ISLAND

Discovery Island occupies the center of the Animal Kingdom and is the first land you reach after exiting The Oasis and crossing a bridge. Most of Discovery Island's shops are decorated in equatorial African architecture, with vibrant hues of teal, yellow, red, and blue. Surrounded by water, the island is connected to the other lands by bridges. A number of animal exhibits are found on Discovery Island, and at the middle of the island is the park's signature landmark, the Tree of Life.

© Daniel M. Brace

THE TREE OF LIFE /
IT'S TOUGH TO BE A BUG ★★★★

APPEAL • BY AGE	Preschool ★★★½	Grade School ★★★★	Teens ★★★★
	Young Adults ★★★★	Over 30 ★★★★	Seniors ★★★★

What it is 3-D theater show. Scope and scale Minor attraction. When to go Before 10:30 a.m., after 4 p.m. Comments The theater is inside the tree. Authors' rating Zany and frenetic; ★★★★. Duration About 7½ minutes. Probable waiting time 12–30 minutes.

The Tree of Life is quite a work of art. Although from afar it is certainly magnificent and imposing, it is not until you examine the tree at close range that you truly appreciate its rich detail. What appears to be ancient gnarled bark is, in fact, hundreds of carvings depicting all manner of wildlife, each integrated seamlessly into the trunks, roots, and limbs of the tree. A stunning symbol of the interdependence of all living things, the Tree of Life is the most visually compelling structure found in any Disney theme park.

In sharp contrast to the grandeur of the tree is the subject of the attraction within its trunk. Starring the cast of Disney/Pixar's *a bug's life, It's Tough to Be a Bug!* is a humorous 3-D presentation about the difficulties of being a small insect. Flik, the main character from *a bug's life,* is the host and shows the audience how many insects perform vital roles in the ecosystem.

Along the way the audience gets to see, hear, smell, and—ick alert!—feel various bugs during the film. (Parents should be aware of this when considering whether the attraction is too intense for small children.) We generally leave just thankful that there wasn't a taste requirement, but unlike the relatively serious tone of Animal Kingdom in general, *It's Tough to Be a Bug* stands virtually alone in providing some much needed levity and whimsy.

CAMP MINNIE-MICKEY

Camp Minnie-Mickey is designed to be the Disney characters' Animal Kingdom head-quarters. A small land, Camp Minnie-Mickey is about the size of Mickey's Toontown

Fair but has a rustic and woodsy theme, like a summer camp. It's also a cul-de-sac, meaning you can't get to any other part of the park without back-tracking to Discovery Island. Camp Minnie-Mickey is home to the park's main character-greeting area and *Festival of the Lion King*, a live stage production featuring Disney char-acters from the popu-lar film.

DISNEY DESIGN with Sam Gennawey

Disney's Animal Kingdom is organized around three groups of animals. The animals of today can be found in Asia, Africa, The Oasis, and Discovery Island. DinoLand U.S.A. is all about animals of the past. Camp Minnie-Mickey represents mythical beasts and legendary creatures. It wasn't always this way. Once upon a time, the camp area was going to be known as Beastly Kingdom with "creatures that ever, or never,

The dragon waterfall on the way to Camp Minnie-Mickey.

were." It would have featured dragons and unicorns. Did you ever notice the dragon's head hanging over one of the Craftsman-style ticket booths, wonder why there's a unicorn section in the parking lot, or see the waterfall that looks like a dragon just off the bridge entering the land?

Budget cuts postponed the con-struction of Beastly Kingdom, and Camp Minnie-Mickey was born. When you cross the bridge into the camp, you are entering a cartoon land where you might find Mickey Mouse on vacation. The real design chal-lenge was creating this environment with living plant materials.

The Imagineers based the landscape, architecture, and street furniture on the resorts of the Adirondack Mountains. By using the language of the Adirondack style, they were able to get a handmade look and feel, which blends nicely with the dense foliage and puts the characters out front. To enhance the camp theme, The Festival of the Lion King theater is meant to look like the camp's assembly hall.

CHARACTER TRAILS

The Character Trails are at the center of Camp Minnie-Mickey, past a series of wooded areas and small shaded streams on your way from Discovery Island. It's a lovely walk, especially in the cooler early morning or late afternoon. In the midday sun you might wonder out loud whether Disney couldn't do this whole "nature" thing in a giant air-conditioned plastic bubble.

You'll find characters at the end of each of several small garden paths. A sign in front of each path tells you which character awaits you at its end in his or her own private reception area. The most typical lineup has Mickey, Minnie, Goofy, and Donald at one queue each, but Daisy often subs for Donald during his lunch break. Goofy and the ducks often get replaced with characters from Disney's latest film if the movie has anything to do with nature, animals, or the environment. Mickey and Minnie are constants.

Budget cuts force the park service into some serious personnel compromises.

FESTIVAL OF THE LION KING ★★★★

! APPEAL
• BY AGE

| Preschool ★★★★½ | Grade School ★★★★½ | Teens ★★★★½ |
| Young Adults ★★★★½ | Over 30 ★★★★½ | Seniors ★★★★★ |

What it is Theater-in-the-round stage show. Scope and scale Major attraction. When to go Before 11 a.m. or after 4 p.m. Comments Performance times listed in handout park map or Times Guide. Authors' rating Upbeat and spectacular; not to be missed: ★★★★. Duration 25 minutes. When to arrive 20–30 minutes before showtime.

This energetic production is part stage show, part parade, and part circus. Disney's official line is that it's inspired by Disney's *Lion King* film. We think it's more like a documentary into the everyday life of Elton John. We're not sure, but here are the details:

First, there's the music, for which Sir Elton won a 1994 Academy Award. By our count, every tune from *The Lion King* is belted out and reprised a couple of times. This is either what's running through Elton's head every day, or is a canny way to build up royalty payments for when he's retired.

Besides the music, there is a great deal of parading around by limber acrobats, a lot of dancing, and some incredible costuming. It's all spectacular, but as you're

sitting through the show, ask yourself whether any of it would seem truly out of place in Elton's living room. Heck, the costumes probably came from Elton's spare closet!

Kidding aside, *Unofficial Guide* readers have been almost unanimous in their praise of *Festival of the Lion King*, and we consider it one of the best stage shows in all of Walt Disney World.

AFRICA

Africa is the largest of Animal Kingdom's lands, and guests enter through Harambe, Disney's idealized and immensely sanitized version of a modern, rural African town. There is a market (with modern cash registers), and table-service dining is available. What distinguishes Harambe is its understatement. Far from the stereotypical great-white-hunter image of an African town, Harambe is definitely (and realistically) not exotic. The buildings of Disney's Harambe—while interesting, maintained, and more aseptic than the real McCoy—would be a lot more at home in Kenya than the Magic Kingdom's Main Street would be in Missouri.

Harambe serves as the gateway to the African veld habitat, Animal Kingdom's largest and most ambitious zoological exhibit. Access to the veld is via the Kilimanjaro Safaris attraction, located at the end of Harambe's main drag near the fat-trunked baobab tree. Harambe is also the departure point for the train to Rafiki's Planet Watch and Conservation Station, the park's veterinary headquarters.

DISNEY DESIGN with Sam Gennawey

Africa represents the most "urban" environment in the Animal Kingdom. Inspired by an island town called Lamu off the east coast of Kenya, the Swahili-style structures represent a village that has learned to benefit by conserving nearby natural resources and becoming a tourist destination. It has a main street, and the safari's entrance next to a baobab tree (a real tree) acts like Cinderella Castle in the Magic Kingdom and draws you forward. The roof over the entrance was weaved by 13 thatchers from Zululand in South Africa. The grass roof is expected to last 30 to 40 years. The Imagineers say it is "so imperfect that it's perfect."

The spark of imagination that solidified this version of Africa as the central theme was a visit to Lake Nakuru, a popular safari park in Kenya. As described by Imagineer Kevin Brown, the group was driving around the park looking for animals in jeeps. A call came over the radio that somebody had spotted a leopard in a tree. By the time Kevin's truck made it to the spot, there were more than 40 vehicles with people hanging out taking photos. This is when the lightbulb went off for Joe Rohde, executive designer and vice president of creative for Walt Disney Imagineering.

As Kevin describes it, "Africa is a theme park—just not a particularly well-run one. We knew the experience we could provide in the Animal Kingdom would be as good as or better than that." So they created the fictional town of Harambe. *Harambe* is Swahili for "let us all pull together." The village is layered in history, with the walls of the ancient fort and canyons behind the Dawa Bar and remnants of the time when the area was under British Colonial control.

The safari is the big draw, and the locals manage the savanna. They collectively fear poaching, which threatens the ecosystem and their livelihood. The historic buildings have been readapted to accommodate the tourist trade with a hotel, a bar, a restaurant, and other necessary facilities. The posters on the walls reinforce the commercial nature of the village.

The family later opened for Bon Jovi at the Meadowlands.

KILIMANJARO SAFARIS (FASTPASS) ★★★★★

! APPEAL
• BY AGE

Preschool ★★★★½	Grade School ★★★★½	Teens ★★★★½
Young Adults ★★★★★	Over 30 ★★★★½	Seniors ★★★★★

What it is Truck ride through an African wildlife reservation. **Scope and scale** Superheadliner. **When to go** As soon as the park opens, in the 2 hours before closing, or use FASTPASS. **Authors' rating** Truly exceptional; ★★★★★. **Duration** About 20 minutes. **Average wait in line per 100 people ahead of you** 4 minutes; assumes full-capacity operation with 18-second dispatch interval. **Loading speed** Fast.

The park's premier zoological attraction, Kilimanjaro Safaris offers an exceptionally realistic, albeit brief, imitation of an actual African photo safari. Thirty-two guests at a time board tall, open safari vehicles and are dispatched into a simulated African veld. Animals such as zebras, wildebeests, impalas, Thomson's gazelles, giraffes, and even rhinos roam apparently free, while predators such as lions, as well as potentially dangerous large animals such as hippos, are separated from both prey and guests by all-but-invisible, natural-appearing barriers. Although the animals have more than 100 acres of savanna, woodland, streams, and rocky hills to call home, careful placement of water holes, forage, and salt licks ensures that the critters are hanging out by the road when safari vehicles roll by, no matter the time of day. (Just to be sure about that, we had the researchers ride the safari for days on end during the summer. Those results showed that you'll see, on average, the same number of large and small critters at any time of day.)

Having traveled in Kenya and Tanzania, Bob will tell you that Disney has done an amazing job of replicating the sub-Saharan east African landscape. The main difference that an east African would notice is that Disney's version is greener and (generally speaking) less barren. Like on a real African safari, what animals you see (and how many) is pretty much a matter of luck. We've tried Disney's safari upwards of 50 times and had a different experience on each trip.

Mr. King of the Jungle loses his naptime spot.

© Disney

OK, we're going to take the class photo now. You guys with the horns, sit up front. Zebra and giraffe, you stand in the back …What do you mean you have to go to the bathroom? OK, but make it quick.

PANGANI FOREST EXPLORATION TRAIL ★★★

! APPEAL Preschool ★★★★ Grade School ★★★★ Teens ★★★★
• BY AGE Young Adults ★★★★ Over 30 ★★★★ Seniors ★★★★

What it is **Walk-through zoological exhibit.** Scope and scale **Major attraction.** When to go **Before 10 a.m. and after 2:30 p.m.** Authors' rating ★★★. Duration **About 20–25 minutes.**

When you're done with Kilimanjaro Safaris, you have the choice of either returning to the village of Harambe in Africa or taking a stroll through the Pangani Forest Exploration Trail. Winding between the domain of two troops of lowland gorillas, it's hard to see what, if anything, separates you from the primates. The trail also features a hippo pool with an underwater viewing area and a chance to view skulls of various creatures. A highlight of the trail is an exotic-bird aviary so craftily designed that you can barely tell you're in an enclosure.

CONSERVATION STATION AND AFFECTION SECTION ★★★

! **APPEAL** **Preschool** ★★★½ **Grade School** ★★★½ **Teens** ★★½
● **BY AGE** **Young Adults** ★★½ **Over 30** ★★★ **Seniors** ★★★

What it is Behind-the-scenes walk-through educational exhibit and petting zoo. Scope and scale Minor attraction. When to go Anytime. Comments Opens 30 minutes after the rest of the park. Authors' rating Evolving; ★★★. Probable waiting time None.

Conservation Station is Animal Kingdom's veterinary and conservation headquarters. Located on the perimeter of the African section of the park, Conservation Station is, strictly speaking, a backstage, working facility. Here guests can meet wildlife experts, observe some of the station's ongoing projects, and learn about the behind-the-scenes operations of the park. The station includes a rehabilitation area for injured animals and a nursery for recently born (or hatched) critters. Vets and other experts are on hand to answer questions.

While there are several permanent exhibits, including Affection Section (an animal-petting area), what you see at Conservation Station will largely depend on what's going on when you arrive. If you trek there during the summer heat only to find nothing of interest, comfort yourself in knowing that Conservation Station has undoubtedly the best air-conditioning in the Animal Kingdom, and that's got to be worth something.

WILDLIFE EXPRESS TRAIN ★★

! **APPEAL** **Preschool** ★★★★ **Grade School** ★★★ **Teens** ★★★
● **BY AGE** **Young Adults** ★★½ **Over 30** ★★★ **Seniors** ★★★

What it is Scenic railroad ride to Rafiki's Planet Watch and Conservation Station. Scope and scale Minor attraction. When to go Anytime. Comments Opens 30 minutes after the rest of the park. Authors' rating Ho-hum; ★★. Duration About 5–7 minutes one way. Average wait in line per 100 people ahead of you 9 minutes. Loading speed Moderate.

This transportation ride snakes behind the African wildlife reserve as it makes its loop connecting Harambe to Rafiki's Planet Watch and Conservation Station. En route, you see the nighttime enclosures for the animals that populate the Kilimanjaro Safaris. Similarly, returning to Harambe, you see the backstage areas of Asia. It's a pleasant, if visually unspectacular, experience.

ASIA

Crossing the bridge from Discovery Island, you enter Asia through the village of Anandapur. Situated near the bank of the Chakranadi River (translation: "the river that runs in circles") and surrounded by lush vegetation, Anandapur provides access to a gibbon exhibit and to Asia's two feature attractions, Kali River Rapids whitewater raft ride and Expedition Everest. Also in Asia is Flights of Wonder, an educational production about birds.

DISNEY DESIGN with Sam Gennawey

Asia is a remarkable land that sprawls from the Flights of Wonder theater all the way to Expedition Everest. Unlike Africa, which features a strong center in Harambe, the little village of Anandapur weaves in and out of the jungle along the floodplains and lower foothills of the Himalayas. Asia is not set in any one country but reflects the design and urban form of rural communities throughout Nepal, India, Thailand, and Indonesia.

Anandapur means "place of delight" in Sanskrit, and the underlying theme is the conflict between the population explosion and traditional respect for animals and wild places. On Discovery Island, nature and the built environment were in balance. In Africa, that balance was being restored, but there is a clear distinction between the urban and rural edge. In Asia, nature seems to have the upper hand, as many structures are being reclaimed, and the foliage is taking over.

The architecture varies from Nepalese, Javanese, and Thai influences. The hand-built feel is everywhere. But the real star of the show is the landscape architecture. One of the designers, Paul Comstock, said, "If you've been in the wild, surrounded by the foliage and flowers, you know you have to go over the top. We had to convince them that landscape was the show." As you move toward Serka Zong (Fortress of the Chasm), the little village at the base of Expedition Everest, you will see a greater use of red, the color of protection. Enhancing the authenticity of place is the use of prayer flags, which are common in Tibetan villages and meant to bring prosperity, long life, and happiness to those who put them on display. The flags also add kinetic energy to the landscape.

The paving materials along the pathways add to the story. Look down (careful) and you will see—imprinted on the rough surface—footprints, bicycle and truck treads, leaves, and animal prints. As you move toward Everest, the bicycle tires fade away as that mode of travel becomes impractical. Here you will find more hoof marks. It's as if you just missed the residents.

Tibetan laundry day.

EXPEDITION EVEREST (FASTPASS) ★ ★ ★ ★ ½

| ! APPEAL | Preschool ★★½ | Grade School ★★★★½ | Teens ★★★★★ |
| • BY AGE | Young Adults ★★★★★ | Over 30 ★★★★★ | Seniors ★★★½ |

What it is **High-speed.outdoor roller coaster through Nepalese mountain village.** Scope and scale **Super-headliner.** When to go **Before 9:30 a.m. or after 3 p.m., or use FASTPASS.** Special comments **44" height requirement.**

Expedition Everest reprises that Disney-story-board staple, the runaway train, although this time the scenery includes bamboo forests, waterfalls, glacier fields, and vertiginous peaks. You're chugging up Mount Everest on an old pack-track in search of the legendary Abominable Snowman. But the track turns out to have collapsed (of course), and as the cars pick up speed—both forward and backward, and in the dark—riders find themselves perilously close to an elephant-sized and pretty irascible Yeti, protector of the Himalayas. The attraction also includes a new and especially intriguing type of queue, designed by uber-Imagineer Joe Rohde: while waiting to load onto the train, visitors walk through a meticulously recreated Himalayan village. Indeed, everyone should at least see it even if they don't wish to ride the coaster itself.

© Barrie Brewer

KALI RIVER RAPIDS (FASTPASS) ★★★½

! APPEAL Preschool ★★★★   Grade School ★★★★½   Teens ★★★★½
• BY AGE Young Adults ★★★★   Over 30 ★★★★   Seniors ★★★★

What it is Whitewater raft ride. Scope and scale Headliner. When to go Before 10:30 a.m. or after 4:30 p.m., or use FASTPASS. Comments Guaranteed to get wet. Opens 30 minutes after the rest of the park. 38" height requirement. Switching-off option available (see page 107). Authors' rating Short but scenic; ★★★½. Duration About 5 minutes. Average wait in line per 100 people ahead of you 5 minutes. Loading speed Moderate.

Whitewater raft rides have been a hot-weather favorite of theme-park patrons for more than 20 years. The ride itself consists of an unguided trip down a man-made river in a circular rubber raft with a top-mounted platform seating 12 people. The raft essentially floats freely in the current and is washed downstream through rapids and waves. Because the river is fairly wide, with numerous currents, eddies, and obstacles, there is no telling exactly where the raft will drift. Thus, each trip is different and exciting. The only certainty, however, is that you will be utterly soaked. At the end of the ride, a conveyor belt hauls the raft up to be unloaded and prepared for the next group of guests.

What distinguishes Kali River Rapids from other theme-park raft rides is Disney's trademark attention to visual detail. Where many raft rides essentially plunge down a concrete ditch, Kali River Rapids flows through a dense rain forest and past waterfalls, temple ruins, and bamboo thickets, emerging into a cleared area where greedy loggers have ravaged the forest, and finally drifting back under the tropical canopy as the river cycles back to Anandapur. Along the way, your raft runs a gauntlet of raging cataracts, logjams, and other dangers.

Disney has done a great job with the visuals on this attraction. The queuing area, which winds through an ancient Southeast Asian temple, is one of the most striking and visually interesting settings of any Disney attraction. And though the sights on the raft trip itself are also first-class, the attraction is marginal in two important respects. First, it's only about three and a half minutes on the water, and second, well...it's a weenie ride. Sure, you get wet, but otherwise the drops and rapids are not all that exciting.

FLIGHTS OF WONDER ★★★★

! APPEAL   Preschool ★★★★   Grade School ★★★★   Teens ★★★★
• BY AGE   Young Adults ★★★★   Over 30 ★★★★   Seniors ★★★★

What it is Stadium show about birds. Scope and scale Major attraction. When to go Anytime. Comments
Performance times listed in handout park map or Times Guide. Authors' rating Unique; ★★★★ Duration 30 minutes. When to arrive 20–30 minutes before showtime.

Both interesting and fun, *Flights of Wonder* is well paced and showcases a surprising number of bird species. The show has a straightforward educational presentation, yet is still riveting. The focus of *Flights of Wonder* is on the natural talents and characteristics of the various species, so don't expect to see any parrots riding bicycles. The natural behaviors, however, far surpass any tricks learned from humans. Overall, the presentation is fascinating and exceeds most guests' expectations.

MAHARAJA JUNGLE TREK ★★★★

! APPEAL   Preschool ★★★½   Grade School ★★★★   Teens ★★★★
• BY AGE   Young Adults ★★★★   Over 30 ★★★★   Seniors ★★★★

What it is Walk-through zoological exhibit. Scope and scale Headliner. When to go Anytime. Comments
Opens 30 minutes after the rest of the park. Authors' rating A standard-setter for natural habitat design; ★★★★. Duration About 20–30 minutes.

The Maharaja Jungle Trek is a zoological nature walk similar to the Pangani Forest Exploration Trail, but with an Asian setting and Asian animals. You start with Komodo dragons and then work up to Malayan tapirs. Next is a cave with fruit bats. Ruins of the maharaja's palace provide the setting for Bengal tigers. From the top of a parapet in the palace, you can view a herd of blackbuck antelope and Asian deer. The trek concludes with an aviary. Labyrinthine, overgrown, and elaborately detailed, the temple ruin would be a compelling attraction even without the animals. Throw in a few bats, bucks, and Bengals, and you're in for a treat.

Did someone say. "Here, kitty, kitty?"

DINOLAND U.S.A.

This most typically Disney of Animal Kingdom's lands is a cross between a paleontological dig and a quirky roadside attraction. Accessible via the bridge from Discovery Island, DinoLand U.S.A. is home to a children's play area, a nature trail, a 1,500-seat amphitheater, and Dinosaur, one of Animal Kingdom's two thrill rides. Also in Dino-Land are a couple of natural-history exhibits, including Dino-Sue, an exact replica of the largest, most complete *Tyrannosaurus rex* discovered to date. Named after the fossil hunter Sue Hendrickson, the replica (like the original) is 40 feet long and 13 feet tall. And no, it doesn't dance, sing, or whistle, but it will get your attention nonetheless.

DISNEY DESIGN with *Sam Gennawey*

The key to appreciating DinoLand is understanding its backstory. A backstory is a Disney specialty and becomes the organizing tool that creates continuity between design elements. A writer provides a story, and all of the design elements and attractions are created to support that story, just like set design for a movie.

In this case, the backstory starts with the famous Dino Institute, filled with mischievous students who have taken over a small roadside stop. Next door, the owners of the gas station, Chester and Hester, have decided to cash in and create a carnival in their parking lot. After all, it was their dog that found the bone that led to all of the excavation in the first place.

Each physical element is created to add to the story in subtle layers. The Dino Institute is a formal structure with a proper plaza and educational trail. Right in front of the institute is the students' contribution: the rambling and ever expanding Restaurantosaurus made up of permanent and temporary additions, including an Airstream trailer. Puns and artifacts are everywhere. Well worth the time to check out.

Even the plant material supports the theme. The area is heavy on primitive plants that include monkey puzzle trees with nasty spines, one of the largest collections of cycads, and 20 different species of magnolias, which go back to the dinosaur era.

Dino-Sue

BONEYARD ★★★½

! APPEAL BY AGE

Preschool ★★★★½ Grade School ★★★★ Teens ★★½
Young Adults ★★ Over 30 ★★½ Seniors ★★

What it is **Elaborate playground.** Scope and scale **Diversion.** When to go **Anytime.** Comments **Opens 30 minutes after the rest of the park.** Authors' rating **Stimulating fun for children; ★★★½.**

This attraction is an elaborate playground, particularly appealing to kids age 10 and younger, but visually appealing to all ages. Arranged in the form of a rambling open-air dig site, the Boneyard offers plenty of opportunity for exploration and letting off steam. Playground equipment consists of the skeletons of Triceratops, Tyrannosaurus rex, Brachiosaurus, and the like, on which children can swing, slide, and climb. In addition, there are sandpits where little ones can scrounge around for bones and fossils.

DINOSAUR (FASTPASS) ★★★★½

! APPEAL   Preschool ★★   Grade School ★★★½   Teens ★★★★
● BY AGE   Young Adults ★★★★   Over 30 ★★★★   Seniors ★★★½

What it is Motion-simulator dark ride. Scope and scale Superheadliner. When to go Before 10:30 a.m., in the hour before closing, or use FASTPASS. Comments Must be 40" tall to ride. Switching-off option provided (see page 107). Authors' rating Really improved; ★★★★½. Duration 3½ minutes. Average wait in line per 100 people ahead of you 3 minutes; assumes full-capacity operation with 18-second dispatch interval. Loading speed Fast.

Dinosaur is a combination track ride and motion simulator. In addition to moving along a cleverly hidden track, the ride vehicle also bucks and pitches (the simulator part) in sync with the visuals and special effects encountered. The plot has you traveling back in time on a mission of rescue and conservation. Your objective, believe it or not, is to haul back a living dinosaur before the species becomes extinct. Whoever is operating the clock, however, cuts it a little close, and you arrive on the prehistoric scene just as a giant asteroid is hurtling toward Earth. General mayhem ensues as you evade carnivorous predators, catch the dino, and make your escape before the asteroid hits.

© Disney

Dinosaur serves up nonstop action from beginning to end with brilliant visual effects. Elaborate even by Disney standards, the attraction provides a tense, frenetic ride that's embellished by the entire Imagineering arsenal of high-tech gimmickry. Although the ride is jerky, it's not too rough for seniors. The menacing dinosaurs, however, along with the intensity of the experience, make Dinosaur a no go for younger children. To our surprise and joy, Dinosaur has been refined and cranked up a couple of notches on the intensity scale. The latest version is darker, more interesting, and much zippier.

THEATER IN THE WILD /
FINDING NEMO, THE MUSICAL ★★★★

! APPEAL   Preschool ★★★★½   Grade School ★★★★   Teens ★★★★
● BY AGE   Young Adults ★★★★   Over 30 ★★★★   Seniors ★★★★

What it is **Enclosed venue for live stage shows.** Scope and scale **Major attraction.** When to go **Anytime.** Comments **Performance times listed in handout park map or Times Guide.** Authors' rating **Not to be missed; ★★★★.** When to arrive **30 minutes before showtime.**

Another chapter in the Pixar-ization of Disney theme parks, Finding Nemo is arguably the most elaborate live show in any Disney World theme park. Incorporating dancing, special effects (including trapezes), and sophisticated digital backdrops of the undersea world, it features onstage human performers retelling Nemo's story with colorful, larger-than-life puppets. To be fair, puppets doesn't adequately convey the size or detail of these props, many of which are as big as a car and require two people to manipulate. An original musical score was written for the show, which is a must-see for most Animal Kingdom guests. A few scenes, such as one in which

Nemo's mom is eaten, may be too intense for some very small children. Some of the midshow musical numbers slow the pace, so the main concern for parents is whether the kids can sit still for an entire show. With that in mind, we advise parents to catch an afternoon performance—around 3 p.m. would be great—after seeing the rest of Animal Kingdom. If the kids get restless, you can either leave the show and catch the afternoon parade, or end your day at the park.

274

PRIMEVAL WHIRL (FASTPASS) ★★★

! APPEAL   Preschool ★★½   Grade School ★★★★   Teens ★★★★
• BY AGE   Young Adults ★★★   Over 30 ★★★   Seniors ★★½

What it is Small coaster. Scope and scale Minor attraction. When to go During the first 2 hours the park is open, in the hour before closing, or use FASTPASS. Comments 48" minimum height requirement. Switching-off option provided (see page 107). Authors' rating "Wild mouse" on steroids; ★★★. Duration Almost 2½ minutes. Average wait in line per 100 people ahead of you 4½ minutes. Loading speed Slow.

Primeval Whirl is a small coaster with short drops and curves, and it runs through the jaws of a dinosaur, among other things. What makes this coaster different is that the cars also spin. It's like being on one of the Magic Kingdom's teacups, mounted on a roller coaster track. Because guests cannot control the spinning, the cars spin and stop spinning according to how the ride is programmed. Sometimes the spin is braked to a jarring halt after half a revolution, and sometimes it's allowed to make one or two complete turns. The complete spins are fun, but the screeching-stop half spins are almost painful. If you subtract the time it takes to ratchet up the first hill, the actual ride time is about 90 seconds. Like Space Mountain, the ride is duplicated side by side, but with only one queue.

The spinning takes a toll on yet another visitor.

© Andrew Petersen

TRICERATOP SPIN ★★

! APPEAL   Preschool ★★★★½   Grade School ★★★★   Teens ★★★
• BY AGE   Young Adults ★★   Over 30 ★★★   Seniors ★★

What it is Hub-and-spoke midway ride. Scope and scale Minor attraction. When to go First 90 minutes the park is open and the hour before closing. Authors' rating Dumbo's prehistoric forebear; ★★. Duration 1½ minutes. Average wait in line per 100 people ahead of you 10 minutes. Loading speed Slow.

Another Dumbo-like ride. Here you spin around a central hub until a dinosaur pops out of the top of the hub. You'd think with the collective imagination of the Walt Disney Company, they'd come up with something a little more creative.

LIVE ENTERTAINMENT

Afternoon Parade Mickey's Jammin' Jungle Parade is comparable to the parades at the other parks, complete with floats, Disney characters (especially those from The Lion King, The Jungle Book, Tarzan, and Pocahontas), skaters, acrobats, and stilt walkers. Though subject to change, the parade starts in Africa, crosses the bridge to Discovery Island, proceeds counterclockwise around the island, and then crosses the bridge to Asia. In Asia, the parade turns left and follows the walkway paralleling the river back to Africa. The walking path between Africa and Asia has several small cutouts that offer good views of the parade and excellent sun protection. As it's used mainly as a walkway, the path is also relatively uncrowded. (*Note:* The paths on Discovery Island get very crowded, making it easy to lose members of your party.)

Here's our advice for watching the festivities: The parade both begins and ends in Africa. At the beginning of the parade, there's a legion of guests vying for a viewing spot in the village of Harambe. As soon as the parade crosses the bridge to Discovery Island, however, the crowd breaks up and leaves Harambe relatively deserted. Because most guests don't realize that the parade cycles back through the village, there's never much of a crowd on hand when the parade rumbles through the second time en route to going offstage. Therefore, if you make your way to Harambe about 20 minutes after the parade time listed in the Times Guide, you should be able to score yourself an excellent vantage point at the last minute.

276 **Animal Encounters** Throughout the day, Disney staff conduct impromptu short lectures on specific animals at the park. Look for a cast member in safari garb holding a bird, reptile, or small mammal. And walk toward them, not away as your natural impulse may suggest.

Goodwill Ambassadors A number of Asian and African natives are on hand throughout the park. Both gracious and knowledgeable, they are delighted to discuss their country and its wildlife. Look for them in Harambe and along the Pangani Forest Exploration Trail in Africa, and in Anandapur and along the Maharaja Jungle Trek in Asia. They can also be found near the main entrance and at The Oasis.

Kids' Discovery Club Activity stations offer kids ages 4 to 8 a structured learning experience as they tour Animal Kingdom. Set up along walkways in six themed areas, Discovery Club stations are manned by cast members who supervise a different activity at each station. A souvenir logbook, available free, is stamped at each station when the child completes a craft or exercise. Kids enjoy collecting the stamps and trying puzzles in the logbook while in attraction lines.

Adults' Discovery Club
The Dawa Bar offers adults age 21 and up an unstructured learning experience as they tour Animal Kingdom's alcoholic beverages. Set up along the walkway in Africa, the

Draft Beer

Safari Amber   6.00
Bud Light   5.25

Two alcoholic beverages per person with valid I.D.

Sales tax not included
Gratuities not included

Bottled Beer

Tusker Lager (Kenya)   6.75
Windhoek Lager (Namibia) 6.75
Yuengling   5.75
Blue Moon   5.75
Budweiser   5.75
Corona

bar is manned by cast members who specialize in exotic drinks. A souvenir logbook, available free and stamped when the adult completes a different drink or shot, would be a fabulous idea if Disney actually implemented it. Adults enjoy collecting the drinks and trying bar food prior to jumping in attraction lines.

Street Performers Street performers can be found most of the time at Discovery Island, Harambe in Africa, Anandapur in Asia, and DinoLand U.S.A. Far and away the most intriguing street performer is the one you can't see—at least not at first. Totally bedecked in foliage and luxuriant vines is a stilt walker named DeVine, who blends so completely with Animal Kingdom's dense flora that you don't notice her until she moves. We've seen guests standing less than a foot away gasp in amazement as DeVine brushes them with a leafy tendril. Usually found at The Oasis or Discovery Island, DeVine is a must-see. If you don't encounter her, ask a cast member when and where she can be found.

COUNTER-SERVICE RESTAURANTS

Counter-service food is a cut above the average at the Animal Kingdom, and both ethnic and standard fare (hotdogs, burgers, etc.) are available. Our two favorites are the Flame Tree Barbeque with outdoor waterfront dining, and the Yak & Yeti Local Food Café for casual Asian fare.

Flame Tree Barbecue

QUALITY Good VALUE B– PORTION Large LOCATION Discovery Island
READER RESPONSES 90% 👍 10% 👎 DINING PLAN Yes

Half slab St. Louis–style ribs; smoked half chicken; smoked-beef and -pork sandwiches; salad with barbecued chicken; child's plate of baked chicken drumsticks or hot dog; fries, coleslaw, onion rings; chocolate cake; Safari Amber beer, Bud Light, and wine. Queues very long at lunchtime, but seating ample and well shaded. Try the covered gazebo overlooking the water.

Kusafiri Coffee Shop

QUALITY Good VALUE B PORTION Medium LOCATION Africa
READER RESPONSES Too new to rate DINING PLAN No

Fruit turnovers, Danish and other pastries, muffins, croissants, bagel with cream cheese, cookies, brownies, cake, fruit cup, yogurt, coffee, cocoa, juice. A good early-morning sugar rush on the way to Kilimanjaro Safaris. Shares space with Tusker House; easy walk-up window.

Picnic in the Park

QUALITY Fair VALUE C PORTION Small–medium LOCATION Varies
READER RESPONSES Too new to rate DINING PLAN Yes

Sandwiches: grilled-chicken wraps, ham grinders, and turkey on focaccia. Entrees: rotisserie chicken and sliced ham. Sides: fruit salad, mac and cheese, pasta salad, mashed potatoes and gravy, potato wedges, tomatoes and cucumbers, coleslaw, and green beans. Bottled water is the only beverage choice. Before 1 p.m., stop by Guest Relations at the front of the park to place your order; after 1 p.m., head to Tusker House in Africa. Choose one of the two meal options available and specify a pickup time, allowing at least two hours between ordering and pickup. When your order is ready, retrieve it at the Kusafiri Coffee Shop.

Pizzafari

QUALITY Fair VALUE B PORTION Medium LOCATION Discovery Island
READER RESPONSES 82% 👍 18% 👎 DINING PLAN Yes

Cheese and pepperoni personal pizzas; chicken Parmesan sandwich; grilled-chicken Caesar salad; breadsticks; Italian deli sandwich; child's mac and cheese or cheese pizza. Hectic at peak mealtimes. The pizza is pretty unimpressive.

Restaurantosaurus

QUALITY Good VALUE B+ PORTION Medium–large LOCATION DinoLand U.S.A.
READER RESPONSES 69% 👍 31% 👎 DINING PLAN Yes

Cheeseburgers; hot dogs; chicken nuggets; Mandarin chicken salad; veggie burger; fries; chocolate cake and carrot cake; coffee, tea, and cocoa; apple and orange juice; beer.

Royal Anandapur Tea Company

QUALITY Good VALUE B PORTION Medium LOCATION Asia
READER RESPONSES 86% 👍 14% 👎 DINING PLAN No

Wide variety of hot and iced teas; lattes; coffee, espresso, and cappuccino; large pastries. Offers about a dozen loose-leaf teas from Asia and Africa.

Tamu Tamu

QUALITY Good **VALUE** C **PORTION** Large **LOCATION** Africa
READER RESPONSES 63% 🖐 37% 🖐 **DINING PLAN** No

Milk shakes. During peak seasons, turkey sandwiches, tuna-salad sandwiches, and burgers on multigrain buns are on the menu at Tamu Tamu. Seating is behind building.

Yak & Yeti Local Food Cafe

QUALITY Fair **VALUE** C **PORTION** Large **LOCATION** Asia
READER RESPONSES 83% 🖐 17% 🖐 **DINING PLAN** Yes

Crispy honey chicken with steamed rice (the best choice), kung pao beef, lo mein, Asian salads. For kids, chicken bites with pork egg roll and mini cheeseburgers with applesauce and carrots. The beef and lo mein don't fare well sitting under a heat lamp until someone orders them.

Animal Kingdom Special Treats Menu

Pluto Dog

Everyone knows that Pluto is a good dog, but this weenie winner proves it. For those on bread-free diets, you can eat the Pluto Dog without the bun by holding the dog upside down by its tail—watch that dripping mustard though! Served with corrugated potato chips.
....$4.50

Buzz Lightbeer

When your mood is heading south and you're looking for a change of attitude, a Buzz Lightbeer will give you a happy lite-beer buzz. Comes in a souvenir mug.
....$6.00.

HOLIDAYS AT WALT DISNEY WORLD

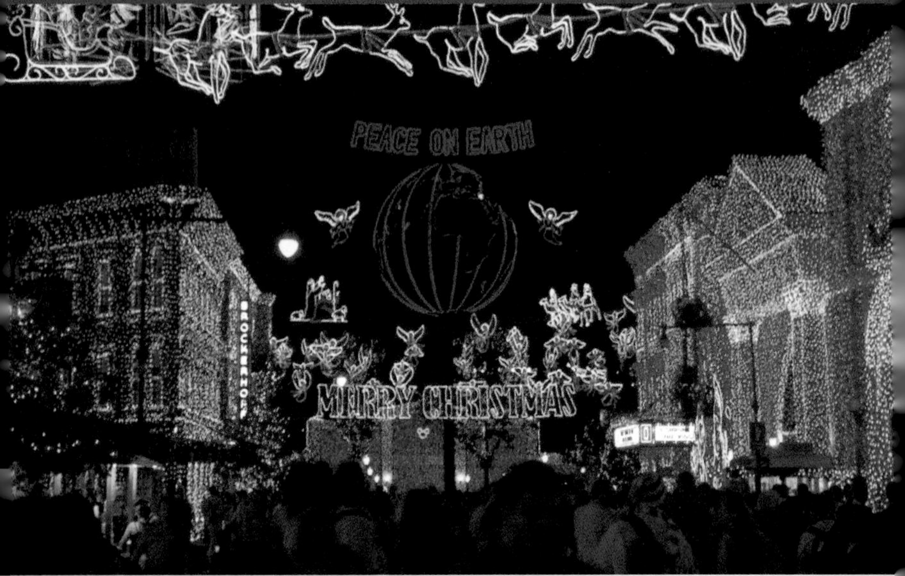

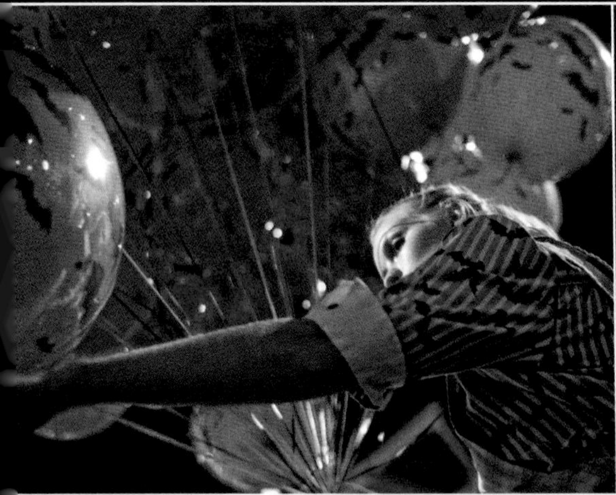

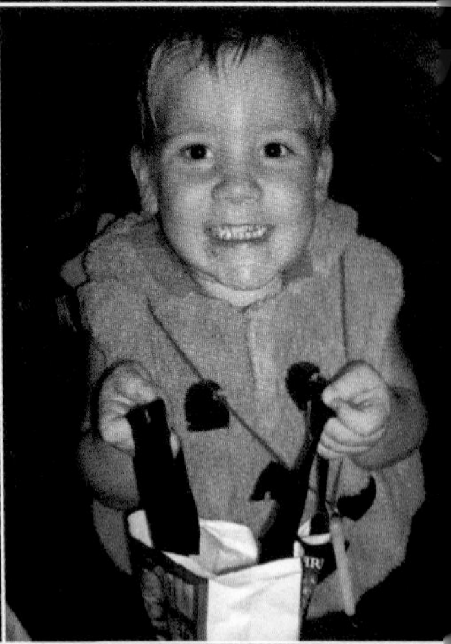

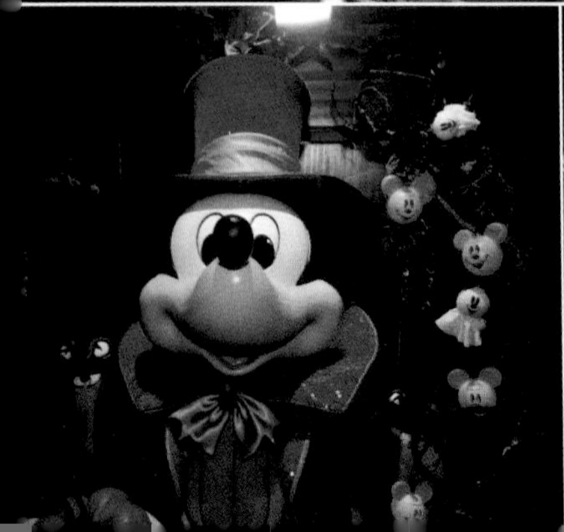

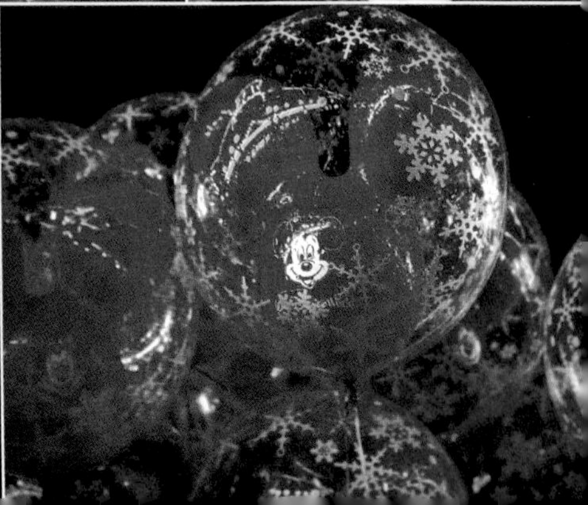

PART 8

DISNEY'S HOLLYWOOD STUDIOS

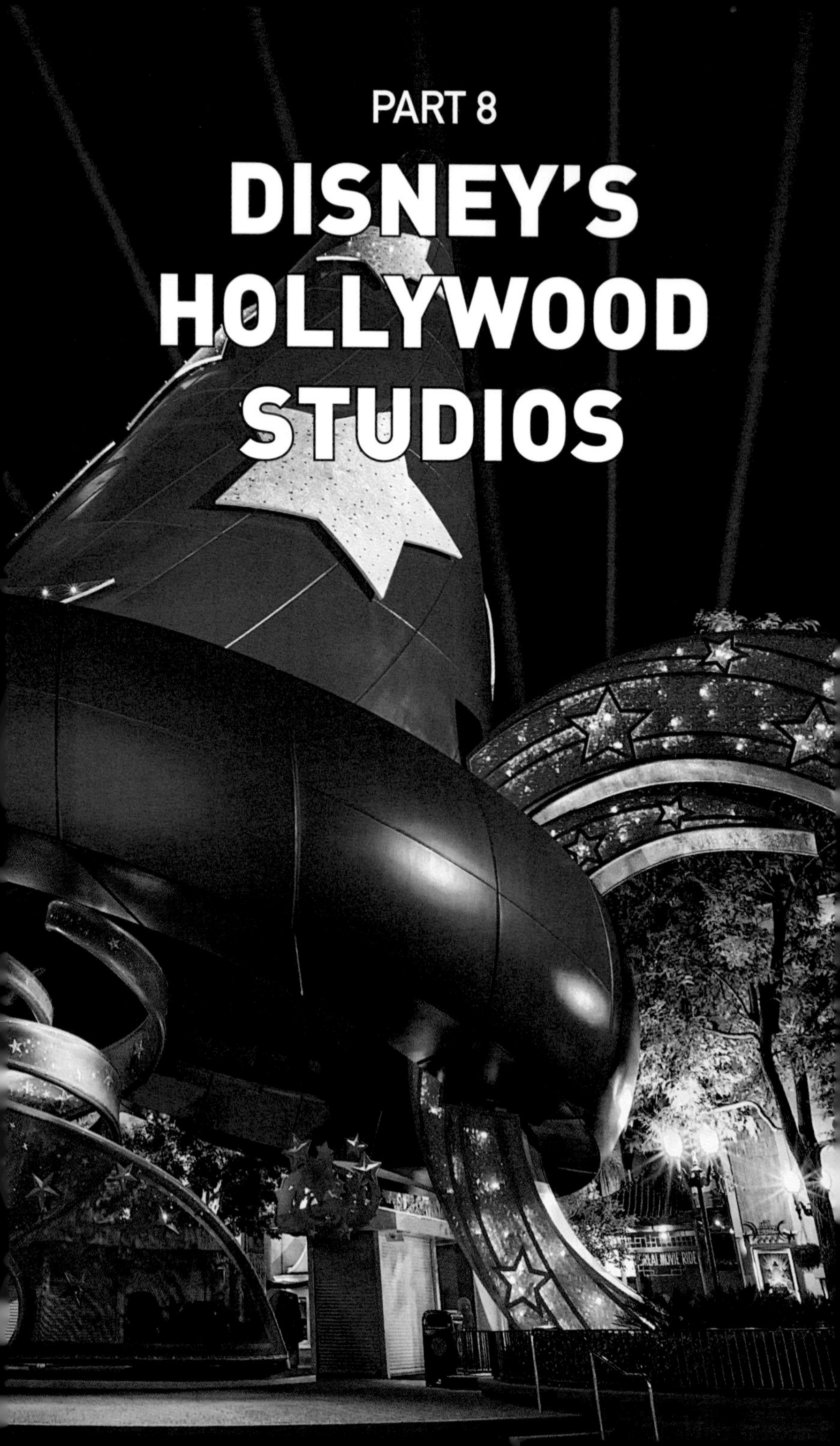

Disney's Hollywood Studios is a theme park dedicated to the process of making films, theater productions, television shows, and music. The park also pays tribute to classic achievements in film and the other arts, especially those that have become part of popular American culture.

Formerly known as Disney-MGM Studios, the Disney Company built the park in response to the creation of Universal Studios Florida, a movie- and film-based theme park, in the late 1980s. When Disney-MGM opened, Disney promoted it as a working television and movie production facility. And for a time it was common to see both animated films (such as Disney's animated *Lilo & Stitch*, *Mulan*, and *Brother Bear*) and television shows in production as you walked through the park. Eventually, however, the costs of running duplicate facilities in both California and Florida became too great, and most Florida work stopped. While the buildings are still present, it's extremely rare to see actual television or film work being done nowadays.

Also gone from the Studios is the MGM name. Disney purchased Pixar Animation Studios after partnering with the company on a series of highly successful films, including *Toy Story*; *A Bug's Life*; *Monsters, Inc.*; *Finding Nemo*; and *The Incredibles*. The cost of continuing an association with MGM, coupled with Pixar's arguably greater popularity, probably convinced Disney to rename the theme park. But rather than replace MGM with Pixar, Disney decided that Hollywood represented a more generic reference to moviemaking and fit in with the timeless theme that the park was supposed to convey. Nowadays, most guests refer to Disney's Hollywood Studios simply as Disney Studios, DHS, or the Studios.

Not to Be Missed at Disney's Hollywood Studios

DHS Backlot Tour	*Fantasmic!*
Jim Henson's Muppet-Vision 3-D	*Lights! Motors! Action!* Extreme Stunt Show
Rock 'n' Roller Coaster	*Toy Story* Mania!
The Twilight Zone Tower of Terror	*Voyage of the Little Mermaid*

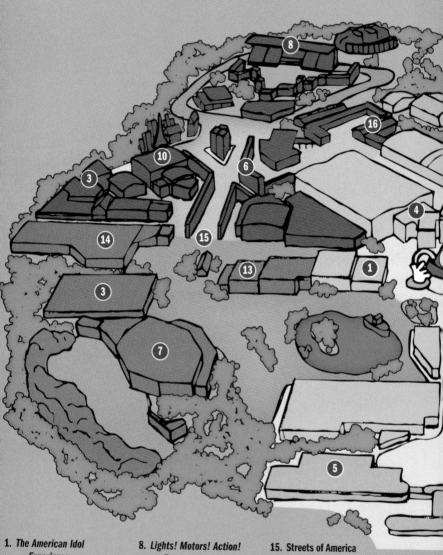

1. *The American Idol Experience*
2. *Fantasmic!*
3. Food and shopping
4. Great Movie Ride
5. Guest Services
6. *Honey I Shrunk the Kids Movie Set Adventure*
7. *Indiana Jones Epic Stunt Spectacular*
8. *Lights! Motors! Action! Extreme Stunt Show*
9. The Magic of Disney Animation
10. *Muppet-Vision 3-D*
11. *Playhouse Disney— Live on Stage!*
12. Rock 'n' Roller Coaster
13. Sounds Dangerous
14. Star Tours
15. Streets of America
16. Studios Backlot Tour
17. Theater of the Stars
18. *Toy Story Mania!*
19. *The Twilight Zone Tower of Terror*
20. *Voyage of the Little Mermaid*
21. *Walt Disney: One Man's Dream*
22. Oscar's

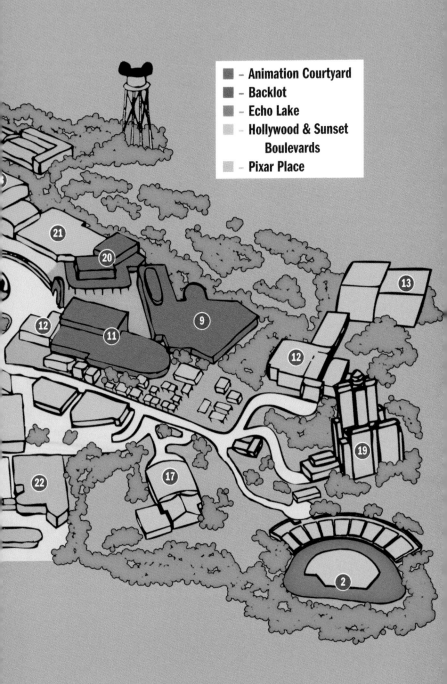

- Animation Courtyard
- Backlot
- Echo Lake
- Hollywood & Sunset Boulevards
- Pixar Place

HOLLYWOOD AND SUNSET BOULEVARDS

Hollywood Boulevard is a palm-lined re-creation of Hollywood's main drag during Los Angeles's golden age. Architecture is streamlined moderne with Art Deco embellishments. Most service facilities are here, interspersed with eateries and shops. Merchandise includes Disney trademark items, Hollywood and movie-related souvenirs, and one-of-a-kind collectibles obtained from studio auctions and estate sales. Hollywood characters and roving performers entertain on the boulevard, and daily parades and other happenings pass this way.

Sunset Boulevard, evoking the 1940s, is a major component of DHS. The first right off Hollywood Boulevard, Sunset Boulevard, provides another venue for dining, shopping, and street entertainment.

DISNEY DESIGN with Sam Gennawey

In 1989, Michael Eisner proclaimed that Walt Disney World's third park would be dedicated to Hollywood, "not a place on a map, but a state of mind," and "a Hollywood that never was—and always will be."

Inspired by early filmmakers who used Los Angeles as the background for their movies, Disney's Imagineers use real building facades and billboards to tell the story of the mythical Hollywood of our collective consciousness. For the architecture, the Imagineers apply a design trick called shrink and edit that takes a real building for inspiration and then changes the scale, color, or detail to support the story. Hollywood Boulevard is filled with such examples.

Your adventure starts at the park entrance as you pass through a reproduction of the Streamline Moderne Pan-Pacific Auditorium, Hollywood's primary convention center from 1935 to 1972. The entry plaza is at the intersection of Hollywood and Prospect Avenue. The central building is the Cross Roads building (1936), which is a tribute to an early Los Angeles mini-mall. It is topped by a five-foot Mickey Mouse, with one of Mickey's ears functioning as a lightning rod.

To the left of the park entrance is Sid Cahuenga's One-of-a-Kind shop, an example of the California bungalow and inspired by the true story of the Janes House, in which a homeowner on Hollywood Boulevard held out against commercial development, and a shopping mall was built around it. Other buildings include an electric substation (1907) from Culver City that is now a performance space, the Baine Building (1926), a J.J. Newberry (1928), a bank on Wilshire Boulevard (1929), the Chapman Market (1929), Max Factor Building (1931), Owl Drug Store (1933), the Darkroom (1938), and many, many others. A highlight is The Hollywood Brown Derby (1929), which is a treasure inside and out.

The two billboards at the entrance, as well as Echo Lake (1920–1945), establish the architectural timeframe for Hollywood and Sunset Boulevards. The Hollywoodland billboard refers to a subdivision that opened in 1923, the same year Walt Disney moved to Hollywood. Adjacent is a billboard for the 1945 Hollywood Canteen, a Hollywood oasis for soldiers fighting in World War II.

Hollywood Boulevard Services

Most of the park's service facilities are on Hollywood Boulevard, including:

Baby Center/Baby Care Needs: At Guest Relations; baby food and other necessities available at Oscar's Super Service

Banking Services: ATM outside the park to the right of the turnstiles

Film and Cameras: At the Darkroom on the right side of Hollywood Boulevard as you enter the park, just past Oscar's Super Service

First Aid: At Guest Relations

Live Entertainment and Parade Information: Available free at Guest Relations and elsewhere in park

Lost and Found: At Package Pick-Up, to the right of the entrance

Lost Persons: Report lost persons at Guest Relations

Storage Lockers: Rental lockers to the right of the main entrance, on the left of Oscar's Super Service

Wheelchair and Stroller Rental: To the right of the entrance, at Oscar's Super Service

THE AMERICAN IDOL EXPERIENCE ★★★★

| ! APPEAL | Preschool ★★★ | Grade School ★★★★ | Teens ★★★★ |
| BY AGE | Young Adults ★★★½ | Over 30 ★★★★ | Seniors ★★★ |

What it is Theme-park version of the TV show. Scope and scale Major attraction. When to go Anytime. Comments Guests must be at least age 14 to perform. Authors' rating Even if you don't watch the show, you'll find someone to cheer for; ★★★★. Duration 20 minutes for daytime preliminary shows, 40 minutes for the nighttime finale. When to arrive 20–30 minutes before showtime.

Based on the wildly popular TV talent search, *The American Idol Experience* is your chance to unleash your song stylings on the world. Your path to superstardom goes like this: Guests audition a cappella in front of a judge, just as in *American Idol*'s first shows of the season. Those who make the cut move on to a second audition and sing, karaoke style, to a prerecorded track. The judge's picks from this round get to perform in one of the attraction's preliminary shows, held several times a day.

During the preliminaries, each contestant repeats his or her song from the second audition in front of a live audience of theme-park guests. As with *Idol*, three judges—in this case, Disney cast members—provide feedback. Don't fret that your operatic rendition of "Boot Scootin' Boogie" will be raked over the coals: For the most part, the Disney panel uses gentle humor to tell you not to quit your day job, although the judge who stands in for Simon Cowell does let fly the occasional zinger ("I can picture you on the cover of *Rolling Stone* . . . standing next to someone who can sing on key").

Audience members decide the preliminary winners, who meet for one last showdown at night. The winner of the finale receives a Dream Ticket—a front-of-the-line pass to try out for *American Idol* in his or her hometown.

We'd never make it on Idol. Besides the whole "not having talent" thing, we're not cute as buttons either.

BEAUTY AND THE BEAST—LIVE ON STAGE/ THEATER OF THE STARS ★★★★

! APPEAL Preschool ★★★★½ Grade School ★★★★ Teens ★★★★
• BY AGE Young Adults ★★★★ Over 30 ★★★★ Seniors ★★★★½

What it is **Live Hollywood-style musical, usually featuring Disney characters; performed in an open-air theater.** Scope and scale **Major attraction.** When to go **Anytime; evenings are cooler.** Comments **Performances are listed in the daily** *Times Guide*. Authors' rating **Excellent; ★★★★.** Duration **25 minutes.** When to arrive **20–30 minutes before showtime.**

Theater of the Stars combines Disney characters with singers and dancers in upbeat and humorous Hollywood musicals. *The Beauty and the Beast* show, in particular, is outstanding. The singing is a cut above most theme-park shows in Disney or elsewhere. The story, necessarily abbreviated from the film, is clear and has no slow moments. The sets and costume design are colorful and dynamic, without being distracting. *Beauty and the Beast* ranks second only to *Aladdin* (at Disney's California Adventure park) in the entire lineup of Disney stage shows.

The theater offers a clear field of vision from almost every seat, and a canopy protects the audience from the Florida sun (or rain). The theater still gets mighty hot in the summer, but you should make it through a performance without suffering a heatstroke.

FANTASMIC! ★★★★★

! APPEAL   Preschool ★★★★   Grade School ★★★★½   Teens ★★★★½
• BY AGE   Young Adults ★★★★★   Over 30 ★★★★½   Seniors ★★★★½

What it is **Mixed-media nighttime spectacular.** Scope and scale **Superheadliner.** When to go **Staged only at night, generally Monday and Thursday.** Comments **Disney's best nighttime event.** Authors' rating **Not to be missed; ★★★★★.** Duration **25 minutes.** Probable waiting time **50–90 minutes for a seat; 35–40 minutes for standing room.**

Fantasmic! is a mixed-media show presented twice weekly when the park is open late. Located off Sunset Boulevard behind the Tower of Terror, *Fantasmic!* is staged on an island opposite a 6,900-seat amphitheater. By far the largest theater facility ever created by Disney, the amphitheater can accommodate an additional 3,000 standing guests for an audience of nearly 10,000. Until recently, *Fantasmic!* was staged nightly and always played to a full house. Presumably as a cost-containment measure, Disney has cut performances to two evenings a week. As you might imagine, trying to cram seven nights of capacity crowds into two nights is not working very well, as a reader from Sandwich, Illinois, reports:

The reduction in *Fantasmic!* shows per week is ridiculous to me. The Studios is an absolute ghost town on nights it doesn't show, and packed to capacity on nights when it does! There has to be a happy medium.

Nonetheless, *Fantasmic!* is far and away the most innovative outdoor spectacle ever attempted at any theme park. Starring Mickey Mouse in his role as the sorcerer's apprentice from Fantasia, the production uses lasers, images projected on a shroud of mist, fireworks, lighting effects, and music in combinations so stunning

that you can scarcely believe what you are seeing. The plot is simple: good versus 291 evil. The story gets lost in all the special effects at times, but no matter; it's the spectacle, not the story line, that is so overpowering. While *beautiful*, *stunning*, and *powerful* are words that immediately come to mind, they fail to convey the uniqueness of this presentation.

Though we do not receive many reports of young children being terrified by *Fantasmic!*, we suggest that you spend a little time preparing your younger children for what they will see. You can mitigate the fright factor somewhat by sitting back a bit. Also, make sure to hang on to your children after *Fantasmic!* and to give them explicit instructions for regrouping in the event you are separated.

THE GREAT MOVIE RIDE ★★★½

!	APPEAL	Preschool ★★★	Grade School ★★★½	Teens ★★★½
.	BY AGE	Young Adults ★★★½	Over 30 ★★★★	Seniors ★★★★

What it is Movie-history indoor adventure ride. **Scope and scale** Headliner. **When to go** Before 11 a.m. or after 4:30 p.m. **Comments** Elaborate, with several surprises. **Authors' rating** Unique; ★★★½. **Duration** About 19 minutes. **Average wait in line per 100 people ahead of you** 2 minutes; assumes all trains operating. **Loading speed** Fast.

Entering through a re-creation of Hollywood's Chinese Theater, guests board vehicles for a fast-paced tour through soundstage sets from classic films, including *Casablanca*, *Tarzan*, *The Wizard of Oz*, *Alien*, and *Raiders of the Lost Ark*. Each set is populated with Disney audio-animatronic characters, as well as an occasional human, all augmented by sound and lighting effects. One of Disney's larger and more ambitious dark rides, The Great Movie Ride encompasses 95,000 square feet and showcases some of the most famous scenes in filmmaking, in some of the largest sets ever constructed for a Disney ride.

We're fans of Great Movie Ride—it's elaborate and well engineered—but that doesn't mean it's perfect. For one thing, many of the film references—which may have been appropriate for audiences in the late 1980s—are hopelessly outdated for many guests under age 40, and certainly most under 30. We think we'd be hard-pressed to find someone in those demographics who's actually seen a James Cagney or Busby Berkeley film (or, for that matter, Disney's *Fantasia*). Perhaps it's time to update the attraction. Or to bring back musicals with swimming starlets. Either one is fine with Bob and Len.

Pucker up!

Our second observation is that the Great Movie Ride would make an excellent drinking game because there is an underlying theme (which we'll explain) throughout most of the scenes. Because drinks aren't allowed on the attraction, we propose the following rules for what we're calling the Great Movie Ride of Love: Begin the ride seated next to your spouse, significant other, or random attractive stranger you meet in line. Kiss said person once for every violent scene, display of a weapon, or reference to death you find in the ride (including deaths you can name from the film, if not shown in the attraction). We're pretty sure you and your sweetie will be giggling like young lovers mere minutes into the ride, and you'll probably be gasping for breath by the finale.

ROCK 'N' ROLLER COASTER (FASTPASS) ★★★★

! APPEAL
• BY AGE

Preschool ★	Grade School ★★★★½	Teens ★★★★★
Young Adults ★★★★★	Over 30 ★★★★★	Seniors ★★★

What it is Rock-music-themed roller coaster. **Scope and scale** Headliner. **When to go** Before 10 a.m., in the hour before closing, or use FASTPASS. **Comments** Must be 48" tall to ride; children younger than age 7 must ride with an adult. Switching-off option provided (see page 107). Note that there is a single-rider line for this attraction. **Authors' rating** Disney's wildest American coaster; not to be missed; ★★★★. **Duration** Almost 1½ minutes. **Average wait in line per 100 people ahead of you** 2½ minutes; assumes all trains operating. **Loading speed** Moderate–fast.

WARNING:
THIS RIDE WILL
MUSS YOUR DO

This is Disney's answer to the roller-coaster proliferation at Universal's Islands of Adventure and Busch Gardens theme parks. Exponentially wilder than Space Mountain or Big Thunder Mountain in the Magic Kingdom, Rock 'n' Roller Coaster is an attraction for fans of high-tech thrill rides. Although the rock icons and synchronized music add measurably to the experience, the ride itself, as opposed to sights and sounds along the way, is the focus. Rock 'n' Roller Coaster offers loops, corkscrews, and drops that make Space Mountain seem like the Jungle Cruise. What really makes this metal coaster unusual, however, is that at first, it's in the dark (like Space Mountain, only with Southern California nighttime scenes instead of space), and second, you're launched up the first hill like a jet off a carrier deck. By the time you crest the hill, you'll have gone from 0 to 57 miles per hour in less than three seconds. When you enter the first loop, you'll be pulling five g's. By comparison, that's two more g's than astronauts experience at liftoff on a space shuttle.

The ride lasts less than two minutes, but there might be enough entertainment in the queue and preshow to make up for any long waits in line. A series of classic concert posters line the halls of the queue, providing the opportunity to point out that you could once see Jimi Hendrix for what it costs to park at concerts these days. Roll your eyes and sigh deeply if your kids say, "Jimi who?" The preshow features Aerosmith in a short video setting up the premise to the ride. It's funny as much for the band's stilted delivery as it is for Steven Tyler's background antics when others are talking.

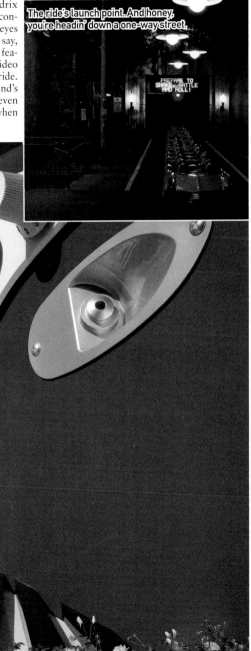

The ride's launch point. And honey, you're headin' down a one-way street.

PREPARE TO SHAKE RATTLE AND ROLL !

THE TWILIGHT ZONE TOWER OF TERROR
(FASTPASS) ★ ★ ★ ★ ★

**! APPEAL
• BY AGE**

| Preschool ★★½ | Grade School ★★★★ | Teens ★★★★½ |
| Young Adults ★★★★★ | Over 30 ★★★★★ | Seniors ★★★★ |

What it is Sci-fi–themed indoor thrill ride. **Scope and scale** Superheadliner. **When to go** Before 9:30 a.m., after 6 p.m., or use FASTPASS. **Comments** Must be 40" tall to ride; switching-off option offered (see page 107). **Authors' rating** Walt Disney World's best attraction; not to be missed; ★★★★★. **Duration** About 4 minutes plus preshow. **Average wait in line per 100 people ahead of you** 4 minutes; assumes all elevators operating. **Loading speed** Moderate.

The Tower of Terror is a different species of Disney thrill ride, though it borrows elements of The Haunted Mansion at the Magic Kingdom. The story is that you're touring a once-famous Hollywood hotel gone to ruin. As at Star Tours, the queuing area immerses guests in the adventure as they pass through the hotel's once-opulent public rooms. From the lobby, guests are escorted into the hotel's library, where Rod Serling, speaking from an old black-and-white television, greets the guests and introduces the plot.

The Tower of Terror is a whopper at 13-plus stories. Breaking tradition in terms of visually isolating themed areas, it lets you see the entire Studios from atop the tower...but you have to look quickly. The ride vehicle, one of the hotel's service elevators, takes guests to see the haunted hostelry. The tour begins innocuously, but at about the fifth floor, things get pretty weird. Guests are subjected to a full range of eerie effects as they cross into *The Twilight Zone*. The climax of the adventure occurs when the elevator reaches the top floor (the 13th, of course) and the cable snaps.

The Tower of Terror is an experience to savor. Though the final plunges (yep, make that plural) are calculated to thrill, the extraordinary visual and audio effects are the meat of the attraction. There's richness and subtlety here, enough to keep the ride fresh and stimulating after many repetitions. Disney tinkers with the Tower of Terror incessantly. Random ride and drop sequences were introduced a few years back, which make the attraction faster and keep you guessing about when, how far, and how many times the elevator will drop. In addition to random sequencing, new visual and auditory effects have been added to the experience lately.

Some of the hotel's permanent guests.
Drop by for a visit. They're dying to meet you.

How great would it be if the Tower were an actual hotel? We'd take the stairs, of course.

VALID PARK
ADMISSION
REQUIRED TO USE
ELEVATOR.

HAVE A NICE DAY.

SERVICE ELEVATOR

Answer: The Indian Ocean, west of Australia and south of the Cocos (Keeling) Islands at latitude –30

If the elevator shaft for the Tower or Terror was drilled right through the center of the Earth, where would it come out?

**degrees, 26 minutes, and 55.22 seconds by longitude
93 degrees, 9 minutes, and 50.62 seconds.**

ECHO LAKE

DISNEY DESIGN with *Sam Gennawey*

The real Echo Lake is a man-made lake near downtown Los Angeles and served as the background for many early silent film comedies. Just like the park's Hollywood Boulevard, the buildings that surround Echo Lake are from Los Angeles. Hollywood & Vine is modeled after a cafeteria (once the Hollywood Post Office) that was within walking distance of all the movie-making action and burned down in 1990. The 50's Prime Time Cafe is influenced by residential buildings by Richard Neutra, Frank Lloyd Wright, and Pierre Koenig. The Streamline Moderne theater and adjacent buildings that house *The American Idol Experience* are based on NBC Radio City (1938) and CBS Columbia Square (1938).

At that time, Los Angeles was filled with what is known interchangeably as programmatic architecture, California Crazy, or duck. A building of this type, as defined by architect Robert Venturi, is one whose "exterior is in the shape of the everyday object they relate to" and is "a building in which the architecture is subordinate to the overall symbolic form." The boat you see in the corner of Echo Lake is a tribute to a 1930 film called *Min and Bill* that won Marie Dressler an Academy Award. The dinosaur at the other end of Echo Lake is Gertie, an animated character who toured along with Winsor McCay on the vaudeville circuit in 1914. His hand-painted film was a huge influence on Walt Disney.

As you walk away from Echo Lake, you also move away from the architectural history of Los Angeles and into a studio back lot. Things become less real. *Indiana Jones Epic Stunt Spectacular* is just a backdrop. The Star Tours facade is a reproduction of the Ewok Village movie set, with no pretension of being anything other than a stage. And the Backlot Express is a prop storage area.

INDIANA JONES EPIC STUNT SPECTACULAR
(FASTPASS) ★★★★

! APPEAL
• BY AGE

Preschool ★★★	Grade School ★★★★	Teens ★★★★
Young Adults ★★★★	Over 30 ★★★★	Seniors ★★★★

What it is Movie-stunt demonstration and action show. **Scope and scale** Headliner. **When to go** First three morning shows or last evening show. **Comments** Performance times posted on a sign at the entrance to the theater; FASTPASSes available seasonally. **Authors' rating** Done on a grand scale: ★★★★. **Duration** 30 minutes. **Preshow** Selection of extras from audience. **When to arrive** 20–30 minutes before showtime.

This stage show showcases professional stuntmen and stuntwomen who demonstrate dangerous stunts with an insider's look at how it's done. Key scenes from the first Indiana Jones film, *Raiders of the Lost Ark*, are re-created on an enormous covered stage, and those scenes provide an opportunity to explain how moviemaking stunt work is done.

Indiana Jones's opening, which reenacts the big rolling ball intro of *Raiders*, is well done and certainly gets the audience's attention. In fact, sets throughout the entire show are elaborate and detailed. Besides the intro, other highlights include the German flying-wing airplane scene and the chase through Cairo's streets, with plenty of fire and explosions. Audience members (selected right before the show begins) get a chance to be extras in some of the scenes that don't involve things blowing up.

Indiana Jones's stunt work ranges from audience participation in fight scenes to large-scale explosions involving elaborate props.

STAR TOURS (FASTPASS) ★ ★ ★ ★

! APPEAL
• BY AGE

Preschool ★★★½	Grade School ★★★★	Teens ★★★★
Young Adults ★★★★	Over 30 ★★★★	Seniors ★★★½

What it is Indoor space flight–simulation ride. **Scope and scale** Headliner. **When to go** First 90 minutes after opening. **Comments** Expectant mothers and anyone prone to motion sickness are advised against riding. Too intense for many children younger than age 8. Must be 40" tall to ride. **Authors' rating** A classic adventure; ★★★★. **Duration** About 7 minutes. **Average wait in line per 100 people ahead of you** 5 minutes; assumes all simulators operating. **Loading speed** Moderate–fast.

Based on the *Star Wars* movie series, this attraction was Disney's first modern simulator ride. Guests ride in a flight simulator modeled after those used for training pilots and astronauts. You're supposed on a vacation outing in space, piloted by a droid (android, a.k.a. robot) on his first flight with real passengers. Mayhem ensues almost immediately. Scenery flashes by, and the simulator bucks and pitches. You could swear you were moving at the speed of light. After several minutes of this, the droid somehow lands the spacecraft.

Do light sabers have an "on" button, or do you just use the Force?

In 2009 Disney announced a new *Star Wars* film for the simulators, to be released in 2011. Film and simulator technology has evolved substantially in the decades since Star Tours debuted, but we confess we're going to miss the voice of the droid pilot, done by Paul Reubens.

An interactive show, ***Jedi Training Academy,*** is staged several times daily to the left of the Star Tours building entrance. Young Skywalkers-in-training are selected from the audience to train in the ways of the Force and do battle against Darth Vader. If all this sounds too intense, it's not—Storm Troopers provide comic relief, and just as in the movies, the Jedi always wins. Check the daily entertainment schedule for showtimes.

MOTION SICKNESS WARNING

Traveling at light speed aboard Star Tours, with a brand-new robot pilot. What could possibly go wrong?

SOUNDS DANGEROUS (OPEN SEASONALLY) ★ ★ ★

! APPEAL   Preschool ★   Grade School ★ ★   Teens ★ ★ ★
• BY AGE   Young Adults ★ ★   Over 30 ★ ★   Seniors ★ ★ ½

What it is Show demonstrating sound effects. **Scope and scale** Minor attraction. **When to go** Before 11 a.m. or after 4 p.m. **Authors' rating** Funny and informative; ★ ★ ★. **Duration** 12 minutes. **Preshow** Video introduction to sound effects. **Probable waiting time** 15–30 minutes.

Sounds Dangerous: Looks closed.

Sounds Dangerous, a film presentation starring Drew Carey as a blundering detective, is the vehicle for a crash course on movie and TV sound effects. While the film itself is funny and well paced and (for once) doesn't hawk some Disney flick or product, time has not been kind to the attraction. Most young guests have no idea whom Drew Carey is, with no television series or major films recently. And the theater itself seems run-down. Readers rank *Sounds Dangerous* the lowest of any attraction at Disney's Hollywood Studios, and it sits with the Magic Kingdom's Stitch's Great Escape! as one of the least popular attractions in Walt Disney World.

If your group needs a break from the heat, however, the air-conditioning still works well. Note that part of the show is presented in the dark so guests can focus on the sound effects, and the darkness disturbs some small children.

Reader Questions We Can't Answer

What did Florida look like when giant poodles ruled the Earth?

BACKLOT

Guests strolling through an elaborate urban street set, with points of interest from San Francisco and New York, appreciate its rich detail. There's never a wait to enjoy the Streets of America; save it until you've seen the attractions that develop long lines. Characters such as Kim Possible and the Power Rangers often make appearances here.

DISNEY DESIGN with Sam Gennawey

The building facades here use a cinematic trick known as forced perspective, and the trick is also used throughout Walt Disney World. Forced perspective is the design pattern that gives buildings the appearance of greater height and scale. It is why the castle looks so grand and Everest looks so tall. In the back lot area, it allows the designers to fit in the New York or San Francisco skylines in such a small space.

Playing with scale is also a feature of the *Honey, I Shrunk the Kids Movie* Set. Realizing that there wasn't enough to do for small children, the Imagineers worked in record time to design and fabricate the attraction. This type of stage area is an example of another cinematic trick used in Disney films.

HONEY, I SHRUNK THE KIDS
MOVIE SET ADVENTURE ★★½

❗ APPEAL
● BY AGE

Preschool ★★★★½   Grade School ★★★★   Teens ★★½
Young Adults ★★   Over 30 ★★½   Seniors ★★★

What it is **Small but elaborate playground.** Scope and scale **Diversion.** When to go **Before 11 a.m. or after dark.** Comments **Opens an hour later than the rest of the park.** Authors' rating **Great for young children. more of a curiosity for adults; ★★½.** Duration **Varies.** Average wait in line per 100 people ahead of you **20 minutes.**

This elaborate playground appeals particularly to kids age 11 and younger. The story is that you have been miniaturized and have to make your way through a yard full of 20-foot-tall blades of grass, giant ants, lawn sprinklers, and other oversize features. This imaginative playground has tunnels, slides, rope ladders, and a variety of oversize props. All areas are padded, and Disney personnel are on hand to help keep children in some semblance of control.

© Disney

JIM HENSON'S MUPPET-VISION 3-D ★★★★½

! APPEAL
• BY AGE

| Preschool ★★★★ | Grade School ★★★★ | Teens ★★★★ |
| Young Adults ★★★★ | Over 30 ★★★★ | Seniors ★★★★ |

What it is 3-D movie starring the Muppets. Scope and scale Major attraction. When to go Before 11 a.m. or after 3 p.m. Authors' rating Uproarious; not to be missed; ★★★★½. Duration 17 minutes. Preshow Muppets on television. Probable waiting time 12 minutes.

Muppet-Vision features the cast of Jim Henson's Muppets demonstrating an improvement to late 1980's 3-D animation. While that might sound boring, the actual plot represents perhaps 10% of the overall film. The rest is a series of classic Muppet gags and skits, featuring the entire cast of characters from Kermit and Miss Piggy, to Gonzo, the Swedish Chef, and the elder grouches, Statler and Waldorf. There are enough funny one-liners and jokes here that you'll be repeating them for the rest of the day. (One of our favorites: In answer to a question about how they got a place in the attraction, Statler and Waldorf answer, "We entered a contest. Yeah, we lost.")

It's a tribute to the show's writers that although the film hasn't been updated in almost two decades, some of the jokes can still get giggles from repeat visitors. If you're tired and hot, this zany presentation will make you feel brand-new. Arrive early and enjoy the hilarious preshow video and stage props.

Bob and Len review *Muppet-Vision 3-D* **for the umpteenth time.**

LIGHTS! MOTORS! ACTION!
EXTREME STUNT SHOW (FASTPASS) ★ ★ ★ ½

❗ APPEAL   Preschool ★★★½   Grade School ★★★★   Teens ★★★★½
• BY AGE   Young Adults ★★★★   Over 30 ★★★★   Seniors ★★★★

What it is Auto stunt show. Scope and scale Headliner. When to go First show of the day or after 4 p.m. Comments FASTPASSes available seasonally. Authors' rating Good stunt work, slow pace; ★★★½. Duration 25–30 minutes. Preshow Selection of audience volunteers. When to arrive 25–30 minutes before showtime.

Don't worry. It's a rental.

This show, which originated at Disneyland Paris, features cars and motorcycles in a blur of chases, crashes, jumps, and explosions. The secrets behind the special effects are explained after each stunt sequence, with replays and different camera views shown on an enormous movie screen; the replays also serve to pass the time needed to place the next stunt's props into position.

While the stunt driving is excellent, the show plods along between tricks, and you will probably have had your fill by the time the last stunt ends. Expect about 6 to 8 minutes of real action in a show that runs 25 to 30 minutes. Because of this, small children may become restless during the show.

Steve's coworker helpfully points out his untied shoelace, preventing a dangerous workplace situation.

STUDIOS BACKLOT TOUR ★★★★

! APPEAL   Preschool ★★★   Grade School ★★★½   Teens ★★★½
• BY AGE   Young Adults ★★★½   Over 30 ★★★½   Seniors ★★★½

What it is Combination tram and walking tour of modern film and video production. **Scope and scale** Headliner. **When to go** Anytime. **Comments** Use the restroom before getting in line. **Authors' rating** Educational and fun; not to be missed; ★★★★. **Duration** About 30 minutes. **Preshow** A video before the special-effects segment and another video in the tram boarding area.

A substantial part of the Studios was, at one time, an active film and television facility, where actors, artists, and technicians occasionally worked on actual productions. Everything from television commercials, specials, and game shows to feature motion pictures has been produced here. Visitors to DHS can take a backstage studio tour to learn production methods and technologies.

The tour begins on the edge of the back lot with the special-effects walking segment and then continues with the tram segment. The first stop on the walking tour is a special-effects water tank, where technicians explain the mechanical and optical tricks that "turn the seemingly impossible into on-screen reality." Included are rain effects and a naval battle. The waiting area for this part of the tour displays miniature naval vessels used in filming famous war movies. A prop room separates the special-effects tank and the tram tour. Trams depart about once every four minutes on busy days, winding among production and shop buildings before stopping at the wardrobe and crafts shops. Here, costumes, sets, and props are designed, created, and stored.

Still seated on the tram, you look through large windows to see craftsmen at work. The tour continues through the back lot, where western desert canyons exist side by side with New York City brownstones. The tour's highlight is Catastrophe Canyon, an elaborate special-effects movie set where a thunderstorm, earthquake, oil-field fire, and flash flood are simulated.

Volunteers in the special-effects water tank.

Catastrophe Canyon provides an ironic laugh to those who realize they left the oven on before heading out on vacation.

ANIMATION COURTYARD

DISNEY DESIGN with Sam Gennawey

In 1989, the Studios were more than just a theme park. It was a real working studio with live production facilities as well as an animation studio. Films such as Mulan, Lilo & Stitch, Brother Bear, and Home on the Range were produced in Florida. You used to be able to take a tour, watch animators working at their desks, and view an informative film that made every adult male in the audience sob uncontrollably. The architecture for this area is based on the work of Kem Weber, who designed Walt Disney's Burbank Studio (1939).

Which of these is not a real Disney princess?

THE MAGIC OF DISNEY ANIMATION ★★½

APPEAL	Preschool ★★★	Grade School ★★★½	Teens ★★★½
BY AGE	Young Adults ★★★½	Over 30 ★★★½	Seniors ★★★★

What it is Overview of Disney animation process, with limited hands-on demonstrations. **Scope and scale** Minor attraction. **When to go** Before 11 a.m. or after 5 p.m. **Comments** Opens an hour later than the rest of the park. **Authors' rating** Not as good as previous renditions; ★★½. **Duration** 30 minutes. **Preshow** Gallery of animation art in waiting area. **Average wait in line per 100 people ahead of you** 7 minutes.

The consolidation of Disney animation at the Burbank, California, studio has left this attraction without a story to tell. Park guests can still get a general overview of the Disney animation process but will not see the detailed work of actual artists, as was possible in previous versions.

The revamped attraction starts in a small theater, where the audience is introduced to a cast-member host and Mushu, the dragon from *Mulan*. Between the host's speech, Mushu's constant interruptions, and a very brief taped segment with real Disney animators, guests are hard-pressed to learn anything about actual animation. The audience is shown a plug for current Disney animated releases, which falls flat.

The audience then moves to another room, this one with floor seating, where another cast member gives guests a verbal description of what used to be the walking tour of the actual animation studio. The cast member supplies bits of Disney character trivia (for example, Buzz Lightyear's original name was Lunar Larry) and fields questions from the audience, but nothing truly enlightening is presented.

Afterward, guests have the option of exiting the attraction or attending the Animation Academy (the limited space is on a first-come, first-served basis). This is by far the most interesting part of the attraction, but not designed for all guests. The animator works quickly, which seems to frustrate younger guests who need more time or assistance to get their drawing right. For those who keep up with the animator, this part gives a good idea of how difficult hand-drawn animation really is.

PLAYHOUSE DISNEY—LIVE ON STAGE! ★★★★

!	APPEAL	Preschool ★★★★½	Grade School ★★★★	Teens ★★½
•	BY AGE	Young Adults ★★	Over 30 ★★★	Seniors ★★½

What it is Live show for children. Scope and scale Minor attraction. When to go Per the daily entertainment schedule. Comments Audience sits on the floor. Authors' rating A must for families with preschoolers; ★★★★. Duration 20 minutes. When to arrive 20–30 minutes before showtime.

The show features characters from the Disney Channel's *Little Einsteins*, *The Book of Pooh*, and *Handy Manny*, as well as Mickey, Minnie, Donald, Daisy, and Goofy. Reengineered in 2007, *Playhouse Disney* replaced live Disney characters with elaborate puppets. A simple plot serves as the platform for singing, dancing, some great puppetry, and a great deal of audience participation. The characters, who ooze love and goodness, rally throngs of tots and preschoolers to sing and dance along with them. All the jumping, squirming, and high-stepping is facilitated by having the audience sit on the floor so that kids can spontaneously erupt into motion when the mood strikes. Even for adults without children, it's a treat to watch the tykes rev up. If you have a younger child in your party, all the better: Just stand back and let the video roll. For preschoolers, *Playhouse Disney* will be the highlight of their day.

VOYAGE OF THE LITTLE MERMAID
(FASTPASS) ★★★★

!	APPEAL	Preschool ★★★★	Grade School ★★★★	Teens ★★★½
•	BY AGE	Young Adults ★★★½	Over 30 ★★★★	Seniors ★★★★

What it is Musical stage show featuring characters from the Disney movie *The Little Mermaid*. Scope and scale Major attraction. When to go Before 9:45 a.m., just before closing, or use FASTPASS. Authors' rating Romantic, lovable, and humorous in the best Disney tradition; not to be missed; ★★★★. Duration 15 minutes. Preshow Taped ramblings about the decor in the preshow holding area. Probable waiting time Before 9:30 a.m., 10–30 minutes; after 9:30 a.m., 35–70 minutes.

Voyage of the Little Mermaid is a winner, appealing to every age. Cute without being silly or saccharine, and infinitely lovable, *The Little Mermaid* show is the most tender and romantic entertainment offered anywhere in Walt Disney World. The story is simple and engaging, the special effects impressive, and the Disney characters memorable.

PIXAR PLACE

DISNEY DESIGN with *Sam Gennawey*

Welcome to the world of Pixar. Headquartered in Emeryville, California, the architecture of their studio is legendary and designed in a very specific way to maximize the creativity and productivity of its employees. The major design criteria for the Studios park were to match those materials and bring a piece of California to Florida. The gateway you pass under is a scale model of the one at the studio, and all of the bricks used were hand-kilned from the same factory to match the look, texture, and color of the ones in California. Characters from *Toy Story* decorate the corridor and play with your perception of scale. If you want to see how the puzzle is put together, look for and check out Andy's instruction hanging on a wall.

MOVIE PROMO SOUNDSTAGE

Disney has been using the soundstage between *Walt Disney: One Man's Dream* and *Toy Story* Mania! to promote the *Chronicles of Narnia* films, but to call this sparse offering an attraction is a stretch. Disney's biggest effort went into building the set's doors in the shape of the wardrobe described in the Narnia books. If you're a C. S. Lewis fan, see the attraction—it has some behind-the-scenes footage and concept art from the films, new props and costumes, and a Prince Caspian greeting area. Otherwise, skip it.

WALT DISNEY: ONE MAN'S DREAM ★★★

! APPEAL   Preschool ★★   Grade School ★★★   Teens ★★★½
• BY AGE   Young Adults ★★★★   Over 30 ★★★★   Seniors ★★★★

What it is Tribute to Walt Disney. **Scope and scale** Minor attraction. **When to go** Anytime. **Authors' rating** Excellent! ★★★ and about time. **Duration** 25 minutes. **Preshow** Disney memorabilia. **Probable waiting time** For film, 10 minutes.

One Man's Dream is a long-overdue tribute to Walt Disney. Launched in 2001 to celebrate the 100th anniversary of Disney's birth, the attraction consists of an exhibit area showcasing Disney memorabilia and recordings, followed by a film documenting Disney's life.

The exhibits chronicle his life and business. On display are a replica of Walt's California office, various innovations in animation developed by Disney, and early models and working plans for Walt Disney World, as well as various Disney theme parks around the world. The film provides a personal glimpse of the man and offers insights regarding both Disney's successes and failures.

Owning a theme park means you get to play with the coolest gadgets.

TOY STORY MANIA! (FASTPASS) ★★★★½

| **! APPEAL** | Preschool ★★★★★ | Grade School ★★★★★ | Teens ★★★★★ |
| **• BY AGE** | Young Adults ★★★★★ | Over 30 ★★★★★ | Seniors ★★★★½ |

What it is 3-D ride-through indoor shooting gallery. Scope and scale Headliner. When to go Before 10:30 a.m., after 6 p.m., or use FASTPASS (if available). Authors' rating ★★★★½. Duration About 6½ minutes. Average wait in line per 100 people ahead of you 4½ minutes. Loading speed Fast.

Toy Story Mania! ushers in a whole new generation of Disney attractions: virtual dark rides. Since Disneyland opened in 1955, ride vehicles have moved past two- and three-dimensional sets often populated by audio-animatronic (AA) figures. These amazingly detailed sets and robotic figures defined the Disney Imagineering genius in attractions such as Pirates of the Caribbean, The Haunted Mansion, and Peter Pan's Flight.

For *Toy Story* Mania! the elaborate sets and endearing AA characters are gone. Imagine long corridors, totally empty, covered with reflective material. There's almost nothing there…until you put on your 3-D glasses. Instantly, the corridor is full and brimming with color, action, and activity, thanks to projected computer-graphic (CG) images.

Conceptually, this is an interactive shooting gallery much like Buzz Lightyear's Space Ranger Spin, but in *Toy Story* Mania!, your ride vehicle passes through a totally virtual midway, with booths offering such games as ring tossing and ball throwing. You use a cannon on your ride vehicle to play as you move along from booth to booth. Unlike the laser guns in Buzz Lightyear, however, the pull-string cannons in *Toy Story* Mania! take advantage of CG image technology to toss rings, shoot balls, and even throw eggs and pies.

Each game booth is manned by a *Toy Story* character who is right beside you in 3-D glory, cheering you on. In addition to 3-D imagery, you experience various smells, vehicle motion, wind, and water spray. The ride begins with a training round to familiarize you with the nature of the games, and then continues through a number of "real" games in which you compete against your riding mate. The technology has the ability to self-adjust the level of difficulty, and there are plenty of easy targets for small children to reach. Tip: Let the pull string retract all the way back into the cannon before pulling it again.

Finally, and also of note, a new generation of "living character" audio-animatronic figures has been introduced in the preshow queuing area of *Toy Story* Mania! A six-foot-tall Mr. Potato Head breaks new ground for an audio-animatronic character by interacting with and talking to guests in real time (similar to Epcot's *Turtle Talk with Crush*).

3-D glasses? Check. Hands on cannon? Check. Disembodied hand creeping around the corner? Check.

LIVE ENTERTAINMENT

When the Studios opened, live entertainment, parades, and special events weren't as fully developed or elaborate as those at the Magic Kingdom or Epcot. With the introduction of an afternoon parade and elaborate shows at Theater of the Stars, the Studios joined the big leagues. In 1998, DHS launched a new edition of *Fantasmic!* (see pages 290–291), a water, fireworks, and laser show that draws rave reviews. Staged in its own specially designed 10,000-person amphitheater, *Fantasmic!* makes the Studios the park of choice for spectacular nighttime entertainment.

WDW live-entertainment guru Steve Soares posts the DHS performance schedule about a week in advance at **pages.prodigy.net/stevesoares.**

Afternoon Parade Staged once a day, the parade begins near the park's entrance, continues down Hollywood Boulevard, and circles in front of the giant hat.

From there, it passes in front of *Sounds Dangerous* and ends by Star Tours. An alternate route begins at the far end of Sunset Boulevard and turns right, onto Hollywood Boulevard.

The Studios' latest parade, Block Party Bash, features floats and characters based on Disney's animated features, including *Toy Story*; *Monsters, Inc.*; and *A Bug's Life*. It's a colorful, high-energy affair with plenty of acrobatics, singing, and dancing. It's also loud beyond belief. *Unofficial Guide* coauthor Len Testa, who considers most Disney afternoon parades to be cliché-ridden mobile musicals affording a high chance of heat stroke, grudgingly concedes that this may be the best of the lot.

High School Musical Pep Rally We can't fault Disney for trying to cash in on the phenomenal success of the 2006 movie *High School Musical*, and the kids who sing and dance their way through this 20-minute recap of the film's major musical numbers do an admirable job. With little dialogue and stage scenery that consists of

nothing more than a few blow-up basketball-shaped balloons and cheesy "Go Wild-cats!" banners, Disney's not given them much to work with. Children will be disappointed at not seeing the actual stars from the movie. Adults will spend more time wondering what the school's feeding these kids to eliminate all traces of teen angst and raging hormones.

Disney Characters Find characters at the Theater of the Stars, in parades, at Al's Toy Barn (near Mama Melrose's on Streets of America), in the Animation Courtyard, on the Backstage Plaza, and along Pixar Place. Mickey sometimes appears for autographs and photos on Sunset Boulevard. Times and locations for character appearances are listed in the complimentary *Times Guide*.

Street Entertainment With the possible exception of Epcot's World Showcase Players, the Studios has the best collection of roving street performers in all of Walt Disney World. Appearing primarily on Hollywood and Sunset boulevards, the cast

of characters includes Hollywood stars and wannabes, their agents, film directors, gossip columnists, various police officers, and Hollywood public-works crews. Performers are not shy about asking you to join in their skits—you may be asked to explain why you came to "Hollywood" or to recite a couple of lines in one of the directors' new films. If you're looking for a spot to rest and a bit of entertainment, grab a drink and seek out these performers.

You never know whom you're going to meet on Hollywood Boulevard, from movie directors to famous actresses to Bob trying to win cab fare back to the hotel.

Theater of the Stars This covered amphitheater on Sunset Boulevard is the stage for production revues, usually featuring music from Disney movies and starring Disney characters. Performances are posted in front of the theater and are listed in the daily entertainment schedule in the handout *Times Guide*.

COUNTER-SERVICE RESTAURANTS

Counter-service food at DHS consists mostly of burgers, hot dogs, pizza, and chicken strips, with the occasional salad tossed in. Slightly more variety can be found at the **ABC Commissary,** which offers fish-and-chips and chicken curry, and at the **Studio Catering Co.**, with a BBQ pork sandwich and Greek salad.

ABC Commissary

QUALITY Fair VALUE B– PORTION Medium–large LOCATION Backlot
READER RESPONSES 61% 👍 39% 👎 DINING PLAN Yes

Asian salad; Cuban sandwich; chicken curry; fish-and-chips; child's chicken nuggets, cheeseburger, or ham-and-cheese wrap; chocolate mousse; strawberry parfait; wine and beer. Offers kosher food.

Backlot Express

QUALITY Fair VALUE C PORTION Medium–large LOCATION Backlot
READER RESPONSES 75% 👍 25% 👎 DINING PLAN Yes

Burgers with fries or carrot sticks, Southwest salad with chicken, grilled turkey and cheese, hot dogs, grilled-vegetable sandwich, desserts. For children, chicken nuggets or sloppy joe with vegetables. Soft drinks and beer. Great burger-fixin's bar. Indoor and outdoor seating.

Catalina Eddie's

QUALITY Fair VALUE B PORTION Medium–large LOCATION Sunset Boulevard
READER RESPONSES 76% 👍 24% 👎 DINING PLAN Yes

Cheese and pepperoni pizzas, hot Italian deli sandwich, salads, carrot or chocolate fudge cake.

Min and Bill's Dockside Diner

QUALITY Fair VALUE C PORTION Small–medium LOCATION Echo Lake
READER RESPONSES 79% 👍 21% 👎 DINING PLAN No

Shakes and soft drinks; beer; chips and cookies; variety of pretzels, including spicy cheese-stuffed and apple-cinnamon. Limited outdoor seating.

Pizza Planet

QUALITY Good VALUE B+ PORTION Medium LOCATION Backlot
READER RESPONSES 74% 👍 26% 👎 DINING PLAN Yes

Cheese, pepperoni, and vegetarian pizzas; salads; cookies and crisped-rice treats. Fresh ingredients.

Rosie's All American Cafe

QUALITY Fair VALUE C PORTION Medium LOCATION Sunset Boulevard
READER RESPONSES 70% 👍 30% 👎 DINING PLAN Yes

Veggie burgers; soups; side salads; fries; child's cheeseburger or chicken nuggets with carrot sticks, grapes, or applesauce; apple pie and chocolate cake; premade sandwiches. Backlot Express is better.

Starring Rolls Cafe

QUALITY Good VALUE B PORTION Small–medium LOCATION Sunset Boulevard
READER RESPONSES 87% 👍 13% 👎 DINING PLAN Yes

Deli sandwiches, salads, pastries, desserts, coffee. Sometimes open for breakfast. Slow service.

Studio Catering Co.

QUALITY Good VALUE B PORTION Small–medium LOCATION Backlot
READER RESPONSES 63% C 37% 👎 DINING PLAN Yes

BBQ pork, grilled chicken with rice and beans, chili-cheese dog, chicken Caesar wrap, Greek salad.

Toluca Legs Turkey Co.

QUALITY Good VALUE B PORTION Medium–large LOCATION Sunset Boulevard
READER RESPONSES 80% 👍 20% 👎 DINING PLAN Yes

Smoked turkey legs; hot dogs; coffee, tea, hot chocolate, bottled soda, and beer.

Disney's Hollywood Studios Special Treats Menu

Ursula Special

This is one mean sandwich! Cooked to order (we like ours a little more well done than the one in the picture), the Ursula Special is the best deal on eight legs anywhere. Move over buffalo wings!
....$5.25

Toy Story Treat

This frozen treat is just the ticket to revive a wilting mouseketeer! Alternating lemon, lime, and raspberry flavors are tucked neatly into a cup modeled on Woody's vest and shirt ensemble. A milk chocolate cowboy hat provides a little caffeine boost to help you get back on the trail. $5.95

Mermaid Po'boy

Don't worry! It's not a real mermaid! In fact, the star of this healthy sandwich is a North Sea red hairing, a fish rarely found on menus in developed countries. Hair makes great dental floss after the meal. Served on a bed of lettuce................................$6.50

Hannah Montana Banana

Health-conscious eaters will love this fruity dessert featuring a natural-blond banana dancing in a simple cherry, cranberry, and beebleberry distilled reduction. Certified by doctors as a complete potassium replenishment product................................$7.95

PART 9

THE
WATER
PARKS

322 The two Disney World water parks—the mixed smooth- and surf-water Typhoon Lagoon, home to the country's most elaborate water coaster, Crush 'n' Gusher, and a huge inland surf pool; and the 66-acre big bear, Blizzard Beach, with the 120-foot free-fall speed slide—aren't only for kids. In fact, the idea of skiing barefoot at 60 miles an hour down 120 feet of water may redefine forever the thrill of victory and the agony of the feet. And both parks have a wide variety of attractions and their own fully developed Disney-quality themes, only without character breakfasts.

Individual water-park tickets are a little less expensive than admission at the four big parks—about $48 for adults, with a few dollars off for annual-pass holders—but hefty enough that you should be sure you want to spend the money instead of hanging out at your hotel pool complex.

You should also do a little advance weather research before planning your water-park outing. The water parks are obviously susceptible to closing for inclement weather, so you might do better to wait and add on a Water Park Fun and More option to your ticket once you arrive; you can do this at any Guest Services counter, your hotel, or any of the theme parks. If you do decide to go for just one day, you can now buy water-park tickets at vending machines using either a credit card or your Disney resort ID card, which helps with what used to be notorious backups at the ticket windows. (There's also an ATM near the entrance, but you can't use cash at the ticket machine, only with live vendors.)

Also consider that the water parks are so popular, especially in the hottest season, that they reach capacity fairly frequently and are then closed to the public; even if you are staying at a resort and have guaranteed access, it means a huge crowd of people splashing and yelling.

Both parks are regularly refurbished, although on a rotating schedule and usually out of season, so if the water parks are among your primary destinations, you may want to check out their status before booking your trip. Call ☎ 407-WDW-MAGIC or go to the water-park Web sites at **disneyworld.disney.go.com/parks** to see their calendars.

Although the watery thrill rides get most of the press, both water parks have quieter, nonstrenuous attractions as well, such as the chair lift at Blizzard Beach or Castaway Creek at Typhoon Lagoon, so the less robust need not write these parks off entirely. But if you suffer from high blood pressure, circulation problems, heart disease, or obesity, or are taking certain medications, you should avoid going on very hot days.

PLANNING YOUR VISIT TO THE DISNEY WATER PARKS

Generally speaking, the regulations and limitations placed on water visits have to do with space—that is, saving it for your fellow swimmers—and safety.

- You can't bring in your own flotation devices, but you can borrow an inner tube or a life vest (for the vest you'll have to leave a credit card or driver's license behind as security deposit).
- You can rent a towel for $2 and rent a locker ($10 for small, $12 for large) with a $5 refundable key deposit.
- Only one cooler is allowed per group, but no glass containers or alcoholic beverages may be brought in. (Both water parks have picnic areas.)
- If you drive, the parking is included. There's also free bus transportation, though on the way back to your hotel, your wet self may have to withstand the attentions of your fellow travelers.
- Oh, and we're not kidding when we say you need to consider your bathing costume. Are you going to sunbathe, or slide? Float the tube or brave the flume? Wear something too flimsy, and you're going to give "decorative" a whole new meaning. Summit Plummet is famous among Disney cast members for the number of bathing-suit tops that come down without their owners (or vice versa), but Slush Gusher and Humunga Kowabunga are just as bad; and men, especially those wearing low-riders, jams, or drawstring shorts, are not immune from exposures of their own. If you're not positive that your suit is up to the test, consult with an experienced cast member; you can always take a few minutes to buy something else to wear in the gift shops. (By the way, bathing suits with exposed metal, buckles, studding, chains, and so on are prohibited on all the rides, but why would you want to risk a branding burn, anyway?)
- Sunscreen and sunglasses are a must; it's not just the light itself, but its reflection off the water and concrete. Don't forget lip protection. And wear water socks rather than flip-flops; these are places to preserve body *and* sole.

▶ **UNOFFICIAL TIP** Picnic areas are scattered around the park, as are pleasant places for sunbathing.

TYPHOON LAGOON

326 Typhoon Lagoon is a theme park in its own right, with a surf pool, a 420-foot-long aquatic roller coaster, flume rides, tube slides, body slides, and a 360,000-gallon tank where you can snorkel with the sharks. Don't think that you can do this in half a day; as at the four main parks, the thrill rides back up pretty quickly. If it's one of the days that the park has Extra Magic Hours, you could aim to get here about the time the morning people (and presumably the worn-out little ones) will be headed out, and then stay into the cool of the evening.

The "story" behind the park is that it used to be a pleasant tropical resort that was upended by, in quick order, a typhoon, an earthquake, and a volcanic eruption. The entrance passage to Typhoon Lagoon is a misty forest and a ramshackle "town" of concession stands. The last disaster left a hapless shrimp boat, the *Miss Tilly* (of home port Safen Sound—get it?), marooned 100 feet in the air atop Mount Mayday, where it periodically blows water out of its stack like a beached whale. (Here's a tip for sunbathers pursuing an even tan: The smokestack goes off every 30 minutes—time to turn over.)

© Allie Wojlaszek

One of the most popular attractions is the **surf pool**, which is the world's largest inland surfing spot (which may be a slightly limited category); its machine-produced "tsunamis" throw up rideable waves close to a six-foot curl every 90 seconds or so, thanks to huge water tanks that fill, discharge, and refill. The pool gets pretty full of surfers of all (and unhappily, little) ability, but it's certainly impressive. These waves are higher than a lot of people ever see at the ocean, so do not wear jewelry, cameras, or any of those "decorative" swimsuits. You may also want to consider a trip to the man spa: One of our all-time favorite letters was from a teenage girl who commented:

> The surf pool was nice except that I kept landing on really hairy fat guys whenever the big waves came.

▶ **UNOFFICIAL TIP** A final warning: The surf pool has a knack for loosening watchbands, stripping jewelry, and sucking stuff out of your pockets. Don't take anything out there except your swimsuit (and hang on to that).

Can't surf—yet? In summer, early-morning surfing lessons are available for $150 from pros at Craig Carroll's **Ron Jon Surf School**. Lessons are before the park opens, and no park playtime is included, but surfboards are provided. Call ☎ 407-WDW-PLAY.

Among the big thriller rides is **Crush 'n' Gusher**, the "decor" of which is supposedly the rusted-out and partially collapsed remains of a fruit-packing plant, which the jungle has started taking over since the typhoon. It's a 400-plus-foot flume slide (actually, three of them, slightly different in length and fervor) with inflatable-raft "cars" that twist and turn like a roller coaster—and run uphill—thanks to powerful water jets.

Crush 'n' Gusher

Humunga Kowabunga is Space Mountain with water, a five-story drop in the dark at about 30 feet per second. It's a little like being buried at sea in a casket, lying on your back with your arms folded. This is everybody's choice source for a record-breaking wedgie. You have been warned.

The three "falls" raft rides at Typhoon Lagoon come in Goldilocks style: father bear, mother bear, and baby bear, though all three are approved for all ages. **Mayday Falls** is a tube ride for solos that is relatively scary, running through tunnels and waterfalls in big sweeping curves; **Gangplank Falls** is a 300-foot waterslide employing the larger four-person rafts. **Keelhaul Falls** is the calmest of the tube rides, although if you get a little weird in caves, you might want to skip even this one.

Storm Slides is sort of Humunga Kowabunga light, with a three-story drop and twisting, on-your-back body slides though waterfalls, geysers, and caves to a bottom pool, only in this case you aren't in a vehicle.

Though it sounds a little taxing, the 360,000-gallon snorkeling tank called **Shark Reef** is a fairly low-key but fun attraction, stocked with smallish and nonthreatening hammerhead and leopard sharks, stingrays, and flocks of tropical fish. The stage set here is an overturned sunken tanker, and all the equipment—snorkeling mask, fins, and wet-suit vest are provided at no charge. (There's a brief introductory lesson, but it's free as well.) If you really want to dive in, you can rent a supplied air tank from Hammerhead Fred's Dive Shop. But plan to do this early in the day, as it's a popular draw.

▶ **UNOFFICIAL TIP** Try Shark Reef in the mornings—afternoons can get crowded, and you may be ushered out of the pool more quickly than in the early hours.

Shark Reef

The calmest areas here are the Sandy White Beach and Castaway Creek. Although **Sandy White Beach** has no age limits, and sometimes parents have to impose a time-out here to avert a total breakdown, its low-key character means that fewer youngsters wind up here, or at least few stay for long. It's like the tanning beach at the Yacht and Beach clubs, with lounge chairs, palm trees, and even hammocks. **Castaway Creek** is a sort of throwback to the old River Country days, a 2,000-foot flowing "river" that is to Typhoon Lagoon as the Walt Disney World Railroad is to the Magic Kingdom. It encircles the rest of the park and serves as easy transportation (there are five places to get on and off), and just cruising around on your mini raft is a wonderful way to see the elaborate scenery.

In addition, there are plenty of areas at the foot of rides worth viewing just for the fun of it, and the Shark Reef tank can be admired through viewing portholes in the wall of the tanker, similar to the view at The Seas in Epcot.

BLIZZARD BEACH

Blizzard Beach, Disney World's newer (it opened in 1995), bigger (66 acres), and slightly bolder (bigger thrills) water park also has a full-blown Disney storyboard "history," though one with a logic only a Floridian could love.

It seems that during an unusual cold snap that dumped a freak blanket of ice over the area, a real-estate developer had the smart idea of making lemonade from lemons by opening a ski resort, complete with a little chalet and ski lifts. But of course the climate eventually reverted, and the entire resort went into meltdown, leaving the stranded alpine village, ski lift, bobsled runs (turned into waterslides), pools of melted ice, and of course the mountain. What's a Disney World theme park without a mountain?

From the air Blizzard Beach looks like a plastic set on a model railroad layout.

This particular peak, which tops out at about 90 feet, is called Mount Gushmore, and the big thrillers—Summit Plummet, Slush Gusher, and Teamboat Springs—all come down along it. (Altogether Blizzard Beach boasts 17 waterslides of various forms.)

The infamous **Summit Plummet**, which measures about 350 feet, starts off with a 120-foot free fall at a 66-degree angle, and generates sliding speeds of close to 60 miles per hour. (The "chicken slide," Blizzard Beach's version of Mission Space's green team, is only 90 feet long.) This is one of those rides that requires very serious elastic or Spandex—see our warnings about Crush 'n' Gusher above—and those with very sensitive backsides, or sunburns, should think twice. In addition, older visitors or those with back or neck problems should think twice about Summit Plummet; many people complain of being shaken up and bruised, especially on the backside, which is undoubtedly part of the fun for kids but not, perhaps, for the rest of us.

▶ **UNOFFICIAL TIP** If you're going primarily for the slides, you'll have about two hours in the early morning to enjoy them before the wait becomes intolerable.

Summit Plummet

Slush Gusher is just about as unnerving (and undressing) as Summit Plummet, but not quite as teeth-rattling in the jarring sense; its 90-foot double-hump slide is like the biggest and wettest camel you ever fell off.

Teamboat Springs is the group ride here, a rousing 1,200-foot-long white-water flume ride something like the Kali River Rapids. The hint for this one is the more weight, the more speed, so make friends in line.

Teamboat Springs

▶**UNOFFICIAL TIP** The more people you load into the raft, the faster it goes. If you have only a couple in it, the slide is kind of a snore.

Downhill Double Dipper could, we suppose, qualify as a romantic encounter, since two people go down side by side 230-foot tube slides, but it might not elicit exactly the sort of screaming you had in mind—even if part of it is in the dark, and those walls of water can be shockers. Each of you is given an inner tube, and the two gates open simultaneously as if you were racing down, which in a way you are: Top speed is about 25 miles an hour.

Check Out the View

For those who remember the old Skyway in the Magic Kingdom—and even those who don't—the ski resort–style, 120-foot chair lift at Blizzard Beach is a must even if you don't feel up to screaming down Summit Plummet. The view is a stunner, and you can spend as much time as you want at the observation deck; there's even a gondola for wheelchair users. Just be prepared to wait in line. On the other hand, if you just want to get up there to get down the fast way, take the stairs.

The Blizzard Beach equivalent of Castaway Creek is **Cross Country Creek**, a 45-minute solo-raft circuit of the park, this one with seven portals and some small surprises (such as dripping "icicles" and small wavelets).

Other attractions include **Snow Stormers**, a pseudo–ski slalom course with riding mats that resemble toboggans; **Toboggan Racers**, which is sort of Snow Stormers light (and gets more kids); and **Melt-Away Bay**, a mild wave pool. There are also some very kid-oriented areas you're not likely to spend much time in, unless you're being paid for babysitting.

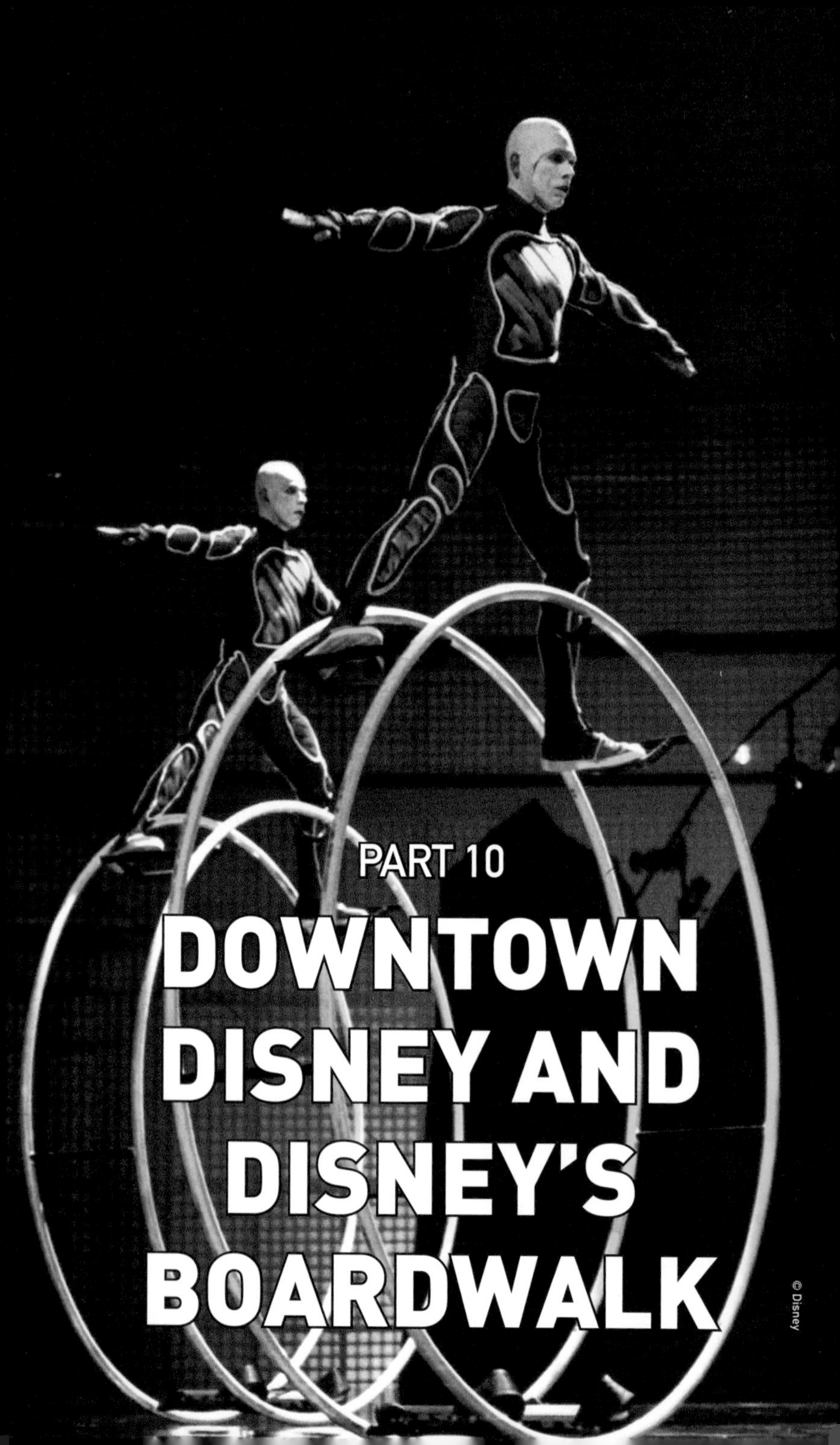

PART 10

DOWNTOWN DISNEY AND DISNEY'S BOARDWALK

© Disney

DOWNTOWN DISNEY

Downtown Disney is a sprawling entertainment, dining, and shopping complex anchored by the Downtown Disney Marketplace to the east, Disney West Side on the west (duh), and Pleasure Island (currently working through an identity crisis) in the middle. The parking lot at Downtown Disney stays open until 3 a.m. Lots stretch alongside all three sections looking rather alike, and, after dark especially, you may have trouble rediscovering your spot. In fact, it happens all the time, so remember to make a note of where you parked.

Disney Marketplace

Downtown Disney Marketplace, the oldest part of Downtown Disney, is long on shopping and dining and short on entertainment. Dining, aside from dockside Captain Jack's Oyster Bar, is, shall we say, beastly. You can choose to dine among animatronic elephants and apes at Rainforest Cafe, or if your manners are truly prehistoric, surrounded by triceratops and pterodactyls at T-REX. Portions are about as big as the critters. Both eateries adjoin gift shops that will appeal especially to Stuckey's shoppers.

Shopping has probably long since replaced baseball as America's national pastime, but only the Walt Disney Company could figure out a way to make it into a whole theme park. Disney Marketplace is the single most complete souvenir mall in Disney World. It's also the longest-running attraction in Disney World, in terms of daily access. The shops there open at 9:30 every morning and stay open until 11 at night, 11:30 on weekends. (Times vary slightly, depending on the season.)

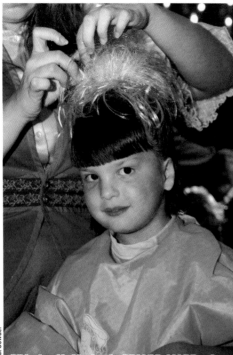

© Paul Gowder

Bibbed and bobbed at the Bibbidi Bobbidi Boutique

A few stores at the Disney Marketplace stock merchandise for the homeowner who doesn't necessarily want to endorse the Disney Company in every room of the house, but most of the shops are Disney-oriented in a really big way—particularly the 12-room **World of Disney**. This is almost a compendium of every sort of character merchandise Disney makes, covering more than 50,000 square feet with toys, accessories, baby bunting, T-shirts, candy, books, videos, and so on. And there's the **Bibbidi Bobbidi Boutique**, where (usually) underage princesses get made up, combed up, curled up, and tiara'd to royal perfection.

If you are shopping for Disney-approved merchandise, you can probably get your entire list of gifts at the Marketplace. (Funniest rarity: the bobblehead of Captain Jack Sparrow, which, at $21, is $2 more valuable than Steamboat Willie, who made it all possible.) But because the Marketplace is a shopping showplace, the smaller stores do have some more interesting products.

This is also the location of the official pin-trading headquarters, **Disney's Pin Traders**, which not only stocks pins but also offers the sole Build-a-Pin facility for collectors who want to merge parts of collectible pins into a custom design. If you haven't been exposed to the pin-trading mania yet, it's half hobby, half a kind of networking. The pins themselves, usually cloisonné or enameled metal, are like large tie tacks, and fasten the same way. They're on sale everywhere in Disney World, themed like the other merchandise to the area, and new designs are added all the time. (Other pins are

338 retired, making some vintage pieces even more desirable.) They cost from $7 to $17, and many people have hats, scarves, or vests virtually studded with them.

The fun part is in the trading, which goes on between guests and cast members, visitors and other visitors, kids and adults, and so forth. Pin trading can even be used as an introduction if you see someone wearing a pin you want to trade for (or pretend to). There is etiquette involved, however; you can only trade one pin at a time. Pins must be intact and with the back attached. Guests may trade two per cast member if the pins are different. Do not try to buy from a cast member, only trade. And look but don't touch; these are, after all, a kind of jewelry.

There's only a limited amount of collectible Mickey at **Team Mickey's Athletic Club**, some of it combined with the ubiquitous Nike swoosh and other logos. If you're desperate for Disney-ized wear with a boutique twist, head into **Tren-D**, but don't be surprised at the prices; Disney has collaborated with young name designers for some of this. **Once Upon a Toy** is a Disney-Hasbro collaboration that is itself a sort of toy: a five-room complex with special Disney versions of Mr. Potato Head and Monopoly games, *Star Wars* figurines, a Lincoln Logs version of the Wilderness Lodge Resort, and Buzz Lightyear Play-Doh sets.

Disney's Wonderful World of Memories caters to the scrapbooking crowd with photo books and bizz items such as the $38 Mickey desk sets. **The Art of Disney** is one of the three or four stores around Disney World where animation cels from Disney films—real, authorized reproductions—and cartoon figurines are sold, but also goes overboard with some rather tacky offerings, sort of the Disney equivalent of velvet Elvises. **Disney's Days of Christmas** store is just what it sounds like. Personally, we think year-round Christmas stores should be abolished because they take all the fun out of the holidays, but if you find stocking-cap ears a hoot, you'll love it.

A much more honestly delightful toy shop is the **LEGO Imagination Center**, a 3,000-square-foot superstore of LEGO toys with fantastic, whole movie sets revolving in window cases, some of which look almost like spoofs of Disney sets. There's a playground, where you'll find tables and stacks of LEGO pieces for kids and less-self-conscious adults to play with. **Mickey's Pantry** has stuff that used to be more unusual—Mickey ears–topped salt-and-pepper shakers, coffee mugs with Mickey (or Minnie) feet, and so on. **Mickey's Mart** is the Disney Dollar Store, so to speak, with four-for-$10 bins.

The most pretentious (or precious, depending on your outlook) shop in the complex may be the **Arribas Brothers** crystal store, which loads up a large room with those "Bohemian" wine goblets with different-colored bowls, beer steins, crystal mermaids, Pegasuses, rainbow dangles, fairy castles, and so on—a lot of which is very much like the crystal sold in various areas of the Epcot World Showcase (but not, perhaps, the glass version of Cinderella Castle for $1,495). If you want a glass slipper, this is the spot.

Pleasure Island

Pleasure Island was originally Walt Disney World's attempt at an entirely adult-only theme park within Disney World, a giant block party of pay-to-play nightclubs. Most of it (the part isolated by a bridge) was closed in 2008, and the area is being reconceived as a more family-friendly attraction.

Currently, there are several restaurants, a cigar bar (the smoking kind), three stores, and a few food and beverage vendors still wearing the Pleasure Island address, though outside the island gates.

The full-service restaurants are **Fulton's Crab House**, **Portobello**, **Paradiso 37**, and **Raglan Road**. Paradiso 37 and Raglan Road have the added benefit of being fun bars that serve late. Ragland Road features live Irish pub music as well as Celtic dancing and is the favorite after-dark haunt of the *Unofficial* research team. Nearby, the 220-foot-long three-decker paddle wheeler that is now Fulton's was formerly called the *Empress Lilly*, named for Walt's widow, Lillian, who personally christened her in 1977.

Raglan Road

Courtesy of Raglan Road

Fuego by Sosa Cigars, next to Raglan Road, is a true anomaly at Walt Disney World, as it is an indoor smoking venue. This is odder than it sounds—after all, Disney artists even managed to erase Rod Serling's ubiquitous cigarettes from the *The Twilight Zone* clips at Tower of Terror—but it does say something about the return of conspicuous (and in our minds, ridiculous) consumption. There are 100 varieties of cigars here, all hand-rolled, including Fuente Fuente Opus X and the house brand Sosa. There is also a handsome bar, made of what looks like a slab of ice, a long martini list, beers, and wine—though who can taste a decent vintage after a cigar? At least Fuego has some outdoor seating, where you can breathe; no smoking allowed there.

Disney's West Side

© Rusty Gaul

Pleasure Island is also home to a **Harley-Davidson** boutique, which may say something about the increasing number of adults who travel on two wheels (or like to look as if they do), and a temporary-tattoo parlor, which says even more about all those overage teen-queen wannabes. And then there's the massage supply store, which says it all.

A truly floating attraction is **Characters in Flight**, a 19-foot-wide hot-air balloon tethered between Pleasure Island and West Side that rises 400 feet into the air to afford passengers a 360-degree view of central Florida. At $16, it's about $2 a minute, but since it's open until midnight, it just might be a romantic getaway.

Disney's West Side

The Marketplace notwithstanding, West Side is the closest thing Disney World has to a downtown with its movie theaters, couple of live-performance venues, handful of restaurants, a little shopping, and so on. The West Side is also where you'll find the five-story **DisneyQuest** virtual theme park and Cirque du Soleil's *La Nouba*.

▶**UNOFFICIAL TIP** Weekday mornings are the least crowded times to visit Disney-Quest.

DisneyQuest

Computers run at least part of nearly all the attractions at Walt Disney World, and at Disney-Quest, computers operate almost everything. Virtually. DisneyQuest has many games designed to attract elementary school–aged kids, but most of the indoor park's attractions seem aimed at teens as well as at 20- and 30-somethings. (Some attractions do have minimum height requirements, ranging from 35 to 51 inches.) However, at $43

Looking up through the beehive levels of DisneyQuest.

a person, some adults may not find it so appealing to kill an evening, and another couple of sawbucks, leaning over yet another computer screen.

But don't dismiss DisneyQuest as just a kids' hangout; it might turn out to be some adults' seriously alternative Disney World. If you have a disability that limits which attractions you can ride, or a temporary stiff neck, or even something as physically irritating as a bad sunburn or poison ivy, you might not be up to some real versions of Disney thrills but would get a kick out of the virtual versions.

DisneyQuest is five stories of fairly convincing interactive computer games involving time travel, space wars, and so on. In several cases it feels like a ride because some of the virtual effects are pretty intense. At the **CyberSpace Mountain** attraction, for instance, "Science Guy" Bill Nye guides you to design your own rad roller coaster with three speeds, three themes (outer space, fire, and ice), and a frightening assortment of corkscrews, loops, and spins—and then your OMG! ride is downloaded for you to experience in a motion simulator.

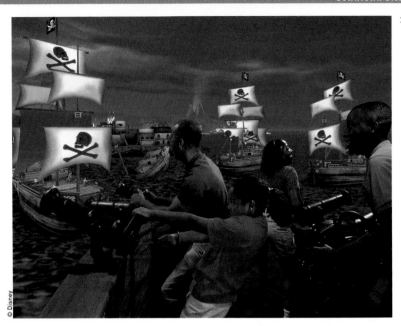

© Disney

DisneyQuest is also rife with Disney self-reference. There are computer versions of *Mighty Ducks* hockey (even after the corporate family divorce), Buzz Lightyear bumper cars, *Pirates of the Caribbean* sea battles, a fairly good re-creation of Aladdin's magic carpet ride through the bazaar (much better than the version in Adventureland and more like the *PhilharMagic* version), and even a leftover salute to the departed ExtraTERRORestrial Alien Encounter.

The DisneyQuest complex is laid out almost exactly as the "physical" parks, such as Magic Kingdom, with a sort of entrance foyer that acts as main street and leads guests to the entrances of the four themed areas (here called zones instead of lands). Weirdly—or Wonderland-ly—you begin at the end; you pay at the entrance, but then move to the departure lounge. Perhaps it's supposed to sound more like a launch pad.

From there you enter a Cyberlator, a transitional attraction (a euphemism for an elevator entry worthy of a Guinness World Record) hosted by the Genie from *Aladdin* that delivers you to an entrance plaza on the third floor called **Ventureport**, and on to the entrances to the four regions: **Explore Zone**, **Score Zone**, **Create Zone**, and **Replay Zone**. But you're not safely oriented yet: in Quest world, zones maze out over multiple levels with stairways, elevators, slides, and walkways linking them in a variety of ways. It's like the Swiss Family Treehouse on speed.

▶**UNOFFICIAL TIP** DisneyQuest is open fairly late—until 10 p.m. on weekdays and 11 p.m. on weekends— and there's food service (pizza, sandwiches, and such) on the fifth floor, and desserts, Internet access tables, and cocktails at the fourth-floor Wonderland Cafe.

Cirque du Soleil's La Nouba

Easily the most impressive attraction on the West Side, and the one that not coincidentally sits at the end of the street like a real-life Cinderella Castle, is the high, white, and handsome theatrical palace that is now a permanent showplace for **Cirque du Soleil** (☎ 407-939-7719 or **www.lanoubaorlando.com**), the Montreal-based acrobatic troupe that has revolutionized the whole concept of modern circus entertainment.

© Disney

The theater is designed to suggest both a castle and an old-fashioned tent, with multiple peaks under which technicians have created a fantastic array of rigging, sound and light equipment, hooks, and hideaways. Inside, its steeply raked seating makes for (nearly) perfect views of every act; the built-in trampolines, elevated stage sections, orchestra balconies, and multilevel trapezes return tumbling to high theater.

This Cirque show is called *La Nouba*, which refers to the party spirit or, depending on your age, "get down," and has a cast of more than 70 acrobats and musicians. (It may seem odd to Cirque novices that a Walt Disney attraction has no animal acts,

© Disney

but that's a Cirque tradition.) The Cirque style of music, usually wordless or sung in a language all its own, is immediately recognizable, as is the sinuous and vivid costume design (which makes the souvenir shop a magnet for fans).

Even with its quite-serious ticket prices—ranging from about $70 to $125—it is worth every penny. La Nouba, in the old Disney phrase, is an e-ticket ride. Anyone who has ever seen a performance by one of the Cirque companies or its alumni spin-offs, such as Cirque Eloise, knows that it is gripping, thrilling, mysterious, enigmatic, funny, exhilarating, and altogether addictive. There are visual and emotional references to classical theater, movies, memories, dreams, and the confluence of desire and fear. This is one place where even the most child-averse vacationers need have no qualms; children are as spellbound as adults.

AMC Cineplex And just in case anyone's forgotten that Disney got its start in the movies, the 24-screen AMC Cineplex near the parking-lot entrance is definitely state-of-the-art, equipped with the George Lucas–designed THX super–sound system and stadium seating. Catch a late flick and let the traffic let up.

West Side Dining

The main street of West Side is studded with name-brand restaurant franchises, few of which are worth seeking out, though there are a few tables with water views, if you can bag one.

Orlando Convention & Visitors Bureau

Probably the best of the eateries, and easily the second-best entertainment venue, is the roadhouse-style **House of Blues** (☎ 407-934-2222 or www.hob .com), which is actually several houses: a restaurant-blues club, a concert hall, and a separate shop. The decor is what might be called voodoo chic, an oversized bayou-country fish shack studded with faux-naif art and gasoline-alley castoffs. It leans to the New Orleans blackened school of food, such as Cajun meatloaf, ribs, voodoo shrimp, and gumbo. The restaurant books live blues bands, which start at 10:30 p.m. Thursday through Saturday, in the bar, and the action runs hot until 1:30 a.m. If there's a name band playing in the club, you'll have to buy a ticket, but if a local group or DJ is performing that night, there's no cover.

The adjoining and much sleeker two-story concert hall, which seats about 150 and stands 1,850 (get in early), brings in a variety of funk, R&B, zydeco, rock, jam, and reggae bands. Concert hall ticket prices can go pretty high, depending on how big a draw the band is. Sunday gospel brunch is a House special in all its cities, a buffet-style meal (two seatings), and the good word in all its glory. Sunday night is service-industry night (affectionately known as SIN), when cast members crowd in to boogie.

Other West Side restaurants include **Wolfgang Puck Cafe** with decor as busily and brightly tiled as a bathroom-fixture warehouse. Pizza, sushi, and pastas (all pretty average) are the headliners. The Wolfgang Puck Cafe's main advantage is that the upstairs bar serves until midnight. Gloria Estefan's **Bongos Cuban Cafe** is somewhat disappointing—though the outside seating can be nice, and you can definitely hear the salsa music from there. There's a Planet Hollywood (otherwise known as Planet Attitude), which has erratic service, no live entertainment, and much the same menu as any other **Planet Hollywood**, meaning blandish and somewhat hefty—and though similar, not as good as the House of Blues.

DISNEY'S BOARDWALK

The BoardWalk is a little like a costume party where the hosts hope you'll dance, but have left the championship fight on the big-screen TV in the rec room just in case you won't. Unlike Pleasure Island or the West Side, which are entirely commercial complexes, the BoardWalk is half resort, half theme park. The BoardWalk Inn and Villas is built over and behind the entertainment and shopping strip, and the theme is the Atlantic City and Long Island resorts of the 1930s.

There are two nightclubs for those age 21 and older, plus **ESPN Club**, open to all ages though heavily bar- and sports TV–oriented, especially later in the evening. The main entertainment venue on the BoardWalk is an elaborate big band–era dance hall called **Atlantic Dance**, which plays the martini-lounge nostalgia theme to the hilt with a ceiling glittering with mirror balls, marble bars, a bandstand, a grand staircase, a balcony to retire to between jitterbugs (and where you can nuzzle in love seats), and lake-view terraces to take in the fireworks. There's no cover charge at Atlantic Dance, no live music, and sometimes no patrons either. The music is heavily 1980s, the golden age of early MTV.

For the dance-challenged in the party, the BoardWalk has a comedy-and-music bar called **Jellyrolls,** a sort of dueling banjos on ivory, with two pianos, two players, and a lot of shouted encouragement. (Although dancing is not the main concept, people often do get down.) Despite the name, which suggests jazz, the music tends to the classic-rock variety (again), but that means that the patrons are sometimes lured into singing along. (Since Jellyrolls attracts some local residents, it occasionally seems like karaoke night at the VFW.) It's a 21-and-up venue with a $10 cover charge but no minimum.

Jellyrolls Dueling Piano Bar: Be Loud. Be Proud.

For the nonmartini crowd, the **Big River Grille & Brewing Works**, a.k.a. The Six Mouse-ka-Beers Bar, can be a draw, but the bar itself is quite small—unfortunate for those who like to talk brewing with the staff. You can sample at least a half-dozen microbrews crafted on the World premises in the huge copper vats visible from the bar. While Walt might blush at the thought of such licentiousness, we think the home-brewed beer here is generally pretty good. All are preservative-free, with four standards available all the time and others that change seasonally. There may be bigger beers served in the World, and there may be more exotic beers, too, but there's something about a beer brewed on the Mouse's turf that makes it seem, well, a bit magical.

Though the ESPN Club and the Big River Grille & Brewing Works offer gut-busting fare, the culinary show pony of the Boardwalk is the **Flying Fish Cafe** with a Coney Island theme and a decidedly adult range of fresh seafood preparations dressed in trendy frills. Try the yellowfin tuna with a citrus zest–and–Szechuan peppercorn crust. Mmmm.

Incidentally, although it's not in one of the official nightlife areas, we direct your attention to **Rix Lounge**, which is a retro Rat Pack lounge with a touch of Hollywood glamour at the Coronado Springs Resort. (If you say the name out loud, you may start hearing "As Time Goes By" in your head.) It may be one reason to trek to Coronado Springs; what stays in Vegas, baby. . . .

PART 11

RECREATION

You would be hard-pressed to come up with any sort of (nonextreme) recreational activity that is not available somewhere in Walt Disney World, with the possible exception of bowling (yet), bungee jumping, and the super slalom (but there are some surprisingly similar virtual games available at Epcot and DisneyQuest). Otherwise, the World is your playground: golf, tennis, croquet, swimming, boating, fishing, skiing, ice-skating, weight lifting, trail riding, rock climbing, running, volleyball, basketball, horseback riding, biking, parasailing, surfing, and scuba diving—even NASCAR driving.

As for bowling: What is said to be the largest bowling complex in the country, a super-deluxe tournament center with 100 lanes, is planned for ESPN Wide World of Sports and scheduled to open in 2011. Beginning in 2013, the center will be home to 13 annual events of the U.S. Bowling Congress; some lanes may be open to the public when not in use.

There are no official skateboard or in-line skating areas at Disney, but none are necessary; there are sidewalks, parking lots, roads, and, though we hate to point it out, stairways everywhere. Other activities available in the World include ballooning (of a sort), parasailing, and gliding (simulated but exhilarating).

In addition, if you or your team are into baseball (at any level), lacrosse, track and field, cricket, rugby, martial arts, field hockey, cheerleading drills, gymnastics, soccer, wrestling, or even foot bag (among other sports!), you should look into the vast number of events at the various ESPN Wide World of Sports venues. Who knows? Perhaps Disney magic can bring out the inner Olympian in you. In any case, the spectating is spectacular.

▶ **UNOFFICIAL TIP** If you plan to include the more traditional sports in your vacation, you should make reservations or tee times as early as you can.

DISNEY RESORT RECREATION

	FITNESS CENTER	WATER SPORTS	MARINA	BEACH	TENNIS	BIKING
All-Star Resorts	—	—	—	—	—	—
Animal Kingdom Lodge and Villas	★	—	—	—	★*	—
Bay Lake Tower	★	★	★	★	—	—
BoardWalk Inn	★	★	★	—	★	★
BoardWalk Villas	★	★	★	—	★	★
Caribbean Beach Resort	—	★	★	★	—	★
Contemporary Resort	★	★	★	★	—	—
Coronado Springs Resort	★	★	★	—	—	—
Dolphin	★	★	★	★	★	—
Fort Wilderness Resort	—	★	★	★	★	★
Grand Floridian Resort & Spa	★	★	★	★	★	—
Old Key West Resort	★	★	★	—	★	★
Polynesian Resort	—	★	★	★	—	—
Pop Century Resort	—	—	—	—	—	—
Port Orleans Resort	—	★	★	—	—	★
Saratoga Springs Resort & Spa–Treehouse Villas	★	—	—	—	★	★
Shades of Green	★	—	—	—	★	★
Swan	★	—	—	★	★	—
Wilderness Lodge and Villas	★	★	★	★	—	★
Yacht and Beach Club Resorts	★	★	★	★	★	—

*Kidani Village only

³⁴⁸ IT'S MORE FUN WHEN YOU'RE WET— WATER SPORTS

Water comes in a lot of forms in Walt Disney World—Bay Lake and Seven Seas Lagoon, Buena Vista Lagoon, the Fort Wilderness waterways, the Disney Village waterways and the Sassagoula River, Barefoot Bay, Crescent Lake, and so on—and not surprisingly, **boating** comes in nearly every variety imaginable, too, from Jet Skis and Sea Raycers to mini speedboats and WaveRunners to 20-foot pontoons for larger parties. There are also canopy boats, rowboats, pedal boats, Water Mice, sailboats, catamarans, speedboats, and kayaks—even outrigger canoes at the Polynesian. (These require at least five passengers, but unlike the others, they're free, perhaps because most amateurs are so clumsy in them that they provide entertainment for other visitors.) Port Orleans has kayaks, and Fort Wilderness has canoes—in fact nearly every resort hotel has some sort of watercraft available, and if not, they can show you where to find one.

The most concentrated site of water sports, if you plan to spend a lot of time playing, is **Sammy Duvall's Water Sports Centre** at the Contemporary Resort, which offers parasailing, wakeboarding, waterskiing, WaveRunners, canopy boats, pontoons, and even inner-tube rentals. For more information, call ☎ 407-WDW-PLAY. Note: You can make a reservation for most activities three months in advance, but you must cancel at least 24 hours ahead of your scheduled time.

Boating

For those who would rather be chauffeured than steer themselves, you can book charter boats and excursions in advance, either for private parties, fireworks viewing, fishing (catch and release only), or picnic lunches. Ask about these activities at the BoardWalk, Yacht and Beach Club resorts, Caribbean Beach, Coronado Springs, Wilderness Lodge, Contemporary, Polynesian, and Grand Floridian hotels, or at Cap'n Jack's Marina at Downtown Disney Marketplace.

The most luxurious water ride in Walt Disney World is the **Grand 1**, a 52-foot yacht that cruises around Bay Lake and Seven Seas Lagoon from the Grand Floridian. An hour's cruise will set you back about $500, but the watercraft has its own kitchen with a microwave, four televisions, air-conditioning, and room for a baker's dozen. And if you schedule it right, maybe you can catch the Magic Kingdom fireworks while on board. Call ☎ 407-824-2682 to schedule a reservation.

Fishing

Bay Lake was originally stocked with 70,000 largemouth bass that have been cheerfully spawning ever since (many are in the eight- to ten-pound range), and you can **pole fish** dockside without a reservation off the Fort Wilderness and Port Orleans Riverside section. Fort Wilderness also has cast rods, worms, wrigglers, and night crawlers for a few bucks. Everything you catch here must also be thrown back. Call ☎ 407-939-BASS for more information.

For something a little more elaborate, you can arrange a **bass-fishing**

expedition on pontoons that leave from a dozen resorts (basically, from every place with a marina) or from alongside Cap'n Jack's at Downtown Disney, and putter along Bay Lake and Seven Seas Lagoon, usually for about two hours. All these excursions—also strictly catch and release—include an experienced guide, rod and reel (if you don't have your own), tackle and bait, and beverages. Rates for two-hour trips are $150 to $255 for parties of up to five; four-hour trips are $225 to $435. (Hiring a tournament-style boat is a little more expensive.) All equipment is provided, but no coolers (or food or beverages) can be brought aboard. Reservations can be made up to 90 days in advance but must be made a day ahead. Call ☎ 407-WDW-PLAY.

Swimming

As for swimming—hello? There isn't a hotel on the place without its own white-sand beach, mini water park, or variety of pools, lap pools, hot tubs, whirlpools, fountains, waterfalls, geysers. . . . The only sad thing is that thanks to man's litigious nature and nature's own caprices, the "real" water of Bay Lake and Seven Seas Lagoons isn't for swimming. Those white-sand beaches are for dry-land activities only.

HOTEL POOL RATING

1. Yacht and Beach Club Resorts	★★★★★ (shared complex)
2. Animal Kingdom Villas (Kidani Village)	★★★★½
3. Port Orleans Resort	★★★★½
4. Saratoga Springs Resort & Spa– Treehouse Villas	★★★★½
5. Wilderness Lodge and Villas	★★★★½
6. Animal Kingdom Lodge and Villas (Jambo House)	★★★★
7. Bay Lake Tower	★★★★
8. Coronado Springs Resort	★★★★
9. Dolphin	★★★★
10. Polynesian Resort	★★★★
11. Swan	★★★★
12. BoardWalk Inn and Villas	★★★½
13. Contemporary Resort	★★★½
14. Grand Floridian Resort & Spa	★★★½
15. All-Star Resorts	★★★
16. Caribbean Beach Resort	★★★
17. Fort Wilderness Resort	★★★
18. Old Key West Resort	★★★
19. Pop Century Resort	★★★
20. Shades of Green	★★★

Waterskiing

Waterskiing can be arranged for about $140 an hour, which covers the boat, a driver-instructor, up to five skiers, and skis if you don't have your own, along with mini surfboards and kneeboards; make reservations at least 24 hours in advance at ☎ 407-824-2621, and specify pickup at Wilderness Lodge, Fort Wilderness, Grand Floridian, Contemporary, or Polynesian resorts.

BACK ON DRY LAND

Tennis

More and more adults play tennis on a regular basis, and some may find that even a short vacation makes them miss their match. But don't worry; even if you didn't come prepared, Disney World is ready. You can rent a tennis racket, tog up in brand-name or souvenir sportswear, and even buy shoes to suit the surface in the respective pro shops. In fact, you can rent a pro as well. If you want to go back home with a new drop shot, this is definitely the place. Not only can you get tennis lessons from a USTA pro on the two clay courts at the **Grand Floridian**, but you can play him for your tuition money: Take two out of three sets, and the lessons ($90 an hour) are free. Lessons can be booked 180 days in advance, and it's probably a good idea to do so. Just to play costs $12.50 an hour per person, but no reservations are accepted, only walk-up time. For lesson reservations or video analysis, call ☎ 407-621-1991. (Ask which facilities have racket rentals.)

Saratoga Springs also has two clay courts located near the Carriage House lobby. These courts are available for free, but only on a walk-up basis; they are open from 9 a.m. to 10 p.m. Several other resorts have courts available: **The BoardWalk**, **Old Key West**, **Yacht and Beach Clubs**, and the **Swan** and **Dolphin** have hard, rubberized surface courts as well, most of them lighted for evening play; inquire when making reservations.

Racecar Driving (or Riding)

Richard Petty Driving Experience   Want to talk thrill rides? We got it. Although it will probably cost you more cash than calories (depending on your adrenalin supply), stock-car enthusiasts can enroll in the Richard Petty Driving Experience that takes place on courses at the one-mile, tri-oval WDW Speedway. Assuming you have a valid driver's license, you can either ride shotgun in a 600-horsepower Nextel Cup–style two-seater stock car at speeds of up to 120 miles per hour or give up the wussy attitude and learn to drive one.

▶ **UNOFFICIAL TIP** You may not have thought about it in these all-too-automatic times, but racecars have manual transmissions, so if you think a stick shift has to do with firewood, forget it.

Just to ride three laps around the track costs about $100. For a little more time and money, you can sign up for the real stuff: an hour of so of serious classroom instruction and track orientation, and eight laps in the driver's seat ($450); instruction and 18 laps (about $850); or you can work your way up to three ten-lap sessions ($1,300). Not all

Orlando Convention & Visitors Bureau

packages are offered every day, and you need reservations, except for the ride-along option, which is first-come, first-served. Oh, and no flip-flops: You must wear closed-toe shoes—which is also fairly obvious if you think about it. For these programs, call ☎ 800-BE-PETTY (237-3889) or go to **1800bepetty.com**. And there are now 20 Petty places in the country, some letting you drive up to 165 miles per hour, so if you really like it, ask about the new Experience Rewards–membership program.

Even faster—up to 180 miles per hour—is the **Indy Racing Experience**, which   351
is similar but allows you to drive (or ride along in) a modified open-wheeled two-
seater like the ones that run the Indianapolis 500. For this encounter you can be no
taller than six-feet, five-inches tall and no heavier than 250 pounds. Whichever type
of car you drive, your instructor will drive the pace car ahead of you and gauge your
nerve and expertise. Prices are fairly similar to the Richard Petty Driving Experience;
for information call ☎ 317-243-7171, ext. 106, or go to racingexperience.com.

Horseback Riding

Let's be frank; nowhere in Walt Disney World are you going to get into any serious gal-
loping or cross-country event. Nevertheless, you can take a guided **trail ride** (at a very
gentle pace), or a more scenic half-hour **carriage ride** at Fort Wilderness for about $45.
The holiday sleigh ride through the backwoods of Wilderness Lodge is quite romantic
(though about twice the price). You can also pick up your carriage at Port Orleans Riverside. Reservations can be made 90 days in advance but must be cancelled at least 24
hours before your scheduled time in order to get a refund; call ☎ 407-WDW-PLAY.

Golf

Disney has been known to promote its golf facilities by calling itself the Magic Link-
dom; though corny, it's not inaccurate. Its five championship courses, three of which
are PGA and/or LPGA Tour facilities, have to stand up to more than 250,000 rounds
of golf every year, along with nearly 400 tournaments. Greens fees on these courses
are about $80 to $150 for resort guests, including electric carts (except at Oak Trail)

© Disney

and practice balls. The new golf carts, incidentally,
are everything you'd expect from Disney and one
of the high-tech wonders of the World: They
come equipped with GPS technology and full-
color monitors so that at each hole you can see
computer-generated three-dimensional images
of the fairways, greens, and hazards and pick up
professional tips and, in some cases, tournament
scoreboard information.

If all this is way beyond your game, private
lessons from PGA and LPGA Tour pros are available for $75 per 45-minute session. A bucket of
balls is $7. If you don't have your own clubs, you
can rent really good ones for about $60 and shoes
for $10.50. If you seriously plan to play golf at
Walt Disney World, you should absolutely stay
at one of the resort hotels. Resort guests can
book tee times up to 90 days in advance, while day guests can only call 60 days in
advance (credit-card number required). Resort guests also get discounted greens fees,
charging privileges, and overnight shipping of clubs from one course to another.

Even better, you can avoid the hassle of driving or hauling your clubs around on
a Disney bus; if you're staying at a resort hotel, round-trip transportation to a Disney
course is free (you pay the cabbie with hotel vouchers).

Remember that high golf season is in a way the opposite of high water-park
season; that is, rates are lower May to January and higher in the spring. If you're just
a regular vacationing duffer, you can also cut costs by signing up for early or twilight
tee times, which may slash rates by half. Fees for replaying the same course on the
same day (if space is available) are half the full rate.

Also note that golf courses are one place where Mickey T-shirts are not appreciated. Proper golf attire is required, meaning a collared shirt for men, Bermuda-length
shorts (nothing torn), and spikeless shoes.

Walt Disney World Golf Course Profiles

To find information about or to book tee times at any of the courses, call ☎ 407-WDW-GOLF.

Palm Golf Course   Designed by Joe Lee, this is Disney's best course. Home to a PGA Tour event, the Palm has numerous lakes coming into play on nine holes, and sand everywhere, with 94 hazards. The highlight, however, is a set of excellent greens. The defining characteristic is a set of holes where water separates tees from landing areas and landing areas from greens, a wet take on desert-style target golf. The signature 18th, with its island green, caps a fine set of finishing holes and has been ranked as high as fourth in difficulty among all holes on the PGA Tour's many venues. But four sets of well-spaced tees make the course playable for all abilities.

Magnolia Golf   Another fine Joe Lee creation, the sweeping, 7,500-plus-yard Magnolia course was renovated in 2005, including new turf. It has 97 bunkers (and the famous Mickey-shaped sand trap at the sixth), elaborate water hazards, and more than 1,500 of its namesake trees. Like the Palm, this course hosts the PGA Tour.

Osprey Ridge Golf   For nature lovers, the Osprey Ridge course may be the most dramatic, set in a polished wilderness—it's actually an Audubon-certified wildlife sanctuary—lined with pine, palmetto, cypress, and bay trees, and named by *Golf Digest* as one of the best courses in Florida, with a four-and-a-half out of five-star rating by *Golf Digest*. The main characteristics of this Tom Fazio course are large, rolling mounds and elevated tees and greens. The greens are huge, making them easy to hit but leaving approaches at four-putt distances where you almost cannot hit the ball hard enough to get it to the hole. Note: Osprey Ridge is scheduled to be made over in the next couple of years as part of the Four Seasons resort complex, so put it on your list.

Lake Buena Vista Golf   There are several memorable holes here, but this layout is the only one at Disney with housing on it—a lot of housing—that detracts from the golf experience. The course is geographically unique among the other layouts, tucked behind Saratoga Springs and Old Key West resorts, and has an Old Florida resort look, with pastel villas, a lighthouse, palmettos, and canals. Narrow fairways and small greens emphasize accuracy over length. This course has hosted PGA, LPGA, and USGA events.

Oak Trail Golf   This pretty little nine-hole walking course has holes as short as 132 yards, which makes it a lot less terrifying for the seriously golf-handicapped, so to speak. On the other hand, it's not an "executive" lunch-hour course—two of the holes are par 5—and it's the only course you can walk. Still, this is where the younger and novice duffers are apt to be.

Miniature Golf

Disney World also has two 36-hole mini golf complexes for less ambitious types, or for those who are still wandering around at night looking for something to do after the fireworks. No doubt Disney designers would have preferred to call it Goofy Golf, but there are older such attractions in Florida than Disney World and, as the Disney corporation knows all too well, trademarks are serious things.

Fantasia Gardens   This miniature-golf complex, tucked behind the Dolphin hotel on Epcot Resorts Boulevard, is two courses in one, both 18 holes and quite prettily landscaped. The setups at Fantasia Gardens are designed to resemble, as you might guess, scenes from *Fantasia*, complete with the hefty hippos and ballerina ostriches, a Sorcerer's Apprentice–style final hole with tipping pails and walking brooms, and so on. Not only that, but there are surfaces and laser beams that react to passing balls with music, special effects, and pop-up scenery. It's more of a game than a golf course.

Its sibling course, Fantasia Fairways, is more truly a miniature-golf course— 353 a traditional-fairway course on a small scale, lavished with topiaries and fountains, and with some impressive back scenery courtesy of Disney's Hollywood Studios.

Prices are about $12 per course, and each is open daily from 10 a.m. to 11 p.m., weather permitting. Got the munchies? There's a snack bar.

Winter Summerland   This complex offers two 18-hole courses near Blizzard Beach: One round, called the Winter Course, is designed to evoke the holidays in Florida, complete with Santa and elves. The other, the Summer Course, has a surfboards-and-sandcastles, "Gidget Goes to Disney World" theme. Hours and prices (and snack bar) are the same as for Fantasia Gardens; call ☎ 407-WDW-GOLF.

Fantasia Gardens' approach-and-putt course

Biking and Running

Although biking may seem more appealing to those with several days to explore Disney World or repeat visitors who'd like to see more of the nature side, it's a great way to see several of the prettiest resort areas. There are bicycles for rent, sometimes tandem bikes too, at Fort Wilderness, Wilderness Lodge, Port Orleans (both Riverside and French Quarter), Coronado Springs, BoardWalk, Old Key West, and Caribbean Beach resorts. There are also four-wheeled surreys, which are like covered bikes, for rent across from the BoardWalk marina. The routes range in length from about a mile around the BoardWalk to nine miles of path at Fort Wilderness. (Remember that most bike paths are also jogging and walking routes, and in some cases might have golf-cart traffic as well.)

Running is obviously popular in a place with so much scenery and sheer space; Disney World is now the site of a popular marathon that takes place on a different course through the theme parks every January, plus half-marathons, triathlons, and assorted races throughout the year. If you're the sort of habitual runner who can't pass a week without a road race, call for local information at ☎ 407-898-1313. For less ambitious joggers, maps are available at each of the hotels that show the nearest trails and access points. Trails are usually no more than three miles long, but most are loops, so you can just go around again. The one between the Wilderness Lodge and Fort Wilderness has fitness stations as well.

Working Out and Other Exercise

Among the most elaborate of the resorts' fitness facilities are those at Saratoga Springs, the Contemporary, Animal Kingdom Lodge, and the Grand Floridian, all of which adjoin spas. Guests at the Polynesian Resort have free access to the Grand Floridian facility. Wilderness Lodge has a fitness center but not a spa. Yacht Club and Beach Club share a fitness center where you can get spa services by advance arrangements; the BoardWalk Inn and Villas have a similar arrangement. Both the Swan and Dolphin hotels have fitness centers—the one in the Swan is slightly larger—and guests have access to the Mandara Spa in the Dolphin. Most of the clubs also have personal trainers available, and in some cases nutritionists for diet advice; check with the specific fitness club.

All health clubs have age limits that require guests to be at least in their teens, and most clubs require even those guests to be with an adult. Some spas have child services, but spas tend to be quieter anyway.

HOTEL FITNESS-CENTER RATING

1. Saratoga Springs Resort & Spa–Treehouse Villas	★★★★★
2. Bay Lake Tower	★★★★½
3. Grand Floridian Resort & Spa	★★★★½
4. Animal Kingdom Lodge and Villas	★★★★
5. BoardWalk Inn and Villas	★★★★
6. Yacht and Beach Club Resorts	★★★★ (shared facility)
7. Contemporary Resort	★★★½
8. Coronado Springs Resort	★★★½
9. Wilderness Lodge and Villas	★★★½
10. Dolphin	★★★
11. Swan	★★★
12. Old Key West Resort	★½

SPECTATOR SPORTS

ESPN Wide World of Sports

The Wide World of Sports includes a retro-ish 9,500-seat, six-luxury-suite lighted baseball stadium, where the Atlanta Braves train and play their home exhibition-season games. It also houses four major-league practice fields, 20 major-league pitcher's mounds, four softball fields, and eight batting tunnels. The 5,000-seat field house holds six basketball courts and a weight room and hosts dozens of competitions and clinics in fencing, wrestling, martial arts, badminton, racquetball, gymnastics, and even coaching and groundskeeping. There's an Olympic-quality track-and-field complex, and an Olympic-tested 250-meter velodrome was disassembled after the 1996 Atlanta Olympics and moved to Disney World. The complex has four convertible fields suitable for football, rugby, soccer, field hockey, lacrosse, and so on; ten tennis courts, including a 2,000-seat stadium center court where the U.S. Men's Clay Court Championships are played; and five outdoor, sand volleyball courts. When that huge 100-lane bowling complex opens, it will also have its own stadium seating (!) and restaurant.

To inquire about events here, call ☎ 407-939-GAME. Many events do sell out, so you should try to call or surf in advance.

© Disney

SPA PLEASURES

Luxury spas are big business, and as far as Disney is concerned, conspicuous consumers R Us, so the place is now fairly rife with pampering possibilities—many of them (naturally) fantastic ones. Exotic scents and aromatherapy (citrus zest, ginger, and coconut milk), body wraps (mud, mineral, or seaweed), and hot stones are almost passé. These days, nearly every facial or body treatment description implies not merely ambience but spiritual healing (the Mystical Forest Therapy massages and facials at Saratoga Springs; the holistic Crystal Hands and Bamboo Harmony massages at the Grand Floridian). Some services at the Mandara Spa in the Dolphin are even rituals.

You can banish cellulite, encourage collagen production, erase sun damage, articulate your spinal column, and even soothe your overfed colon—not an impractical suggestion in these indulgent parts. But luxury spa services aren't cheap, here or anywhere else. Ask at your hotel lobby what services they have—most of the fitness centers also have whirlpools, saunas, or steam rooms, massages by appointment, and tanning booths—and decide how fragrant you need to be.

A couple of tips: If you have a preference for a male or woman massage therapist, advise spa personnel when you call. Be sure to discuss any physical ailments or allergies with any therapist, whatever the service; it's a good idea to mention this when booking as well. And ask whether a gratuity has already been added to your bill, and if so, what percentage. That way, if you have a really good experience and want to leave a few dollars more, you won't be going overboard.

There are four spas on the Walt Disney World campus. The spa at **Saratoga Springs** (☎ 407-827-4455; relaxedyet.com) and the spa at the **Grand Floridian** (☎ 407-824-2332; relaxedyet.com), which are both operated by Niki Bryan Spas, are in their own buildings; the **Mandara Spa** in the Walt Disney World Dolphin (☎ 407-934-4772; mandaraspa.com) is on the main lobby level. The fourth spa is in the **Buena Vista Palace** (☎ 407-827-3200; buenavistapalace.com), which is one of the Downtown Disney Resort Area hotels just across the highway from Downtown Disney Marketplace. All are nearly equal in their quality of ingredients and variety of services. Personal service at the Buena Vista and Mandara spas is a touch above the rest. The overall facilities at Saratoga Springs are fine; check out the machine that sucks all the water out of your bathing suit. The spa at the Grand Floridian is generally the most expensive, and though clean and attractive, is beginning to show its (relative) age; locker rooms are spare. Rates at the Buena Vista Palace are at the lower end of the scale.

INDEX

PHOTO CREDITS

If you would like to express your opinion in writing about Walt Disney World or this guidebook, complete the following survey and mail it to:

Unofficial Guides Reader Survey
P.O. Box 43673
Birmingham, AL 35243

Inclusive dates of your visit: _____

Members of your party:

	Person 1	Person 2	Person 3	Person 4	Person 5
Gender:	M F	M F	M F	M F	M F
Age:					

How many times have you been to Walt Disney World? _____

On your most recent trip, where did you stay? _____

Concerning your accommodations, on a scale of 100 as best and 0 as worst, how would you rate:

The quality of your room?   The value of your room?

The quietness of your room?   Check-in/check-out efficiency?

Shuttle service to the airport?   Swimming pool facilities?

Did you rent a car?_____   From whom?_____

Concerning your rental car, on a scale of 100 as best and 0 as worst, how would you rate:

Pick-up processing efficiency?_____   Return processing efficiency?____

Condition of the car?_____   Cleanliness of the car?_____

Airport shuttle efficiency?_____

Concerning your dining experiences:

Estimate your meals in restaurants per day? _____

Approximately how much did your party spend on meals per day? _____

_____

Favorite restaurants in Walt Disney World: _____

_____

Did you buy this guide before leaving? _____ While on your trip?_____

How did you hear about this guide? (check all that apply)

Loaned or recommended by a friend ☐   Radio or TV ☐

Newspaper or magazine ☐   Bookstore salesperson ☐

Just picked it out on my own ☐   Library ☐

Internet ☐